Moodle 1.9 Extension Development

Customize and extend Moodle by using its robust plugin systems

Jonathan Moore

Michael Churchward

BIRMINGHAM - MUMBAI

Moodle 1.9 Extension Development

First published: April 2010

Production Reference: 1220410

Published by Packt Publishing Ltd.
32 Lincoln Road
Olton
Birmingham, B27 6PA, UK.

ISBN 978-1-847194-24-4

www.packtpub.com

Cover Image by Parag Kadam (paragvkadam@gmail.com)

Credits

Authors

Jonathan Moore

Michael Churchward

Reviewer

Anthony Borrow

Acquisition Editor

Rashmi Phadnis

Development Editor

Ved Prakash Jha

Technical Editors

Chris Rodrigues

Hithesh Uchil

Indexer

Hemangini Bari

Editorial Team Leader

Akshara Aware

Project Team Leader

Priya Mukherji

Project Coordinator

Ashwin Shetty

Proofreader

Dirk Manuel

Graphics

Geetanjali Sawant

Production Coordinator

Aparna Bhagat

Cover Work

Aparna Bhagat

About the Authors

Michael Churchward is currently the President and CTO of Remote Learner, a Moodle partner based in the U.S. and Canada. Mike has been a developer of Moodle since 2004, and contributes both core code and add-on functions to the open source project. Mike and his development team are currently working on other extensions to Moodle, and helping to define the new Moodle 2.0 architecture.

Michael began his career building computer-based simulations of internal aircraft systems used in the training of ground and maintenance crews. Since then, he has been involved in many types of software and computer-based learning. Programming Moodle became a natural extension of that career.

Michael lives with his family in a small town in south-western Ontario, and thanks all of them for their patience while he was writing this book.

I thank the Moodle community for their energy and input; my wife, Janet; my sons, William, Cole, and Janson for their constant encouragement; and lastly my parents, Bob and Lorane for pointing me in the right direction.

Jonathan Moore is the Vice-President for Business Development at Remote Learner. Jonathan began working with Moodle in 2003. Over the past four years, Jonathan has worked with dozens of clients, delivering Moodle customizations. Jonathan has a Bachelor of Science degree in Information Technology.

Jonathan formerly served as the Director of Technology for Winfield Public Schools. He served in this capacity for almost ten years, and has developed a broad set of educational technology and project management skills over the course of his career. His student technology program, Student Technology Assistance Team (STAT), was recognized nationally by CompTIA as the best rural student technology program. Earlier in his career, Jonathan worked as a full-time developer, and studied computer science prior to pursuing Information Technology. Jonathan started working with open source technology in 1993 with an early release of Slackware Linux, and has used and supported a variety of open source technologies in educational settings.

Jonathan lives with his wife, in Lenexa, Kansas, a suburb of Kansas City.

I wish to thank my co-author, Michael Churchward, for taking on this crazy project to write a book while growing a company. Thanks for taking this leap of faith. I would also like to thank my wife for putting up with a cranky writer this past year, my parents for emphasizing the importance of literacy, Bryan Williams and the rest of our leadership team for their support, and finally the staff of Winfield Public Schools for providing a wonderful place to grow.

About the Reviewer

Anthony Borrow, S.J. is a Jesuit of the New Orleans Province, who has been active in the Moodle community for five years. Anthony has an M.A. in Counseling from Saint Louis University. Anthony has worked on the design and implementation of various database systems since 1992.

Anthony serves the Moodle community as its CONTRIB Coordinator. In that role, Anthony has presented at various MoodleMoots (conferences) across the United States, and has provided in-house training opportunities for institutions learning how to implement Moodle. Anthony has taught at Dallas Jesuit College Preparatory and provides technical advice to the Jesuit Secondary Education Association (`http://jsea.org`) and the Jesuit Virtual Learning Academy (`http://jvla.org/`).

Anthony is the co-author of the Honduras chapter of *Teen Gangs: A Global View*.

Table of Contents

Preface

Moodle has evolved into one of the most widely-used Learning Management Systems in the world, with over 35,000 installed sites and 25 million users. Much of its popularity is due to its ability to be extended by developers, by using its open source architecture. Understanding how to develop on the Moodle platform provides an organization using Moodle the flexibility to expand its functions.

This book will teach you the inner workings of Moodle, and provide you with the ability to develop code the "Moodle way". You will learn to develop standard Moodle plugins, such as activities and blocks, by creating functioning code that you can execute in your own Moodle installation.

This book will expose you to all of the core code functions in Moodle in a progressive, understandable way. You will learn what libraries are available, what the API calls are, how Moodle is structured, and how it can be expanded beyond the plugin system.

Approach

This is a practical, hands-on book that will allow you to build plugins as you learn. All of the technologies that you need are freely-available in the open source world.

You will begin by gaining an understanding of the basic architecture that Moodle uses to operate in. Next, you will build your first plugin, a block. You will carry on building other Moodle plugins, gaining knowledge of the "Moodle way" of coding, before plunging deeper into the API and inner libraries. Lastly, you will learn how to integrate Moodle with other systems, by using a variety of methods.

By the time you have finished this book, you will have a solid understanding of Moodle programming, and will have the knowledge to extend its functionality in whatever way you want.

What this book covers

Chapter 1, *Moodle Architecture*, introduces some of the important concepts of Moodle architecture: how Moodle is structured, and how Moodle works.

Chapter 2, *Creating and Modifying Blocks*, covers how to create a basic block in Moodle, one of the easiest and most common customizations. Moodle blocks are plugins that display content in the right-hand or left-hand side column of a Moodle site. Several basic Moodle programming concepts that are used throughout the book are introduced.

Chapter 3, *Creating and Modifying Filters*, covers the basic concepts of creating a Moodle filter. The Moodle filter system is a method of processing the contents of the Moodle database (typically, user-entered content) prior to display, so that it can be modified in some beneficial way.

Chapter 4, *Creating and Modifying Activity Modules*, covers how to create a Moodle activity that can send results to the gradebook. Moodle activities are plugins that provide instructional activities for learners. One or more activities of each type can be added to courses, and each activity typically has a graded component that sends its results to the Moodle gradebook.

Chapter 5, *Customizing the Look and Feel*, elaborates on the common methods of customizing the look and feel of a Moodle site. This chapter will discuss how to tell the difference between a requirement that needs programming and one that can be completed by a theme designer.

Chapter 6, *Developer's Guide to the Database*, covers both the overall structure of the Moodle database and the coding methods used to access and store information there. Moodle supports a variety of SQL databases to store program information.

Chapter 7, *Developing Pluggable Core Modules*, covers useful programming concepts and considerations for the core Moodle system and modules. Some common ways by which popular modules can be modified are explored in this chapter.

Chapter 8, *Creating Moodle Reports*, covers a variety of methods of adding to Moodle's built-in reports. Moodle has an excellent logging system, but often users find they need to write a custom reporting module in order to get the data in the exact format that they desire.

Chapter 9, *Integrating Moodle with Other Systems*, covers four common types of integrations: user authentication, user enrollment, performance results, and Single Sign On. A common customization request for Moodle is to integrate with a third-party system.

Chapter 10, *Writing Secure Code*, covers various security concerns and best practices when developing code for Moodle.

Chapter 11, *Sending Notifications to Users*, discusses methods of messaging and notifying users through e-mail, RSS, and others.

Chapter 12, *Constructing and Displaying Pages by Using the pagelib Library*, covers the basic concepts of using pagelib. The pagelib library is used in the construction of display pages in Moodle.

Chapter 13, *Building Forms with formslib*, covers how to use the formslib library for customizations. The formslib library controls Moodle forms, user input, and input sanitation.

Chapter 14, *Development for the Adventuresome: Web Services*, covers two separate Moodle implementations for web services: one SOAP-based and one XML-RPC-based. The SOAP library allows remote manipulation and creation of courses, users, user enrollments, and user grades. The XML-RPC library provides a secure channel and full Moodle API exposure to the trusted site. This chapter will explore basic concepts of using both libraries.

Who this book is for

This book is written for technologists who are interested in expanding Moodle's functions through programming, either for their own organizations or to contribute to the open source project.

This book is aimed at programmers already familiar with Moodle's basic technologies: PHP, MySQL, and HTML/CSS.

You will need an understanding of PHP in order to follow along with coding activities in the book.

Conventions

In this book, you will find a number of styles of text that distinguish between different kinds of information. Here are some examples of these styles, and an explanation of their meaning.

Code words in text are shown as follows: "Finally, we display our table using the `print_html` member function"

A block of code is set as follows:

```php
<?php
  function learningisfunlink_filter($courseid, $text) {
    return $text;
  }
?>
```

When we wish to draw your attention to a particular part of a code block, the relevant lines or items are set in bold:

```
function get_content() {
  if ($this->content !== NULL) {
    return $this->content;
  }//if
  $context = get_context_instance(CONTEXT_SYSTEM);
  require_capability('moodle/site:doanything', $context);
  $this->content           =  new stdClass;
    $this->content->text   = 'Hello World!';
  return $this->content;
}//function get_content
```

New terms and **important words** are shown in bold. Words that you see on the screen, in menus, or dialog boxes for example, appear in the text like this: "Click on the **Notifications** link in the **Site Administration** block."

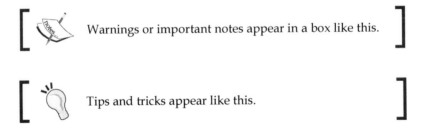

Warnings or important notes appear in a box like this.

Tips and tricks appear like this.

Reader feedback

Feedback from our readers is always welcome. Let us know what you think about this book—what you liked or may have disliked. Reader feedback is important for us to develop titles that you really get the most out of.

To send us general feedback, simply send an e-mail to feedback@packtpub.com, and mention the book title in the subject of your message.

If there is a book that you need and would like to see us publish, please send us a note in the **SUGGEST A TITLE** form on www.packtpub.com or send an e-mail to suggest@packtpub.com.

If there is a topic that you have expertise in and you are interested in either writing or contributing to a book on, see our author guide on www.packtpub.com/authors.

Customer support

Now that you are the proud owner of a Packt book, we have a number of things to help you to get the most from your purchase.

Downloading the example code for the book

Visit https://www.packtpub.com//sites/default/files/downloads/4244_Code.zip to directly download the example code.

Errata

Although we have taken every care to ensure the accuracy of our content, mistakes do happen. If you find a mistake in one of our books—maybe a mistake in the text or the code—we would be grateful if you would report this to us. By doing so, you can save other readers from frustration and help us to improve subsequent versions of this book. If you find any errata, please report them by visiting http://www.packtpub.com/support, selecting your book, clicking on the **let us know** link, and entering the details of your errata. Once your errata are verified, your submission will be accepted and the errata will be uploaded on our website, or added to any list of existing errata under the Errata section of that title. Any existing errata can be viewed by selecting your title from http://www.packtpub.com/support.

Piracy

Piracy of copyright material on the Internet is an ongoing problem across all media. At Packt, we take the protection of our copyright and licenses very seriously. If you come across any illegal copies of our works, in any form, on the Internet, please provide us with the location address or website name immediately, so that we can pursue a remedy.

Please contact us at copyright@packtpub.com with a link to the suspected pirated material.

We appreciate your help in protecting our authors and our ability to bring you valuable content.

Questions

You can contact us at questions@packtpub.com if you are having a problem with any aspect of the book, and we will do our best to address it.

1
Moodle Architecture

Moodle is an open source **Learning Management System (LMS)**. It can be used to deliver online learning in a variety of settings. These settings include virtual schools, K12, higher education, corporate universities, charter schools, and commercial training, to name but a few. Moodle is designed to be used primarily as an asynchronous learning tool, where learners study at different times. However, it also includes synchronous tools. Moodle is used both as the primary delivery vehicle for courses as well as a supplemental tool for face-to-face learning. To put it simply, Moodle is a teacher's toolkit to help improve learning. Moodle is designed in a community with teachers interacting directly with programmers. Moodle's intuitive and simple interface is the result of this collaboration.

Moodle originally stood for Modular Object-Oriented Dynamic Learning Environment. From a programmer's perspective, the "M" in Moodle is a very important concept. Modularity is designed throughout Moodle. This lets a developer make significant modifications to Moodle without having to modify its code. This is a very important capability in terms of reducing the amount of time taken to make modifications when new versions of Moodle are released. Writing modular plugins for Moodle will be a large focus of this book.

You can learn more about general Moodle functionality and history on the Moodle Documentation site at `http://docs.moodle.org/en/About_Moodle`.

This chapter introduces some of the important concepts of Moodle architecture; how Moodle is structured and how Moodle works. This chapter introduces the following concepts:

- Components of the system (operating system, web server, PHP interpreter, database, and browser)
- Directory and system structure (Moodle code, database, and file storage)
- Installation (how to install, what happens during installation, and how to upgrade)

- Program execution (the major calling structure, included libraries, execution paths, and separation of function/display/data)
- Configuration (from the interface, from the `config` file, and from the database)
- Application Programming Interface (a brief description of what the major libraries do)
- Other common libraries (PEAR, ADOdb, YUI, and XMLDB)
- Access control for users, courses, and other security objects

As you can see from the list, we will be covering a lot of ground in this chapter. Let's get started with a discussion of the technology stack that drives Moodle.

Understanding the stack

Moodle is an example of a "LAMP" application. LAMP originally stood for Linux, Apache, MySQL, and Perl. Over time, the various components of the acronym have shifted. For example, PHP has become the predominate language for "LAMP" applications. In truth, any of the components can be exchanged for another. However, the title has stuck to refer to applications written in web scripting languages, using an SQL database to store information. With the increasing popularity of running open source web applications on both Windows and Mac OS X, two new terms have been coined, respectively: WAMP and MAMP. See the following figure, which illustrates components of the system in Moodle:

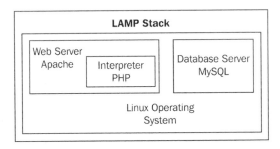

Moodle is written in PHP, and the current version as of this writing (Version 1.9) requires PHP Version 4.3.0 or higher. Version 2.0 of Moodle, which is currently in development, will require PHP Version 5.2.8 or higher.

Database

Moodle's database layer is written using the PHP ADOdb library, which was created to provide a standardized method of accessing various database systems, using a consistent programming interface. PHP native database libraries are database specific and as a result are difficult to use to write a program that can support multiple database servers. Thanks to its use of ADOdb, Moodle provides support for a variety of databases including: MySQL, PostgreSQL, Microsoft SQL, and Oracle. Moodle supports a much longer list of databases for the purpose of external system integrations, by using its plugin architecture. While Moodle does enjoy broad database support, in practice, most systems are deployed using MySQL. As a practical result of this, more eyes are looking at MySQL installations; it has the fewest bugs, with the broadest set of third-party additions. PostgreSQL is the second most popular backend and has a strong following amongst performance enthusiasts and large deployments (tens of thousands or more users). Microsoft SQL and Oracle installations are primarily used by organizations with a pre-existing investment in one of these architectures. Because of their smaller user base, they are not as well tested. It is also more difficult to find good support for using these database types with Moodle. Many third-party add-on modules do not work under these systems without patching.

Database version requirements for Moodle 1.9:

- MySQL 4.1.16
- PostgreSQL 8.0
- Microsoft SQL 9.0
- Oracle 9.0

Proposed database requirements for Moodle 2.0:

- MySQL 4.1.16 or
- PostgreSQL 8.0 or
- Microsoft SQL 9.0 or
- Oracle 9.0
- SQLite 3 (experimental)

The latest version of these requirements can be viewed at the following URL: http://docs.moodle.org/en/Environment#Moodle_version_1.9.

Note that the specifications for the Moodle 2.0 database layer can be found at the following location: http://docs.moodle.org/en/Development:DB_layer_2.0.

Operating system

Moodle can run on any operating system that supports the required version of PHP and the database. Moodle is generally installed on one of the three major operating systems: Windows, Mac OS X, or Linux (or Unix/Unix-like operating systems). As compared to Linux, both Mac OS X and Windows operating systems suffer from less efficient performance for large-scale deployments. For Windows, this is due to a less-optimized PHP stack, and for Mac OS X it is due to poor process forking performance, which both Apache and MySQL rely on for high concurrency. Windows Server 2008 is reported in press releases by both Microsoft and Zend, the creator of PHP, as having improved PHP performance. In a development environment, you can use any of these operating systems as an excellent platform. In a production environment, each operating system will have different performance characteristics.

Web server

Moodle will typically work with any web server that supports running the appropriate versions of PHP. In practice, the most used web server is Apache, which is available for most operating systems. **Internet Information Services (IIS)** is another popular web server for hosting Moodle. There are also a growing number of advocates for Lighthttpd as a web server, and this is reported in the Moodle community forums (http://moodle.org/forums/) as working well with Moodle. Lighthttpd has a growing number of advocates due to its low memory design. It is extremely popular for its use with virtual environments (VMware, Xen, and Amazon Elastic Compute Cloud), where memory footprint is more of a concern.

Moodle as a web application has support and development constraints that are different from the norm. This is due to the way in which Moodle is used. A user interacting with Moodle will have a higher than normal amount of clicks, and Moodle generates many SQL queries as it builds a page. Moodle is very efficient at what it does. However, what it does is fairly complex. This means, as developers, we need to be aware of the type of architectures that our modifications will likely be used within. It also means that we need to be aware of the performance implications of our coding. The following figure illustrates several common configurations used for Moodle in a production environment. Moodle is deployed in a broad range of settings—anywhere from a single teacher running it on his or her desktop all the way up to multi-machine clusters of high performance servers:

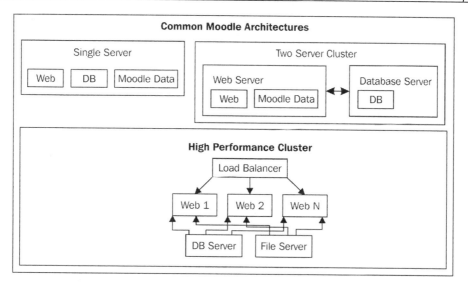

Moodle, as is common with the standard PHP application model, scales at particular points. The first scaling point is the database, which can easily be moved to a separate physical server. After that, we can bring in additional frontend web servers by using a load balancer. When using multiple web servers we will also need shared storage for our Moodle data. Session data can be stored in either Moodle data or in the database. The database server is the point where Moodle's scalability is most limited. To scale the database it is necessary to bring in a faster database server, replacing the older server. Currently, there is no standard method for scaling a single Moodle installation across multiple master database servers, as we do with the web application servers. It is also common practice to use Moodle with a PHP accelerator such as eAccelerator or APC. It's important to test your code in these environments to make sure that it functions correctly.

Directory and system structure

As shown in the following figure, each working Moodle system can be divided into three separate areas: Moodle code, the Moodle database, and Moodle data.

Three Areas of Moodle		
Moodle Code Apache/IIS/Lighthttpd	Moodle Database MySQL/PostgreSQL/Microsoft SQL/Oracle	Moodle Data Local disk, NFS, GFS, SAN, etc.

Moodle code

Because PHP is an interpreted language, the Moodle code is stored as source code files on the web server. When a particular file is requested on the server, the PHP interpreter parses the code on the fly, and the resulting output is sent out via the web server software. As mentioned earlier, the "M" in Moodle stands for "Modular", and its directory structure reflects that. Each top-level folder represents a major component of Moodle. Many of the main components support plugin modules. Each plugin has its own folder inside the component's folder. In some cases, modules will also have support for additional plugins. An example of this is the quiz activity module, which supports modular question types. From the end user point of view, modules are installed by copying the module into the appropriate folder location on the server. Moodle detects the new module the next time that an administrator logs into the system, locates the module's SQL code, runs it, and finally displays the results.

Upgrades work in much the same way with Moodle, tracking the database version and automatically upgrading the database as needed. All of this easy interface for end users comes at the cost of some elbow grease for the developer.

The following screenshot is a directory listing of a recent Moodle 1.9 installation:

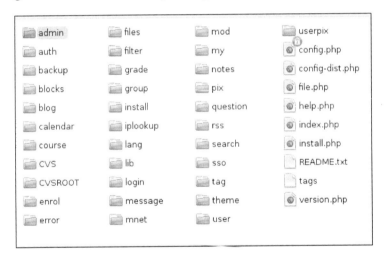

We will not cover all of the directories in the main folder at this time. However, we will explore the functions of some of the important folders used by developers who make modifications to Moodle. Moodle uses a simple nomenclature for modules, where all of the modules are enclosed in their own folder, and the name of the folder is the name that Moodle displays in its interface when referring to the module.

admin:

This folder stores the PHP files that control the administrative user's interface. They also contain the `cron.php` file, which is run as a batch process to perform system maintenance tasks such as message delivery and course backups. We will often hook into the `cron.php` process to perform batch operations.

auth:

The `auth` folder contains all of the authentication modules for Moodle. Each module will have its own directory in this area. Authentication modules control the creation of users, user profile data, and user access to the system. Authentication modules are great for automating system administration, and as a result are a common customization project.

backup:

This folder contains the core course backup facilities for the system. These are not system-wide backup facilities but functions for the backup, restore, and import of courses. Each individual course module is responsible for its own backup code and makes use of these functions as needed. Each module is self-contained, allowing us, as developers, to add modules cleanly to Moodle without having to modify the core code.

blocks:

`blocks` are used to display boxes of information in either the right-hand side or left-hand side column of the Moodle page. This is one of the simplest module types to make, and also tend to work across multiple versions of Moodle with little or no modifications.

course:

This component of Moodle has obvious importance, given that Moodle is organized around courses. As developers, we are most likely to modify or add course formats and reports. Custom course formats can be used to change the layout of courses.

enrol:

The `enrol` folder contains all of the enrollment modules for Moodle. Enrollment modules control the creation and management of course-level role assignments (enrollments). Enrollment modules are another key automation hook.

files:

The `files` component allows Moodle to incorporate files into the system. This includes file uploads, access control, and the viewing of files. `files` will see a major rewrite in Moodle 2.0. Moodle 2.0 will allow storing and using files in external file repositories such as Alfresco, Box.net, and Google Docs.

filter:

The Moodle filtering system is a text/regular expression-based search-and-replace facility. The filter system is fed user-entered content from the database during page creation. Filters match and modify the page before it is displayed. For example, there is a `math` filter that supports auto conversion of TEX markup language to equation graphics. The Multimedia Plugins filter finds references to common media types and wraps the text in the appropriate embed and/or object tags, in order to automatically embed the media, along with player controls, into the page. This is a very powerful capability. However, it needs to be carefully developed, with performance implications in mind.

lang:

The `lang` folder stores the core system language strings. This is the foundation of Moodle's localization and language support. All of the strings displayed to the end user are mapped via this facility. Language string mappings are also stored in the Moodle data `lang` folder. This structure allows for easy local customization of language files.

The following is a small section of the `/lang/en_utf8/moodle.php` language file. Notice how each string that is displayed to the end user is mapped to a string hash by using a key value that is descriptive of the strings purpose (in English):

```
$string['abouttobeinstalled'] = 'about to be installed';
$string['action'] = 'Action';
$string['actions'] = 'Actions';
$string['active'] = 'Active';
$string['activeusers'] = 'Active users';
```

lib:

The `lib` folder stores the core system library functions. As we develop modules and customizations, we will use classes and functions defined in this folder.

mod:

The `mod` folder stores activity modules such as assignment, quiz, wiki, forum, and lesson modules. Learning activities are the core of any course delivered using Moodle. Activity modules are more challenging to create than blocks, because they back up, restore, and store grades. Oh, and of course, they have to teach something to the learner.

my:

`my` is a light-weight portal area in Moodle. It provides a listing of courses a learner is assigned, including a summary of upcoming course activities. The user can also add and remove blocks on his or her portal page. `my` provides a good location to display custom information with minimal core changes to Moodle. For example, we use `my` as a dashboard location in many of our customization projects.

theme:

The `theme` folder stores all of the built-in Moodle themes and any custom themes installed on the system. Themes are a combination of CSS, HTML, and PHP. Each theme has its own folder. The theme system is useful for defining the visual skin, header, and footer of the Moodle page. It is, however, limited in how much of the Moodle page it can modify. For example, certain components of the Moodle page are hardcoded to display in a certain way.

Moodle database

The Moodle database is organized into roughly 200 related tables. The default installation option prepends `mdl_` in front of each table name. Each major component of the system typically has one or more tables, each starting with the component's name. For example, there are two tables related to the `config` component: `mdl_config` and `mdl_config_plugins`. As programmers, we will have to manipulate the database on a regular basis. It's also important for us to be able to treat the entire database as an entity, copying and moving instances of an entire Moodle database for the creation of staging and testing areas as we develop our code. We generally do this by using command-line utilities such as mysqldump and MySQL.

Moodle data

Moodle data is the file storage location for user-uploaded content. Moodle data also stores the session data for users logged into the system, if file-based sessions are being used. Moodle data also stores optional language packs that can be downloaded from Moodle's administration interface. Moodle structures the data in this folder by either the user or by the course. Most of the data by file count and size will be in the courses. Each course has a folder, which is named with an integer value. The integer value is set to the internal database ID of the course in question. We can easily determine these values by navigating to a course via the Moodle web interface and inspecting its URL. For example, examine this URL for a course on my local test Moodle

`http://localhost/workspace/moodle19/course/view.php?id=3.`

Note the `id=3` at the end of the URL. If we have uploaded any files to this course, there will be a folder `path_to_moodledata/3`. Within a course folder, Moodle will store module data in the `moddata` folder. When a module needs to store files, it saves them here in a folder with the same name as the module. For example, the wiki module will have a folder here named `wiki`. Additionally, Moodle will create a folder called `backupdata` if any course backups have been created. Any files that have been uploaded directly by a user using the course files interface will be loaded into the root of this folder. Users can also create their own folders and sub folders within the root folder.

Moodle 2.0 uses an entirely new organizational model for user-uploaded files, which is based on a hashing algorithm. The primary goal of this new method is to support efficient use of disk storage space and greater flexibility for using files across multiple courses.

Installing Moodle

There are many ways to install Moodle. One of the simplest ways is to download one of the all-in-one installers from `http://moodle.org`. These are labeled as **Moodle for Windows** and **Moodle for Mac OS X** under the **Downloads** menu at `http://moodle.org`. These all-in-one installers contain both Moodle and all of the necessary server software, including Apache, PHP, and MySQL. While these packages are not recommended for production use, they can provide a convenient starting point for a developer new to Moodle.

To manually install Moodle, download the Moodle source code files from `http://moodle.org`. You will find a variety of download packages. Each package is labeled with the version number. Major versions of Moodle are numbered in tenths: 1.6, 1.7, 1.8, and so on. Major versions focus on adding new features and bug fixes, which require major system changes to be implemented. Each major release has a number of minor point releases. For example: 1.9.1, 1.9.2, 1.9.3, and so on. Minor point releases focus on bug fixes and security updates. Finally, there are 'plus' releases that contain nightly or weekly fixes.

From a developer's perspective, it makes sense to use the official CVS feeds to get Moodle's source code. This allows for easier updates and code merges, as well as integrating with many popular development tools. See `http://docs.moodle.org/en/CVS_for_Administrators`.

Once you have the source code, it needs to be copied to your server's web root. You should then create a folder (outside of the web root) for Moodle data, which is writable by the web server software. From your SQL server, create an empty database for Moodle to use. Finally, once this is done, you should enter the server's address and path to Moodle into your web browser. This will initiate the Moodle web installer and walk you through the rest of the installation options. During the installation you will be asked to enter details for your database. Once these have been entered, Moodle will connect to the database and create all 200+ tables. At the end of the installation it will write a `config.php` file to your Moodle directory with the values that you entered during installation. The following screenshot illustrates the first screen of the Moodle installer, where we select our default language:

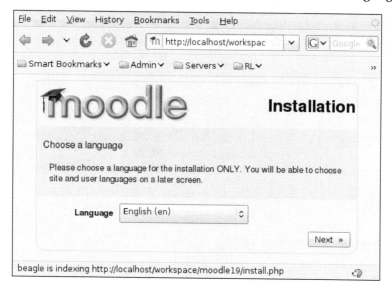

Upgrades follow the same basic pattern. Download the new code, copy it on the server in place of the old code (note that in most cases, you can copy the new code over the top of the old folder contents), and then visit the Moodle site in your web browser. Moodle will detect a version change by comparing the version tags stored in its configuration database against the ones reported in the module code, and then initiate the upgrade. Each module is responsible for its own database upgrades.

The final consideration for our development environment is to have a development tool for writing our code. While it is perfectly possible to write PHP code in any text editor (and many do), a popular option is to use the PHP plugin for Eclipse, or NetBeans. Detailed instructions for optimizing this setup can be found at `http://docs.moodle.org/en/Setting_up_Eclipse_for_Moodle_development`.

Moodle program execution

Moodle has many entry points—scripts that are called for execution. These are the files that are called by the browser to execute Moodle's functions. While there are many, the main ones are:

- `/index.php`: The front page
- `/login/index.php`: The login page
- `/admin/index.php`: The main administration page
- `/course/view.php`: A course page
- `/mod/*/view.php`: A module page

Let's walk through a typical script, and follow the execution path. For the walkthrough, we will use the main course display script, `/course/view.php`. For this example, let's assume that we are using `http://localhost/course/view.php?id=23`.

Before we jump in, let's analyze the URL a bit. The portion up to `/course` will be the URL of your Moodle site. The `/course/` portion is the directory in Moodle that contains the course-handling scripts. The meat of the URL is the portion `view.php?id=23`. This script displays a course page. The course it displays is identified by the `id=23` parameter, where 23 is the data ID of the course in question. If you look in the `course` data table in the database for your Moodle site, you will find an entry with the 'id' field equal to 23. The very first executable line we see in the script is:

```
require_once('../config.php');
```

Executing config.php

All of the entry scripts include the same important file: `config.php`. This is the only file in Moodle that must be included by specifying the exact literal path. This file performs a number of initial parameter assignments in the global `$CFG` variable. This provides the minimal amount of information to run the rest of the system; among this information are the database, web URL, script directory, and data storage directory definitions.

Lastly, and most importantly, `config.php` includes `/lib/setup.php`.

`config.php` performs some basic, important variable assignment, whereas `setup.php` performs all of the initial program execution required to complete the execution environment setup. This includes defining several other important global variables, including $SESSION, $COURSE, $THEME, and $db.

Next, it sets up and connects your database according to the settings defined in `config.php`. Moodle uses the open source ADOdb libraries to manage database functions. These functions are loaded through the inclusion of `/lib/adodb/adodb.inc.php`.

Next, some critical library files are included that will be used by pretty much every other function in Moodle. These libraries include the functions required to manage multibyte strings, HTML output, Moodle data, access controls, events, groups, and general purpose Moodle and PEAR libraries.

The remainder of the file sets up some other critical global variables, loads configuration variables from the database, sets up caching, sessions, environment variables, themes, language, and locales.

Including Moodle libraries

After including `config.php`, our script includes some other library files:

```
require_once('lib.php');
require_once($CFG->libdir.'/blocklib.php');
...
```

This uses the PHP construct `require_once`, in case any of the files were included elsewhere first. Any file not located in the same directory is fully specified using directory definitions defined in `config.php`. You will notice `lib.php` has no directory specification, as it is located in the same directory as `view.php`. Likewise, the remaining files have full paths using directory definitions set up by `config.php`. You will notice the use of $CFG->libdir and $CFG->dirroot. The first is the defined file path to the main library directory (usually the `lib` subdirectory of the Moodle file path), while the second is the defined Moodle file path. Next, our script checks for, and loads, any parameters that it expects to get from the URL:

```
$id        = optional_param('id', 0, PARAM_INT);
$name      = optional_param('name', '', PARAM_RAW);
...
```

It does this by using the Moodle `optional_param` function, which loads the specified variable with a named parameter value if one is present, or a default value if not. If the parameter is required for the script to work properly, then the function `required_param` should be used instead. Both of these functions validate the data based on the specified arguments, and will generate errors or warnings if something other than what was expected is passed in. This is critical to securing user input in case of any additions to Moodle. See Chapter 10, *Writing Secure Code* for more information.

Getting our data

Next, our script loads the specific records that it needs from the database:

```
if (! ($course = get_record('course', 'id', $id)) ) {
    error('Invalid course id');
}
```

This can be done with either a database call, as above, or a specific API call.

At this point, our script has enough information to check if the user has permissions to access its basic functions. This is done by loading contexts, checking the user login, and verifying capabilities:

```
preload_course_contexts($course->id);
if (!$context = get_context_instance(CONTEXT_COURSE,
        $course->id)) {
    print_error('nocontext');
}
require_login($course);
```

Much of the capability verification is performed by the `require_login` function. It verifies that the user is logged in (if necessary — some courses may not require that) and redirects them to the login function if required. It also loads and checks specific capabilities, including whether or not the user has access to the course. It also verifies enrollment and redirects the user to the enrollment function if necessary.

Displaying in Moodle

Next, our script will perform the necessary programming required to carry out its functions. Once it has finished this, it will begin the display process. The main functions for display are the `print_header` and `print_header_simple` functions. The following script uses the `print_header` function from the PAGE object it set up:

```
$PAGE->print_header(get_string('course').': %fullname%', NULL, '',
                $bodytags);
```

This function starts the HTML output by writing the HTTP headers, the theme information, requested JavaScript files, and other header section information. Then it begins with the body section.

The body output is handled by the specific course format. Whatever format has been specified for the course in question in its settings, handles the body output. This is done as follows, by including the file `format.php` from the subdirectory of the format in question:

```
require($CFG->dirroot .'/course/format/'. $course->format .'/
        format.php');
```

If the course used the `topics` format (for example), then the file would be `/course/format/topics/format.php`. This file handles the specific course page output, including the blocks and main content. It uses library functions found in `/course/lib.php` to output the section's content. Lastly, the script outputs the footer:

```
print_footer(NULL, $course);
```

This function closes the body and completes the output to the screen. In most cases, this will be the last function executed for a script.

Configuring Moodle

Moodle is a highly-configurable application, with many complex settings in many areas of its functionality. These settings can be modified by Moodle administrators through:

- Direct code in the main `config.php` file
- The `mdl_config` table via administrative code and interfaces
- The `mdl_config_plugins` table via plugin administration

During program execution, all of the main configuration values are stored in the `$CFG` global variable. `$CFG` is a generic structure. Each configuration variable is an element of the `$CFG` structure. For example, the `$CFG->theme` contains the text name of your site's selected theme.

The elements of `$CFG` are loaded by direct assignment, and from values stored in the database `mdl_config` table. The primary point of direct assignment takes place in `/config.php`. Here, the initial, necessary configuration settings are made.

There are minimal assignments that must be defined in this file. You are prompted for these values when you install Moodle, and you can change them afterwards by editing this file. The minimal settings are as follows:

```
$CFG->dbtype    = 'mysql';      // mysql or postgres7 (for now)
$CFG->dbhost    = 'localhost';  // eg localhost or db.isp.com
$CFG->dbname    = 'moodle';     // database name, eg moodle
$CFG->dbuser    = 'username';   // your database username
$CFG->dbpass    = 'password';   // your database password
$CFG->prefix    = 'mdl_';       // Prefix to use for all table names
$CFG->dbpersist = false;        // Should database connections be
                                //  reused?
$CFG->wwwroot   = 'http://example.com/moodle';
$CFG->dirroot   = '/home/example/public_html/moodle';
$CFG->dataroot  = '/home/example/moodledata';
$CFG->directorypermissions = 02777;
$CFG->admin = 'admin';
```

There are other optional settings that can be made in this file. Review your /config-dist.php file to see all of these settings.

Historically, any configuration settings that did not have a UI available to set these were set via code statements in this file. These often include new, experimental features.

The remainder of the $CFG elements are set from the database. This is done through a call to the library function get_config (located in the /lib/moodlelib.php library file) from /lib/setup.php, which is included as the last action of config.php. The important thing to know about the function get_config is that it will not overwrite any $CFG setting that has already been set. This means you can overrule any database setting by hardcoding it into config.php. Also, config.php clears out the $CFG structure before it does anything else. This guarantees that nothing sets any configuration variables before config.php and setup.php.

Setting configuration variables

As a developer, you can set and use configuration variables for your functionality. You can set a configuration variable through the set_config function. The set_config function takes a name, a value, and an optional plugin name as arguments. The name becomes the element of the $CFG structure and the passed value becomes its value. Additionally, this will be stored into the database mdl_config table, so that it can be loaded on every program execution from then on. You can also specifically request a configuration variable at any time, by using the get_config function, but you won't need to, because it will be loaded into the $CFG structure once it has been set.

The one issue that you need to consider when creating your own configuration variable is that the variable name you choose must be unique. Your variable becomes meaningless if you choose one that already exists. As most customizations you will be developing are likely to be plugins (modules, blocks, and so on), Moodle provides an alternate way to store configuration variables that are plugin specific.

Plugin configuration variables are loaded into the plugin structure itself, rather than into the $CFG global structure. This means that the configuration variable name only needs to be unique to the plugin. Plugin configuration variables are stored in the mdl_config_plugin table, with the name of the plugin. They can be set and retrieved by using the same set_config and get_config functions as before.

Generally, configuration variables are set by using administration interfaces. Most of the Moodle configuration variables are set through the various settings pages in the **Site Administration** menu block, which is visible on the home page of your Moodle site. In future sections, you will learn how the plugins add their interfaces to this structure. The following screenshot displays an example of Moodle's **Site Administration** block:

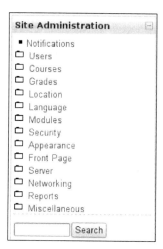

Moodle's API

Moodle's API is a mix of library functions and classes. Moodle was originally based on the version 4 series of PHP, and as such, most of its API is built around functions defined in PHP library files. However, some of the newer constructs of Moodle use object-oriented structures and as such provide extensible classes.

Most of Moodle's main libraries are kept in the /lib/ directory. All of these files generally adhere to the naming convention [function]lib.php. Some of the examples are textlib.php and weblib.php. These library files contain Moodle's API.

Almost all of the core libraries are included in the execution stream when you load `config.php` via its inclusion of `/lib/setup.php`. The `setup.php` file includes these via the following lines:

```
require_once($CFG->libdir .'/textlib.class.php');
// Functions to handle multibyte strings
require_once($CFG->libdir .'/weblib.php');
// Functions for producing HTML
require_once($CFG->libdir .'/dmllib.php');
// Functions to handle DB data (DML)
require_once($CFG->libdir .'/datalib.php');
// Legacy lib with a big-mix of functions.
require_once($CFG->libdir .'/accesslib.php');
// Access control functions
require_once($CFG->libdir .'/deprecatedlib.php');
// Deprecated functions included for backward compatibility
require_once($CFG->libdir .'/moodlelib.php');
// Other general-purpose functions
require_once($CFG->libdir .'/eventslib.php');
// Events functions
require_once($CFG->libdir .'/grouplib.php');
// Groups functions
```

These by no means define all of the functions available in Moodle, and in fact each of these libraries may include other libraries. However, the core of the functions that you will need are contained within these libraries. In fact, the ones that you will need to look at the most are:

- `moodlelib.php`
- `weblib.php`
- `dmllib.php`
- `accesslib.php`
- `grouplib.php`

There are many other libraries that you will use, as you start to carry out specific functions. Most of these are stored in the `/lib/` directory. However, others may be in specific functional areas such as `/course/` and `/blocks/`.

Many of the specific libraries define classes that you can use. Libraries such as `/lib/pagelib.php` and `/lib/formslib.php` define classes that are designed to be extended in order to handle output to screen. `pagelib.php` defines specific page types, with all of the functions necessary to manage page output and create your own page types. Likewise, `formslib.php` defines Moodle's implementation of the PEAR QuickForm classes in order to handle web-based forms.

There is no single, all-encompassing document for all of Moodle's API. However, you can find out more about each specific area in the developer documentation at Moodle Docs. A good place to start is `http://docs.moodle.org/en/Development:` `Developer_documentation#Core_components_that_affect_everything`.

Another resource that can help is the Moodle code cross reference. This is an online resource that is generated from the code and inline comments in order to produce documentation. It is generated automatically by using PHPXref. The reference can be found at `http://docs.moodle.org/en/Development:Code_Cross-Reference`. Note that it may not be up-to-date and maintained. Still, it does provide an easy overview.

Other important libraries

Moodle relies on a number of libraries, both internal and external. Several of these are explained below:

PEAR

PEAR stands for PHP Extension and Application Repository. As such, it's not a single library but a set of tools for getting and updating PHP libraries and modules.

ADOdb

ADOdb is a database library that provides a unified programming interface for a large variety of databases. Although Moodle supports a limited core set of databases for its direct backend, ADOdb really shines through in the supported databases for both the external database authentication and the enrollment plugins.

YUI

The **Yahoo! User Interface (YUI)** library is written in JavaScript, and is used to create rich web interfaces using AJAX, DOM, and DHTML. The Moodle course editing interface relies on this library for drag-and-drop placement of course elements.

XMLDB

XMLDB was added to Moodle as part of the initiative to add Microsoft SQL and Oracle backend support for Moodle. XMLDB rationalized all of the database configuration files to XML schemas, so that the same files could be used across all four supported backends. This extended upon the capabilities available from ADOdb, providing a single code base for accessing all databases supported, while still providing appropriate performance.

Access control, logins, and roles

As open as Moodle is, it is tight with its security. It goes to great efforts to make sure that anyone accessing the system is supposed to be accessing the system, and they are supposed to be accessing it the way they are trying to.

Moodle has a powerful access control and permission system. At the core of the access system is the user account. Although it is possible to grant access to any visitor to your site without authenticating them, it doesn't allow them to do many interesting things. We will assume that you want to know who your users are, and that you will want them to have their own accounts.

A user account provides individual access via a username and password combination. These accounts are created by using authentication plugins. The bare minimum authentication is manual, where a user is created using the administration interface. The next, most common authentication is the e-mail-based system that allows users to create their own accounts using e-mail verification. In either case, a unique username and e-mail address are required as well as a password. Passwords in Moodle are encoded with an MD5 hash function to make them unreadable and difficult to guess.

To get into the system, a user enters their username and password, and if correctly entered, they are granted access to the site. Logging in uses PHP's 'cookie' functions to set cookies into the current session and help identify the user throughout the site visit.

Moodle permission contexts

Permissions can be assigned within six contexts: site/global, course category, course, blocks and activities, user, and front page. There are seven built-in roles: administrator, teacher, non-editing teacher, student, course creator, authenticated user, and guest, all of which can be assigned in any one or more of the above contexts. Any number of customized roles can be created through the list of over 200 system capabilities. Each capability can be assigned one of four access levels: Not Set, Allow, Prohibit, and Prevent. Each user can have multiple roles that inherit permissions from all of the context levels applicable to a given access request from the user. The combination of these provides a powerful and flexible solution for administrators.

The standard system roles are:

- **Administrator**: System administrator has all permissions
- **Course creator**: Can create course shells and can be limited to a course category

- **Teacher:** Can teach a course, develop, and update course content
- **Non-editing teacher**: Can teach a course but can't edit course content
- **Student**: Can take a course
- **Authenticated user**: Any logged in user has this role
- **Guest**: Access permission for non-logged in users

An infinite number of custom roles can be generated by using the Moodle GUI and role definition screens.

To check and force a login from inside your code, a call to `require_login` is used. This function allows you to check if the user is logged in, and forces them to log in if this is required by the element that they are trying to access. For example, you can create a specific activity in a course that requires the user to be logged in. If the user is not logged in, then they will be redirected to the correct login function. This function also remembers what the user was accessing, so they can be returned there once they have successfully logged in.

Contexts are elements in the system associated with the defined context levels. On the code-side, contexts are defined in `/lib/accesslib.php` as follows:

```
define('CONTEXT_SYSTEM', 10);
define('CONTEXT_USER', 30);
define('CONTEXT_COURSECAT', 40);
define('CONTEXT_COURSE', 50);
define('CONTEXT_GROUP', 60);
define('CONTEXT_MODULE', 70);
define('CONTEXT_BLOCK', 80);
```

This means every instance of any of these levels is a context. There is only one 'SYSTEM', but there are many of the others, such as users, courses, and modules.

Capabilities

Capabilities are associated with context levels, and are specific access rules that can be granted to roles. Examples of capabilities are:

- `moodle/site:manageblocks`: Can manage blocks at the site context level
- `moodle/user:viewdetails`: Can view details of a user at the user context level
- `moodle/course:view`: Can view a course at the course context level

As developers, we can create capabilities to control access to our new functionality. Careful consideration should be given as to which context is the best location for a new capability. Capabilities should generally be placed at the lowest context level at which they can function. We will cover these topics in more detail as we work, in the chapters ahead.

Moodle roles

Roles are specific identifiers that are associated with all contexts. Roles are primarily used to group capabilities for a context, so that these capabilities can be given to users. Capabilities are assigned to roles in specific contexts, either by default or by specific assignment (overriding).

Assigning roles

Lastly, users can be assigned to roles in specific contexts. This assignment gives them the accesses defined by the capabilities in that role for that context.

So, to summarize:

- Contexts are specific elements in Moodle
- Roles are associated with all contexts
- Capabilities are assigned to roles in a given context
- Users are assigned roles in a given context

It is the role assignment at the context level being checked, and the capability that role has at that context, which determines whether a user can perform the requested action.

As you develop code for Moodle, you will need to keep this functionality in mind, so that you can design and build the access control that you want for your functions.

Summary

In this chapter, you have started the journey towards becoming a proficient Moodle developer, by studying Moodle's overall architecture. You should now be comfortable with the underlying system requirements to run Moodle, and the major elements that make up a Moodle installation. You have also looked into the process to install and upgrade Moodle with some discussion of our development environment. You have also gained some insights into the program execution for Moodle and the key PHP files that serve as entry points to the system. You have also understood the fundamentals of how Moodle stores its configuration. You now know a bit about both the core internal libraries of Moodle and some of the external library dependencies. Finally, you took a look at Moodle's security and access model.

In the next chapter, you will learn how to create and modify blocks.

2
Creating and Modifying Blocks

Moodle blocks are plugins that load in the right-hand side or left-hand side column of a Moodle site and display information to the user in a rectangular block. Each side column can have zero, one, or multiple blocks loaded. If a column contains no blocks, the column will not be displayed. This allows Moodle to support one, two, or three column page layouts. Examples of built-in Moodle blocks include: HTML content, calendars, menus, and course lists, amongst others.

This chapter covers how to create a basic block in Moodle. This is one of the easiest and most popular customizations. Several basic Moodle programming concepts will be introduced that are used throughout the book. Here are some of the new skills that you will develop:

- Creating a block from scratch
- Managing language files
- Working with capabilities
- Adding instance configuration
- Adding scheduled actions to a block
- Reviewing a real world block
- Using a block as a code container

Creating a block from scratch

We will start our exploration of block plugins by revisiting a programming classic, `Hello World`. Our first block will be about as simple a block as possible, simply displaying the text `Hello World`.

Because our block will be called Hello World, let's start by creating a folder in the `block` folder of our development site called `helloworld`. Inside of this folder, create an empty PHP file called `block_helloworld.php`. Note that the pattern is `module-type_module-name.php`.

We start by creating a new class `block_helloworld` that extends the `block_base` class. Then we create a new `init` function for this class. We set the two required values: the block title and the block version, as follows:

```php
<?php
class block_helloworld extends block_base {
  function init() {
    $this->title   = get_string('helloworld', 'block_helloworld');
    $this->version = 2009050700;
  }//function init
```

Assigning content to our block

Once we have created the `init()` function, all that is left in order to have a functioning block is to assign some content to our block for display in the `get_content()` function. Block content is stored in `$this->content`:

```php
  function get_content() {
    if ($this->content !== NULL) {
      return $this->content;
    }//if
    $this->content       =  new stdClass;
    $this->content->text  = 'Hello World!';
    return $this->content;
  }//function get_content
}//class block_helloworld
?>
```

Now try out the results of our new code, by logging into Moodle with an administrator account. Click on the **Notifications** link in the **Site Administration** block. Moodle then notifies us that it has installed the `[[helloworld]]` block.

Now let's turn on editing, and from the drop-down list of blocks we will see our new block `[[helloworld]]` at the bottom of the list. We then click on it to add an instance of the block to our current page. The results will look similar to the following screenshot:

Adding a language file

Like other plugins in Moodle, blocks can have their own language files to manage their display strings. They are contained within a special `lang` directory within the block's file structure. Moodle uses a hierarchical structure for its language folders. This is designed to allow for parent and child language folders and packs. Language packs are a collection of all of the core language strings needed to support a language. Moodle has an integrated language pack installer, which is used to add language packages for core Moodle. A good example of a parent language folder is `en_utf8`. The name `en_utf8` indicates this is the language folder for English with Unicode encoding. A child language for English is the US dialect. This is designated with the folder name `en_us_utf8`. Moodle allows the child language to inherit strings defined in the parent language. This lets us rapidly develop language support for dialects by minimizing the work to defining only the strings that are different for the sub-dialect. Any strings not defined in the child language will simply be pulled from the parent.

The official documentation for language packs can be found at:

`http://docs.moodle.org/en/Language_packs`

Let's create a folder called `lang` within the `helloworld` folder. Next, we create another folder inside this called `en_utf8`. Each language will have its own folder within `lang`. Inside this folder, create a file with the same name as the block's primary PHP file. In our case, we will call this `block_helloworld.php`. Moodle stores all of its localization strings within a hash array called `$string`. We define our first value for the `$string` hash as follows:

```
<?PHP
$string['helloworld'] = 'Hello World';
?>
```

Our block and block management page (shown in the following screenshot) should now look a lot better:

Hello World		Calendar	2	2007101509	👁		Delete
📷 ✖ ✖ ⬆ ➡		Course/Site Description	0	2007101509	👁		Delete
Hello World!		Courses	3	2007101509	👁		Delete
		Flickr	0	2007101509	👁	Yes (change)	Delete
Blocks		Global Search	0	2008031500	👁		Delete
Add... ⌄		HTML	2	2007101509	👁	Yes (change)	Delete
		Hello World	1	2009050700	👁		Delete

Working with capabilities

In *Chapter 1, Moodle Architecture*, we covered an overview of Moodle's role and permission system. Now we will get a chance to see the system in action. In a later section, we will also add our own access permissions to Moodle.

Testing for built-in capabilities

We use two Moodle core functions to test for a capability, in this section of code. First, we call the `get_context_instance()` function with the site or global context, `CONTEXT_SYSTEM`. The function `get_context_instance()` will return a context object to us for the requested context type, in this case the system context. Once the context is loaded, we use the `require_capability` function to test if the user has the `moodle/site:doanything` capability (essentially, the ability to do anything and everything on the site). `require_capability` tests the current user's capabilities to see if they have the specified capability in the specified context. If they don't, the page is redirected to an error page:

```
function get_content() {
   if ($this->content !== NULL) {
     return $this->content;
   }//if
   $context = get_context_instance(CONTEXT_SYSTEM);
   require_capability('moodle/site:doanything', $context);
   $this->content          =  new stdClass;
   $this->content->text    = 'Hello World!';
   return $this->content;
}//function get_content
```

If we test this same code while logged in as a non-administrative user, we start to see some issues with how the error is handled. This is an example of using `require_capability` incorrectly. When the permission fails, we end up with a partially-rendered Moodle screen. The block bleeds out of its side column and the rest of screen is not printed. The following screenshot illustrates what this looks like if the block is placed in the left-hand side column and viewed by a non-administrative user:

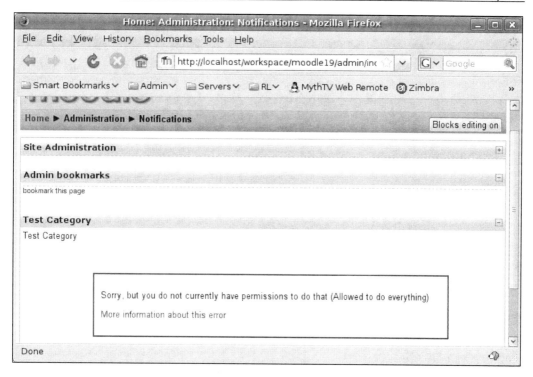

The `require_capability` function is more appropriate for blocking access to an entire page of content. If we want to handle missing capabilities elegantly for a block, we should use the function `has_capability`. Using the following syntax leads to output that works correctly whether or not the user has the required permission. In this case, we use the `has_capability` function, which accepts a capability and a context. It returns a response indicating whether or not the user has access to the capability. We then route the results into an `if/else` clause, which outputs different information to the user depending on whether the capability is present or not.

```
$context = get_context_instance(CONTEXT_SYSTEM);
$this->content = new stdClass;
if (!has_capability('moodle/site:doanything', $context)){
  $this->content->text = 'Not Admin!';
}// if
else {
  $this->content->text = 'Secret Message to Admins!'
}// else
return $this->content;
```

This method is very useful when you want to display different values to the user depending on which capabilities they have access to.

Hiding a block based on capabilities

In many cases, we are only going to want to display the block if the user has a particular capability. By performing some simple restructuring, our `get_content()` function provides this functionality. By moving the creation of the `$this object` and its return value into the `if` statement, we remove the block display if the user doesn't have the `moodle/site:doanything` capability:

```
$context = get_context_instance(CONTEXT_SYSTEM);
if (has_capability('moodle/site:doanything', $context)){
  $this->content          =  new stdClass;
  $this->content->text    = 'Secret Message to Admins!';
  return $this->content;
}// if
```

This method leads to a much cleaner page display, and maximizes the data displayed to the user on any given screen.

Adding your own capability

Let's add a capability, by creating a folder called db within our module. Inside the folder, we create a file called `access.php`. This file is then used to define your capabilities. Here is an example of a simple read capability definition. Capabilities are defined as arrays. Note that the key assignment is the name of the capability `block/helloworld:view`. The other values in the array assignment are used to specify which context the capability applies to, the type of capability, and finally default values for legacy roles.

```
<?php
$block_helloworld_capabilities = array(
   'block/helloworld:view' => array(
       'captype'       => 'read',
       'contextlevel' => CONTEXT_SYSTEM,
       'legacy' => array(
               'guest'           => CAP_PREVENT,
               'student'         => CAP_PREVENT,
               'teacher'         => CAP_PREVENT,
               'editingteacher' => CAP_PREVENT,
               'coursecreator'  => CAP_PREVENT,
               'admin'           => CAP_ALLOW
       )
   )
);
?>
```

In order to make this change take effect, we need to increment our version value in the `block_helloworld.php` file. The format for Moodle version numbers is an integer value of the date (year + month + day) plus two digits to indicate the micro version. The higher the number, the newer the version of the module. Let's set the date of our module to year 2009, month 05, and day 07. This also happens to be the third update to the code for today, so we add a micro version of 03. The following code illustrates the assigning of this version number:

```
$this->version = 2009050703;
```

Note that, as a result of these changes, we should also add some additional strings, as follows, to our language file:

```
$string['helloworld:view'] = 'View Hello World Block';
$string['blockname'] = 'HelloWorld';
```

Let's have a look at the results of these changes, by viewing a role definition in the following screenshot:

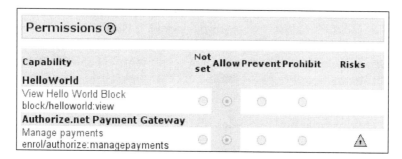

Checking for our new capability

Now that we have added our new capability, we can use it in our block code instead of the `moodle/site:doanything` capability. In this new section of code, the line testing the capability is changed as follows, to use the new one that we created:

```
function get_content() {
  if ($this->content !== NULL) {
    return $this->content;
  }//if
  $context = get_context_instance(CONTEXT_SYSTEM);
  if (has_capability('block/helloworld:view', $context)) {
    $this->content        = new stdClass;
    $this->content->text  = 'Hello World!';
    return $this->content;
  } //if
```

Note that this new capability will work anywhere that we might apply a block: on the front page, on the administration page, in the My Moodle page, within course pages, and so on. However, because we have defined the capability in CONTEXT_SYSTEM only users with a role assigned at the site level will be able to view this block.

In testing, we will find that this block is visible to administrative users, because we set the admin legacy role to have CAP_ALLOW in our access.php file. However, any other built-in roles, even if assigned at the site level, will not see this block, because they have received the CAP_PREVENT permission—unless we manually change their role definition.

We can find further details on the latest methods for programming access permissions at http://docs.moodle.org/en/Development:Roles#Programming_Interface.

Adding instance configuration

We will now add some real functionality to our block by adding the ability to configure what the block will display. This is done by adding another function to the block class. Moodle makes it very simple to add this functionality. With just a few lines of code we will add a full WYSIWYG editing capability for entering the text to be displayed by our block. When completed, our simple Hello World block will have most of the functionality of the built-in HTML block, plus it will have its own capability to control access to who sees the resulting information.

To begin, let's tell Moodle that our block allows each instance to be configured. We do this by adding the instance_allow_config function, and having it return true:

```
function instance_allow_config() {
    return true;
}//function
```

Note that all Moodle modules also support **Global Configuration**, which is covered in *Chapter 3, Creating and Modifying Filters*, on Filter Modules.

Capturing your configuration content

Now we make a config_instance.html file. Add the following text to this file. The first line references and prints a new text string that we will have to add to our language file for the block. This illustrates how simple it is to reference an arbitrary new string in our code. It is important that any code that we create uses this string rather than hardcoding the text in the code. This is necessary for our code to function properly for localization to other languages. The next line prints a textarea input box with the contents, if any, of this instance of the block. The last line displays Moodle's integrated WYSIWYG editor, which is based on the HTMLArea JavaScript editor (this editor is scheduled to be replaced in Moodle 2.0, in order to provide better browser support):

```
<?php print_string('configcontent', 'block_helloworld'); ?>
<?php print_textarea(true, 10, 50, 0, 0, 'text', $this->config->text);
?>
<input type="submit" value="<?php print_string('savechanges') ?>" />
<?php use_html_editor(); ?>
```

Note that this is not a complete HTML form; Moodle pulls in this partial form information and turns it into a complete and functional form for us.

Displaying your content

Finally, we have to edit one line in our `get_content` function. Our original text assignment was:

```
$this->content->text = 'Hello World!';
```

Let's change it to the following new line, which will grab the text entered into the configuration editor and display it in the block:

```
$this->content->text = $this->config->text;
```

In the following screenshot, we see how this new configuration provides not just the ability to enter arbitrary text, but also to format that text by using Moodle's WYSIWYG editor:

The end result of these new changes can be seen in the following screenshot. Notice the edit icon next to the block display, which was added as a result of adding the `instance_allow_config()` function. This version of the block is found in the `helloworld_final` source code folder. While we are still using roughly the same text, we have made it larger, and have formatted it to be bold and italic:

We now have a fully-functional and usable block. At this point, the title Hello World may be the wrong name for our block. With the latest changes it is actually very similar to the core HTML block, but with the addition of its own dedicated capability to control access. Modifying the HTML block to add new capability controls is actually a common project. The HTML block is very powerful because it's the Swiss army knife of blocks. It's not always the most elegant solution to a problem, but it's often possible to put together some HTML in this block in order to quickly and easily make changes to the Moodle interface. Adding a capability control that allows the block to be visible or invisible to certain groups of users adds just enough flexibility to meet a whole new class of common use cases. We can take this basic template and change the context for the capability to work in different situations. This is especially useful if you need to toggle the visibility of a course sticky block, which doesn't currently work with role overrides. This also illustrates how Moodle's API allows us to add a lot of functionality with a small amount of code.

Adding scheduled actions to our block

Moodle's `cron.php` is an administrative process that is run on a scheduled basis to perform maintenance tasks such as e-mail delivery and backups. It is typically run once in every 5 to 15 minutes on most sites. Occasionally, while working with blocks or other plugins, it will be necessary to add some of your own processing to `cron.php`. This is a convenient way of making sure that your module can run background processes without giving the end user a series of complex instructions for a separate cron entry.

To add cron support to our block we just have to set the cron interval in the `init()` function with the following line of code, and define a `cron()` function in our block class:

```
$this->cron = 5;
```

The value assigned to `$this->cron` is the number of seconds between cron runs. It is important to note that no matter what this is set to, the module cron code will only run as frequently as the main site is set to run.

To complete our functionality, we add a `cron()` function. We are just going to print a line of output to confirm that everything is working as expected, as seen in the following code. As we continue to gain new Moodle programming skills, we will expand on this functionality to carry out more useful functions:

```
function cron(){
   print("Hello World is running its cron process.\n");
}//function cron
```

We can test our function by manually running cron by loading `http://my_moodle_domain/admin/cron.php` into our web browser.

Let's review the output of `cron.php`. Note the section "Starting blocks", where we see the output of the print command that we added to the block's `cron()` function.

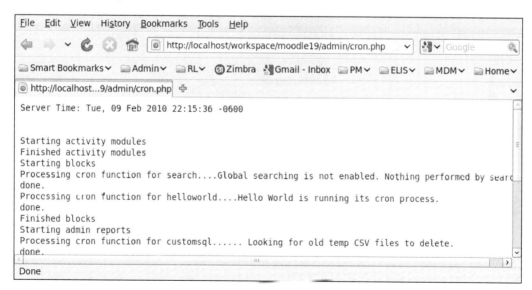

Although this output isn't particularly useful, it does demonstrate how to connect our module with the cron system in order to perform arbitrary actions on a programmed interval. To see a real world example of this concept in action, see the grade categorization block in the Moodle plugin database at: `http://moodle.org/mod/data/view.php?d=13&rid=2068`.

Reviewing a real world block

In this section we will take a look at a real world block. This block was originally created for a large college. It's called the **Instructor Contact Block**. It is designed to make it easier for students to communicate with their instructors. Although we won't cover every line of code, there are a couple of things to pay special attention to. First, we will see a real world example of creating a new block to improve Moodle's functionality. Secondly, we will see how to access some information from a user profile and display it on the screen. Additionally, we will take a quick look at how to gather some configuration data for our block.

Let's have a look at the overall results of the Instructor Contact Block. The following screenshot shows an example of the block configured for an instructor in a course:

The next screenshot shows the settings screen for this block:

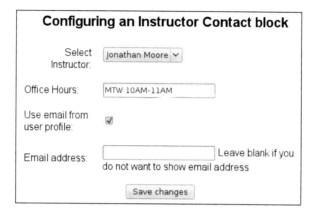

We will now look in more detail at the code that generates this configuration screen.

Reviewing block_instructor_contact.php

Let's start by looking at the main block file, `block_instructor_contact.php`. For space and complexity reasons we will not examine every line of code. This block uses more of the Moodle API to perform its operations. Below we examine parts of the `get_content()` function. Note that we reference the global arrays `$COURSE`, and `$CFG`. We use the `$COURSE` array to reference information from our course, such as pulling up a list of assigned instructors. Also notice that we use `require_once` to include a library file for the block. We can do this any time that we want to separate out library functions that we will use across multiple files in a module, or even from other modules:

```
function get_content() {
  global $COURSE, $CFG;
  require_once($CFG->dirroot . '/blocks/instructor_contact/lib.php');
```

Let's look a little further down in the `get_content` function. In this section, we introduce the `get_complete_user_data()` function, which is used to pull information from the assigned instructor's profile.

```
if (!empty($this->config->selectinstructor)) {
  $user = get_complete_user_data('id', $this->config->
                                 selectinstructor);
```

A little further into the file, we see the end results of pulling the user's data. We can now read the instructor's e-mail address for display, by using $user->email. Note that in the full source code for this block we pull several fields from the profile. Also note that some faculty members wished to have the ability to provide an alternate e-mail address from the one in their profile. The if-else if structure of this section of the code first checks if an alternate value has been provided in the block configuration:

```
if (!empty($this->config->emailoverride)) {
   $email = $this->config->emailoverride;
}//if
else if (!empty($this->config->emailuserdefault)) {
   $email = $user->email;
}
```

Configuring the instructor contact block

The instructor contact block also uses config_instance.html, just like our Hello World block. We load the global $COURSE array so that we can use it in a get_context_instance() function call. We will use the resulting context later in this file to grab a list of all of the instructors for the course:

```
global $COURSE;
$context = get_context_instance(CONTEXT_COURSE, $COURSE->id);
```

In this section, we check for data in two configuration fields. Note the similarity with the method that we use in the Hello World block:

```
$officehours = (!empty($this->config->officehours)) ?
   $this->config->officehours : '';
$emailoverride = (!empty($this->config->emailoverride)) ?
   $this->config->emailoverride : '';
```

Because a course may have more than one instructor, our Instructor Contact Block needs to have an option to pick which instructor's information to display. An instructor is defined as any user with the capability gradereport/grader:view. To get our list of instructors we call the get_users_by_capability function. We then take the results and iterate with a foreach loop to create a pull-down menu for the user to select which instructor's information to display.

```
$users = get_users_by_capability($context,'gradereport/grader:view',
'u.id, u.username, u.firstname, u.lastname',
'u.lastname ASC, u.firstname ASC', '', '', '', '', false);
foreach ($users as $user) {
   if ($this->config->selectinstructor == $user->id) {
```

```
      echo '<option value="'.$user->id.'" selected="selected">' .
      fullname($user) . '</option>';
    }
  else {
    echo '<option value="'.$user->id.'">' . fullname($user) .
'</option>';
```

We can see in the case of our real world block that there is a bit more complexity. We also see how to access some additional functionality that Moodle provides to plugin authors.

Using a block as a code container

Sometimes we will want to make additions to Moodle that don't necessarily have a user interface, or at least a block interface. In these situations we can still benefit from creating a block. Firstly, the block is one of the simplest plugins that we can make for Moodle. Secondly, blocks have a simple, well-understood installation procedure. Moodle also provides many facilities for plugins, such as configuration and database storage. And finally, it gives us a simple and standardized method for dealing with version upgrades.

Let's take a look at the repository block, which is part of a suite of additions to Moodle that we call the **Enterprise Learning Intelligence Suite (ELIS)**. The repository block is never used to display content. It simply acts as a storage container for capabilities associated with the Alfresco integration. The Alfresco integration itself is a separate set of functions contained in its own directory. Alfresco is a popular and powerful open source document management system written in Java.

Creating a block stub for our container

Let's take a look at some code. In this first section of code we are looking at the block's main file, `block_repository.php`. This file uses the **PHPDoc** format for commenting code, which can be used with tools like **PHPXref** to automatically generate documentation. In our initial function, we again define the minimum values for a block: title and version:

```
<?php // $Id: block_repository.php,v 1.2 2009/04/22 15:14:08 jfilip
Exp $
/**
 * Class for the repository control block.
 *
 * @version $Id: block_repository.php,v 1.2 2009/04/22 15:14:08 jfilip
Exp $
 * @author Open Knowledge Technologies - http://www.oktech.ca/
```

```
   * @author Remote Learner - http://www.remote-learner.net/
   * @author Justin Filip <jfilip@oktech.ca>
   */

 class block_repository extends block_base {
   function block_repository() {
     $this->title   = get_string('blockname', 'block_repository');
     $this->version = 2009042100;
     } //function block_repository
```

In the final section of our main file, we make sure that our block content is set to blank values so that the block will never display on screen:

```
 function get_content() {
   if($this->content !== NULL) {
     return $this->content;
   }
   $this->content = new stdClass;
   $this->content->text   = '';
   $this->content->footer = '';
   return $this->content;
 }
```

Creating capabilities for our container

As we can see, there is not much happening in the main block file. This is evidence of the fact that we are just using the block structure as a container. Next, let's take a look at the functional component of the block, which is defined in the db folder. We have a single file defined called access.php. This functions just as it does in our Hello World block. We simply define an array of access capabilities. Note that in the case of this block, we are using the riskbitmask value in the array. This provides the administrator with information about the risk associated with giving this capability to a particular role:

```
 $block_repository_capabilities = array(
     'block/repository:createsitecontent' => array(
        'riskbitmask' => RISK_XSS| RISK_DATALOSS,
        'captype' => 'write',
        'contextlevel' => CONTEXT_SYSTEM,
        'legacy' => array(
           'admin' => CAP_ALLOW
        )
     ),
```

Summary

In this chapter you have added to your arsenal of Moodle coding techniques the ability to create new blocks. You have learned how to manage language files to add localization support to your plugins. You have also learned much about how to leverage Moodle's permission system by using and even adding capabilities. You created your first data input screen to capture user input and redisplay it, in a Hello World block. You also explored how Moodle schedules tasks to be completed: in the background, on a set interval. Finally you looked at a couple of real world examples of blocks in action, including using a block as a container.

In the next chapter, you will learn about filters.

3
Creating and Modifying Filters

Moodle filters modify content from the database as it is output to the screen, thus adding function to the display. An example of this is the **multimedia** filter, which can detect references to video and audio files, and can replace them with a "mini-player" embedded in the content. This chapter will cover the basic concepts of creating a Moodle filter, which includes:

- How a filter works
- Using the API to create filter code
- How to use language files
- How to create configuration settings

How a filter works

Before trying to build a filter, it would help to understand how it works. To begin with, any text written to the screen in Moodle should be processed through the `format_text` function. The purpose of this function is to process the text, such that it is always safe to be displayed. This means making sure there are no security issues and that any HTML used contains only allowed tags.

Additionally, the output is run through the `filter_text` function, and this is the function we are interested in. This function takes the text destined for the screen, and applies all enabled filters to it. The resulting text will be the result of all of these filters.

`filter_text` applies each enabled filter to the text in the order defined in the filter configuration screen (shown in the following screenshot). The order is important; each filter will be fed the output of the previous filter's text. So it is always possible that one filter may change the text in a way that impacts the next filter.

Manage filters

Active filters

Name	Disable/Enable	Up/Down	Settings
Multimedia Plugins	👁	↓	Settings
Multi-Language Content	👁	↑	Settings
Database Auto-linking	👁		
Glossary Auto-linking	👁		
Resource Names Auto-linking	👁		
Wiki Page Auto-linking	👁		
Activity Names Auto-linking	👁		
Algebra Notation	👁		
Word Censorship	👁		Settings
Email Protection	👁		
TeX Notation	👁		Settings
Tidy	👁		

Changes in table above are saved automatically.

Building a filter

Now it's time to build our own filter. To begin with, let's come up with a requirement.

Let's assume that our organization, called "Learning is Fun", has a main website at `http://2fun2learn.org`. Now, we need any instance of the phrase **learning is fun** to be hyperlinked to the website URL every time it appears on the screen, as in the forum post shown in the following screenshots:

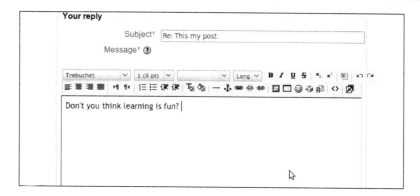

We can do this by implementing a policy with our content creators that forces them to create hyperlink tags around the phrase every time they write it. However, this will be difficult to enforce and will be fraught with errors. Instead, wouldn't it be easier if the system itself could recognize the phrase and create the hyperlink for us?

That's what our filter will do.

Getting started

We need a name for our filter. It is the name that will be used for the directory the filter will reside in. We want a name that will describe what our filter does and will be unlikely to conflict with any other filter name. Let's call it "learningisfunlink".

To start with, create a new subdirectory in the `/filter` directory and call it `learningisfunlink`. Next, create a new file called `filter.php`. This is the only file required for a filter.

Open the new `filter.php` file in your development environment. The filter only requires one function, which is named after the filter name and suffixed with `_filter`. Add the PHP open and close tags (`<?php` and `?>`), and an empty function called `learningisfunlink_filter` that takes two arguments: a course ID and the text to filter. When completed, you should have a file that looks like this:

```php
<?php
  function learningisfunlink_filter($courseid, $text) {
    return $text;
  }
?>
```

We now have the bare minimum required for the filter to be recognized by the system. It doesn't do what we want yet, but it will be present.

Creating the language file

Log in to the site (that makes use of your new filter) as an administrator. On the main page of your site, look for the **Modules | Filters** folder in the **Site Administration** block. Click on the **Manage filters** link. If you have the default filter setup, you will see your new filter near the bottom of the list, called **Learningisfunlink**, as shown in the following screenshot:

Manage filters

Active filters

Name	Disable/Enable	Up/Down	Settings
Multimedia Plugins	👁	↓	Settings
Multi-Language Content	👁	↑	Settings
Database Auto-linking	👁		
Glossary Auto-linking	👁		
Resource Names Auto-linking	👁		
Wiki Page Auto-linking	👁		
Activity Names Auto-linking	👁		
Algebra Notation	👁		
Word Censorship	👁		Settings
Email Protection	👁		
Learningisfunlink	👁		
TeX Notation	👁		Settings
Tidy	👁		

Changes in table above are saved automatically.

Now, even though the name is reasonably descriptive, it will be better if it were a phrase similar to the others in the list; something like **Main website link**.

To do this, we need to create a new directory in our `/filter/learningisfunlink` directory called `lang/en_utf8/` (the `en_utf8` is the language specific part—English in this case). In this directory, we create a new file called `filter_learningisfunlink.php`. This name is the concatenation of the phrase `filter_` and the name of our filter.

In this file, we need to add the following line:

```
$string['filtername'] = "Main website link";
```

This language string defines the text that will be displayed as the name of our filter, replacing the phrase **Learningisfunlink** that we saw earlier with **Main website link**. This file will contain any other strings that we may output to the screen, specifically for this filter.

Once we have created this file, returning to the **Manage filters** page should now show our filter with the name that we provided for it in our language file.

 At the time of writing, a bug was found to exist within the plugin filter language directories that prevented the language string from being displayed in the filters table. Refer to `http://tracker.moodle.org/browse/MDL-17684` for more information. If you really want this to work properly, copy the filter language file into your main language directory and remove the text `filter_` from the filename.

Creating the filter code

We now have a filter that is recognized by the system and that displays the name we want it to. However, we haven't made it do anything. Let's create the code to add some functionality.

Remember, what we want this filter to do is to search the text and add a hyperlink pointing to our website for all occurrences of the phrase "learning is fun". We could simply perform a search and replace function on the text and return it, and that would be perfectly valid. However, for the sake of learning more about the Moodle API, we'll use some functions that are set up specifically for filters. To that end, we'll look at two code constructs: the `filterobject` class and the `filter_phrases` function, both of which are contained in the `/lib/filterlib.php` file.

The `filterobject` class defines an object that contains all of the information required by the `filter_phrases` function to change the text to the way the filter wants it to be. It contains the phrase to be filtered, the tag to start the replacement with, the tag to end the replacement with, whether to match case, whether a full match is required, and any replacement text for the match.

An array of `filterobjects` is sent to the `filter_phrases` function, along with the text to search in. It's intended to be used when you have a number of phrases and replacements to apply at one time, but we'll use it anyway.

Let's initialize our filter strings:

```
$searchphrase = "learning is fun";
$starttag = "<a href=\"http://2fun2learn.org\">";
$endtag = "</a>";
```

Now, let's create our `filterobject`:

```
$filterobjects = array();
$filterobjects[] = new filterobject($searchphrase, $starttag, $endtag);
```

Lastly, let's pass the structure to the `filter_phrases` function, along with the text to be filtered:

```
$text = filter_phrases($text, $filterobjects);
```

Our function now has the code to change any occurrence of the phrase "learning is fun" to a hyperlinked phrase. Let's go test it.

Activating the filter

In our test course, let's add some text containing the phrase "learning is fun" and see how the filter works. The easiest way to do this is to add a label. Turn on editing in your course and select **Insert a label** from the **Add a resource...** drop-down menu. Enter the text **Don't you think learning is fun in this course?** into the editor box and save the link. Our label should now be displayed with the text that we entered, but our phrase isn't hyperlinked.

The reason that our filter isn't working is that we first need to activate it. Navigate back to the main page of your site, open the **Modules | Filters** folder in the **Site Administration** block, and click on the **Manage filters** link. Look for the row with our filter in it, and click on the closed eye icon in the **Disable/Enable** column. This will change the icon to an open eye, indicating that our filter is now enabled, as shown in the following screenshot:

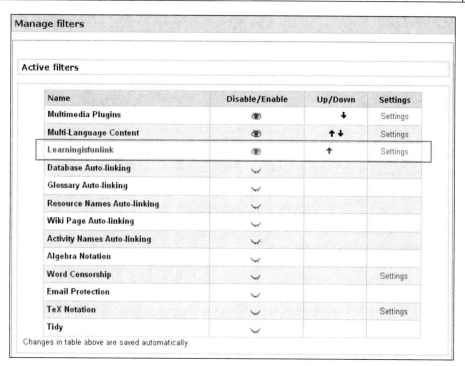

Return to the course where we added our label and see if the filter is now working. We should now see our phrase **Don't you think learning is fun in this course?** with the **learning is fun** part linked to our site. This is the active filter at work!

Adding configuration settings

Our filter now does what we want it to do. However, what if we want to link a different phrase, or change where the phrase is linked to? We'd need to recode the filter. Instead, let's add some configurable settings.

Navigate back to the **Manage filters** page via the **Site Administration** block. Notice that many of the filters have a **Settings** link in the last column. If you click on any one of the links, you will see a form that lets you enter configuration information for that filter. We need to create one for our filter that lets us specify a phrase to link and the URL to link to.

To create configuration settings for our filter, we need to add a file called
`filtersettings.php` to our filter directory. Create this file in our `/filter/`
`learningisfunlink` directory. Once you have created this file, if you go back to
the **Manage filters** page you will see that our filter now has a **Settings** link. Moodle
has noticed the file and created the link for us. Now we just need to make it do
something useful.

Moodle provides a library specifically for these types of `settings` files. These
functions are contained in a number of class definitions in the `/lib/adminlib.php`
file. Look through the file to familiarize yourself with what's there.

Our `settings` file will be included into a main function. We need to add our options
to this function. We do this by adding what we need to a `$settings` variable that
Moodle has set up for us. This variable is an object of the class `admin_settingpage`
and is created in the `/admin/settings/plugins.php` file, which is the file that
includes our `settings` file.

We need to add a couple of form text inputs that will allow us to configure our filter.
We will do this using the `admin_setting_configtext` class. Add the following lines
to the `filtersettings.php` file:

```
$settings->add(new
admin_setting_configtext('filter_learningisfunlink_phrase',
get_string('phrase','filter_learningisfunlink'),
get_string('phraseconfig', 'filter_learningisfunlink'),
get_string('phrasedefault', 'filter_learningisfunlink')));
$settings->add(new
admin_setting_configtext('filter_learningisfunlink_link',
get_string('link','filter_learningisfunlink'),
get_string('linkconfig', 'filter_learningisfunlink'),
get_string('linkdefault', 'filter_learningisfunlink')));
```

These functions define the text inputs, so that the values will be stored in the
specified configuration variables: `filter_learningisfunlink_phrase` and
`filter_learningisfunlink_link`.

We've also used some new language strings here, so add the following lines to the
`/filter/learningisfunlink/lang/en_utf8/filter_learningisfunlink.php` file:

```
$string['link'] = "URL";
$string['linkconfig'] = "URL to link phrase to";
$string['linkdefault'] = "http://2fun2learn.org";
$string['phrase'] = "Phrase";
$string['phraseconfig'] = "Phrase to hyperlink";
$string['phrasedefault'] = "learning is fun";
```

Now, navigate back and look at the `settings` file by clicking on the **Settings** link for our filter on the **Manage filters** page. You should see a form, as shown in the following screenshot:

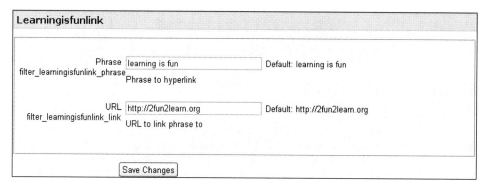

That's all we needed to do. We can now change these settings to anything we want, and save them. You can verify this by making changes, saving them, moving away from the page, and then going back to it. The settings should then reflect what you saved.

Using our settings

We have added functionality that allows us to configure our filter with our own phrase and link, but our code still has these settings hardcoded. In order for these to be useful, we need to use them in our code.

Open up our main filter file (`/filter/learningisfunlink/filter.php`) and change the first three lines of code to the following:

```
global $CFG;
if (!isset($CFG->filter_learningisfunlink_phrase)) {
  set_config( 'filter_learningisfunlink_phrase',
  get_string('phrasedefault', 'filter_learningisfunlink'));
}
if (!isset($CFG->filter_learningisfunlink_link)) {
  set_config( 'filter_learningisfunlink_link',
  get_string('linkdefault', 'filter_learningisfunlink'));
}
$searchphrase = $CFG->filter_learningisfunlink_phrase;
$starttag     = "<a href=\"{$CFG->filter_learningisfunlink_link}\">";
$endtag       = "</a>";
```

Our saved settings are now part of Moodle's global $CFG object variable. The name that we gave them in the settings file is the property of the $CFG object that we use. So for our use, we need to look at $CFG->filter_learningisfunlink_phrase and $CFG->filter_learningisfunlink_link.

The first two if structures check to see if we have saved the configuration settings yet. If not, they are saved with the default values stored in our language file. The next two lines use these settings instead of the old hardcoded strings. Our filter should now work with our configured settings.

Try it out! Change the link value and then look at the label that we created in our test course. The link should now be whatever you specified in the settings. Change the phrase to something different, such as "fun in this course". Now look at the label and see which part of the phrase is linked.

You now have a flexible filter that can link any specified text to any specified URL!

Summary

In this chapter you have learned about filters and created a working example. You have used Moodle's filter API to easily manage text filtering. And, you have learned how to create and use filter configuration settings. You should study other filter examples in Moodle to see the many other things that filters can do.

In the next chapter, we will learn about activity modules and create our own.

4

Creating and Modifying Activity Modules

Moodle activities are plugins that provide instructional activities for learners. One or more activities of each type can be added to courses, and these typically have a graded component that sends results to the Moodle gradebook.

This chapter covers how to create a fully-functional Moodle activity. Topics include:

- Creating an activity using the NEWMODULE template
- Files required for an activity module
- Form setup
- Talking to the gradebook
- Groups support
- Upgrading the database
- Course reset
- Backup and restore

The scope of creating an activity module

As we start to make an activity module, it's important to note that activity modules are inherently more complex than both blocks and filters. An activity module has roughly ten required PHP files, over a dozen functions, three sub folders, and an icon graphic. This is in sharp contrast to the other module types that we created in earlier chapters. Following is a listing of the structure of an empty activity module. We will flesh out each component of the listing as we progress through the chapter:

- `./README.txt`
- `./lib.php`

- `./restorelib.php`
- `./lang`
- `./lang/en_utf8`
- `./lang/en_utf8/foo.php`
- `./lang/en_utf8/help`
- `./lang/en_utf8/help/newmodule`
- `./lang/en_utf8/help/newmodule/index.html`
- `./lang/en_utf8/help/newmodule/mods.html`
- `./version.php`
- `./mod_form.php`
- `./backuplib.php`
- `./submit_form.php`
- `./view.php`
- `./icon.gif`
- `./index.php`
- `./db`
- `./db/access.php`
- `./db/upgrade.php`
- `./db/install.xml`

See `http://docs.moodle.org/en/Development:Modules` for the official project documentation on activity module development.

Included in this chapter's source code files is an empty template folder for starting a new activity module. The folder is named NEWMODULE.

Most new modules are created by using the NEWMODULE template, which is a contributed module. This means that the module is not part of the Moodle core distribution, but has been donated to the Moodle project under the same GPL. The module can be downloaded from `http://moodle.org/mod/data/view.php?d=13&rid=715&filter=1`. NEWMODULE is a useful starting point for creating our activity. However, it does miss a few important functional requirements. The most notable of these is the lack of backup and restore functionality. The code in this chapter, while based on NEWMODULE, also includes adapted components from other core modules, especially in places where NEWMODULE is incomplete. This method of examining the core code, as a way to learn how Moodle works, is common practice in the Moodle development community. In the next section, we will describe the features of the module that we will be creating in this chapter.

Our module—activity Foo!

We are going to call our sample module activity "Foo!". It will include support for gradebook connectivity, course groups, course reset, and backup and restore. Another design element of this chapter's activity module is to be as simple as possible, while still being fairly comprehensive. Even though backup and restore support is very important for a good user experience, many third-party modules do not include this due to it not being included in NEWMODULE. However, most experienced Moodle administrators will not use an activity module if it does not provide working backup and restore. If we want our activity to be widely used, it is important to make sure backup and restore works. Following is a screenshot of the finished Foo! activity. In the next section, we will get started with the template.

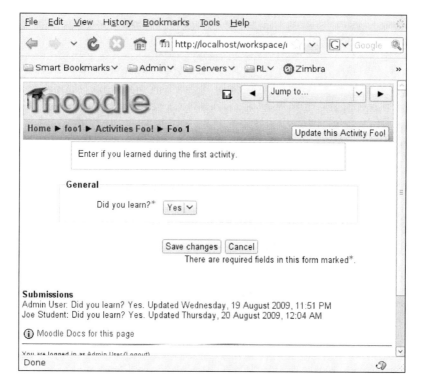

Getting started with the NEWMODULE template

Let's start by downloading a copy of the NEWMODULE template. You can do this either by using the source code included with the book, or by accessing the contributed downloads at `http://moodle.org/`. Note that the code for NEWMODULE is included in the chapter's source code folder, in order to provide a comparison of the version used to develop this example. New development should be done by using the newest version of the module provided at the specified link. Next, we will rename the folder to the name of our new module. We are going to name our folder `foo`. Then, we need to use our development environment to perform a global search and replace on the folder's contents. Note that it is a common feature of development environments to be able to replace a particular string throughout an entire directory structure. What we want to do is find any text 'newmodule' and replace it with the text 'foo'. Alternately, if our development environment doesn't support global search and replace, then we could perform a search and replace on each document as we go through each file, or we can make the changes manually as we review the text of the sample code. Next, we need to rename the language file to the module name. Look in the `lang/en_utf8` folder for a file named `newmodule.php`. We need to rename it to `foo.php`. Now, we are ready to move the entire folder into the `/mod` folder of our development site. In the next section, we start by making the form for creating new activity instances. Let's start coding!

Completing mod_form.php

The file `mod_form.php` provides the form when a new module instance is created. This form captures the user input for any settings that we want to save on creation of a new activity. We will be creating our form by extending the `moodleform_mod` class. This is the standard method for providing a new activity form.

The following two lines of code include the necessary library file that defines the `moodleform_mod` class, and then creates our extended class `mod_foo_mod_form`. The general form of this definition is `mod_<MODULE NAME>_mod_form`:

```
require_once ($CFG->dirroot.'/course/moodleform_mod.php');
class mod_foo_mod_form extends moodleform_mod {
```

Following is an example of a form generated with the `moodleform_mod` class. This is from the settings page for the assignment module from the Moodle core:

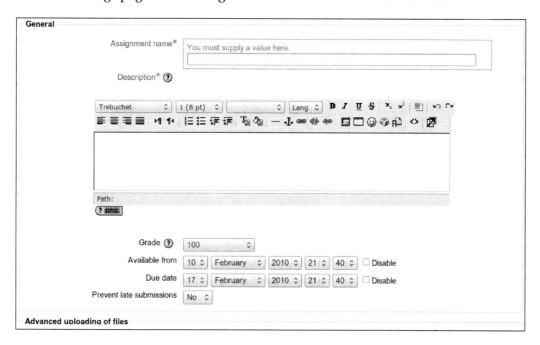

Our form will define some general elements: instructions, title or name, grade, outcomes, group mode, visible indicator, and grade category. Note that all of this is accomplished by defining a single function `definition`:

```
function definition() {
global $COURSE, $CFG;
```

Next, we define an instance of our new class and define elements of the instance, which will control how our form displays and what input elements it contains:

```
// Create form instance
$mform  =& $this->_form;
```

This section of code creates the form header and will be present in any form that we create by using the Moodle forms library. Note that the forms library is discussed in greater detail in *Chapter 13, Building Forms with formslib,* when we discuss formslib.

```
$mform->addElement('header', 'general', get_string('general', 'form'));
```

Next we will cover how to define our input values.

Defining input values

In this section of code, we set the name of the activity. Note that the input element is controlled by the value of the `setType` element, and any UI rules are defined by setting `addRule`. Also, note that the value set for the second parameter, `name` in this case, should be set to the corresponding field name in our database. The form library will take care of making sure that the values entered go into the correct place in the database as long as the field name is set correctly:

```
$mform->addElement('text', 'name', get_string('fooname', 'foo'),
                   array('size'=>'64'));
$mform->setType('name', PARAM_TEXT);
$mform->addRule('name', null, 'required', null, 'client');
```

Next we see an example of using the `htmleditor` element to gather the instructions for our activity:

```
$mform->addElement('htmleditor', 'instructions',
                   get_string('instructions', 'foo'));
$mform->setType('instructions', PARAM_RAW);
$mform->addRule('instructions', get_string('required'), 'required',
                null, 'client');
```

Here we set up a help button for the `instructions` form element:

```
$mform->setHelpButton('instructions', array('questions', 'richtext'),
                      false, 'editorhelpbutton');
```

In this section, we gather date data to control when the activity is available to learners:

```
// Dates available settings
$mform->addElement('date_time_selector', 'timeavailable',
                   get_string('timeavailable', 'foo'),
                   array('optional'=>true));
$mform->setDefault('timeavailable', 0);
$mform->addElement('date_time_selector', 'timedue',
                   get_string('timedue', 'foo'),
                   array('optional'=>true));
$mform->setDefault('timedue', 0);
$mform->addElement('date_time_selector', 'timeavailable',
                   get_string('timeavailable', 'foo'),
                   array('optional'=>true));
$mform->setDefault('timeavailable', 0);
$mform->addElement('date_time_selector', 'timedue',
                   get_string('timedue', 'foo'),
                   array('optional'=>true));
$mform->setDefault('timedue', 0);
```

In the next few lines, we make use of the `modgrade` element to create a menu that lets the user select the point value for the activity. This value will be used to set the points earned in the gradebook:

```
$mform->addElement('modgrade', 'scale', get_string('grade'), false);
$mform->disabledIf('scale', 'assessed', 'eq', 0);
```

Using common form elements

Finally, we wrap up the form by setting some common module elements. The values set in the `features` array are passed into `standard_coursemodule_elements`, which controls the display of multiple form elements. This method is a real time saver versus manually making the form elements:

```
$features = array('groups'=>true, 'groupings'=>true,
                  'groupmembersonly'=>true,'outcomes'=>false,
                  'gradecat'=>false, 'idnumber'=>false);
$this->standard_coursemodule_elements($features);
$this->add_action_buttons();
```

We have completed our new instance form and can now move on to the `version.php` file. The following screenshot shows an example of how Moodle renders this form:

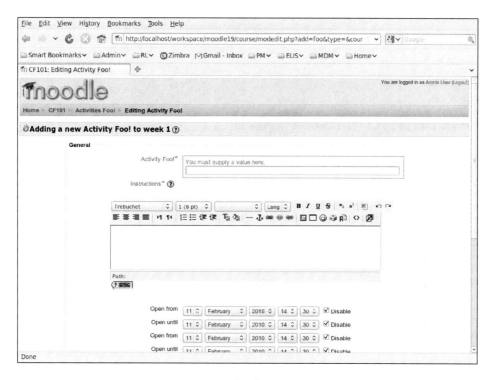

Making version.php

This file works exactly as we have discussed in prior chapters. It is used to manage database upgrades and enforce required versions of Moodle. This file takes on greater importance for activity modules because they are more data intensive than earlier modules. In the code sample below, we define the current version of the module and the version of Moodle required to run the module:

```
$module->version  = 2009060103;
$module->requires = 2007101509;
$module->cron     = 0;
```

In our next section, we will cover how to add a custom icon to the module.

Setting icon.gif

In this chapter, we use an icon of a fire to represent activity Foo!. A fire symbol is used tongue-in-cheek to emphasize that new and untested code can be dangerous. The icon used is from `http://ekstasis.net/web/htr/icon_sites` and is licensed under the LGPL. It was resized from a 32x32 icon to the standard 16x16 size for Moodle. The icon appears as shown below:

With the new icon in place, it's time to set up our module's database!

Generating install.xml

`install.xml` defines the database structure for the module. It is recommended that we start with the basic `install.xml` file from the NEWMODULE template. From there, we can use either an XML editor or a text editor to customize the database to our specific needs.

Using the XMLDB editor

The recommended method to edit the database structure is to use the XMLDB editor from the **Site Administration | Miscellaneous** menu. This editor allows us to quickly and easily make changes. Although we could easily hand-edit the file, the XMLDB editor makes it an easier and less error-prone process. The editor is especially useful for making upgrades to our database schema as we release new versions of the module. It provides both a new XML file and the PHP code to run in our `update.php` file. We will cover the `update.php` file in an upcoming section. Following is a screenshot of the XMLDB editor in action.

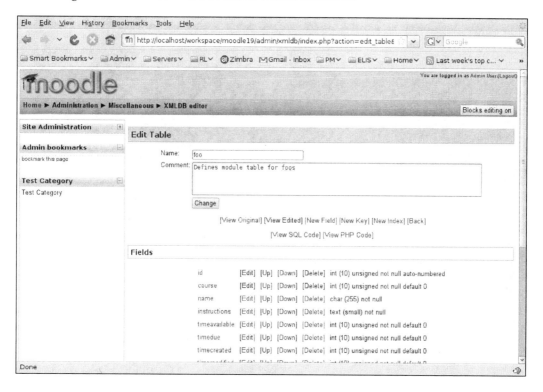

Defining our activity database

Every activity module is required to have at least one table. The table name must be the same as the module name. In our case, that is `foo`. Using the default Moodle `config.php` settings, we end up with a table named `mdl_foo`. Generally, each module table will have at least the following fields defined: `id`, `name`, `intro`, and `modifiedtime`. These are the minimal fields required. Our sample module will define a few more fields needed for the purposes of module Foo!, but they are not mandatory requirements for other modules that we might create. The additional fields include: `course`, `timeavailable`, `timedue`, and `scale`.

The initial section defines the database tables. It uses a standard nested XML structure. The <TABLES> tag denotes the table definition section. Each table starts with a <TABLE> tag. Each field is indicated by a starting <FIELD> tag. The field characteristics are defined within the <FIELD> tag using notations that should be familiar to anyone who has worked with SQL before:

```
<TABLES>
  <TABLE NAME="foo" COMMENT="Defines module table for foos"
    NEXT="foo_responses">
   <FIELDS>
   <FIELD NAME="id" TYPE="int" LENGTH="10" NOTNULL="true"
    UNSIGNED="true" SEQUENCE="true" ENUM="false" NEXT="course"/>
```

Defining the foo_responses table

Next, we need to add a new table not included in the NEWMODULE template, called foo_responses. This table contains the following fields: id, fooid, userid, response, and timemodified. It is used to track the actual response data for our module. This table will store one record for each user response in each foo activity instance:

```
<TABLE NAME="foo_responses" COMMENT="foos submitted by users"
    PREVIOUS="foo">
   <FIELDS>
   <FIELD NAME="id" TYPE="int" LENGTH="10" NOTNULL="true"
    UNSIGNED="true" SEQUENCE="true" ENUM="false" NEXT="fooid"/>
   <FIELD NAME="fooid" TYPE="int" LENGTH="10" NOTNULL="true"
    UNSIGNED="true" DEFAULT="0" SEQUENCE="false" ENUM="false"
    PREVIOUS="id" NEXT="userid"/>
   <FIELD NAME="userid" TYPE="int" LENGTH="10" NOTNULL="true"
    UNSIGNED="true" DEFAULT="0" SEQUENCE="false" ENUM="false"
    PREVIOUS="fooid" NEXT="response"/>
   <FIELD NAME="response" TYPE="text" LENGTH="small"
    NOTNULL="true" SEQUENCE="false" ENUM="false"
    PREVIOUS="userid" NEXT="timemodified"/>
   <FIELD NAME="timemodified" TYPE="int" LENGTH="10"
    NOTNULL="true" UNSIGNED="true" DEFAULT="0" SEQUENCE="false"
    ENUM="false" PREVIOUS="response"/>
   </FIELDS>
    <KEYS>
      <KEY NAME="primary" TYPE="primary" FIELDS="id"/>
    </KEYS>
    <INDEXES>
      <INDEX NAME="userid" UNIQUE="false" FIELDS="userid"/>
    </INDEXES>
  </TABLE>
</TABLES>
```

Defining log types

In the next section, we define the database statements that are used to store user log data for a user's interaction with the module. The defaults are to create a view, add, and update action for each module. You can add additional action types for more logging, as required. In the case of activity Foo!, we only need the defaults:

```
<STATEMENTS>
  <STATEMENT NAME="insert log_display" TYPE="insert"
   TABLE="log_display" COMMENT="Initial insert of records on table
   log_display">
    <SENTENCES>
      <SENTENCE TEXT="(module, action, mtable, field) VALUES
                     ('foo', 'view', 'foo', 'name')" />
      <SENTENCE TEXT="(module, action, mtable, field) VALUES
                     ('foo', 'add', 'foo', 'name')" />
      <SENTENCE TEXT="(module, action, mtable, field) VALUES
                     ('foo', 'update', 'foo', 'name')" />
```

Note that we need to increment our version in `version.php` each time we update this file. We also have to create a new section in the `update.php` file if the module has already been distributed to users. During development, we can either create the appropriate section in `update.php`, or we can delete the module from Moodle and let it reload from scratch. A reload will cause the module to recreate the database using the new format. However, this has the unfortunate side effect of deleting any existing test module instances that you may have already created.

Creating access.php

As with the other module types that we have discussed, the `access.php` file controls which capabilities can be assigned for user access. For our `foo` module we are going to create two capabilities: one to allow response submission `mod/foo:submit`, and another capability to view all responses. Note that while our example doesn't implement this due to space reasons, it is good practice to include a capability to control who can do the grading. These are in the exact same format as the prior examples.

Updating index.php

The `index.php` file lists all of the instances of our activity that are present in the course. These are typically displayed in a tabular format with one row per activity instance, and with a column each for name, intro, and possibly some response data. For activity Foo!, we are displaying the value stored in the response for the individual user to the question "Did you learn?". Again, we will just focus on the changes being made to the template to make this happen.

Adding clean language strings

There are a few places in the NEWMODULE template where strings are hardcoded in the output. We need to change these to use `get_string`. Around line 44 of the `/mod/foo/index.php` file, we need to make a one-line correction. This is very important to allow your module to support localization for other languages:

```
notice(get_string('thereareno', 'moodle', $strfoos),
       "../../course/view.php?id=$course->id");
```

We have covered Moodle's language file system in depth in Chapters 1, 2, and 3, so we won't reprint the entire `foo.php` language file in this chapter. To see a detailed listing of the language file, refer to the `/mod/foo/lang/en_utf8/foo.php` file in the source code download.

Looking up response data

Around line 50 of the template, we need to add some code to look up our response data. First, we set up our SQL query to find all of the responses submitted for this course for the current user, and an array to store the results. This SQL query is adopted from code from the core 'choice' module. Remember this when making queries to weigh performance issues, such as whether a join is required and whether indexes have been created for commonly queried fields. We should also consider the portability of the query between Moodle's supported databases:

```
$sql = "SELECT foo_a.*
       FROM {$CFG->prefix}foo foo_b, {$CFG->prefix}foo_responses foo_a
       WHERE foo_a.fooid = foo_b.id AND
           foo_b.course = $course->id AND foo_a.userid = $USER->id";
$responses = array () ;
```

Next, we call the `get_records_sql` function to grab our response records, and then we use a `foreach` loop to format the array so that we have the `$ra->fooid` element set:

```
if (isloggedin() and !isguestuser() and $allresponses =
   get_records_sql($sql)) {
  foreach ($allresponses as $ra) {
    $responses[$ra->fooid] = $ra;
  }
  unset($allresponses);
}
```

Displaying our table of activities

Next, we need to swap out the `foreach` loop from the template with the one that follows, which prints our table of activities. First, we set up the `foreach` loop to cycle through each value in the array `$foos`:

```
foreach ($foos as $foo) {
```

Now, we need to see if there has been a response submitted for this particular activity, and if one has, assign it to `$response` for later display:

```
if (!empty($responses[$foo->id])) {
  $response = $responses[$foo->id];
} else {
  $response = "";
}
```

Here we assign the actual response value to `$fa`, a temporary variable that we will reference in the actual output statements:

```
if (!empty($response->response)) {
    if( $response->response == "1" ) {
      $fa = $yes;
    }
    else {
      $fa = $no;
    } $response->response;
  } else {
    $fa = $no;
  }
```

Displaying course sections

Courses are divided into sections, typically weeks or topics, depending on the course format selected. In the following code, we deal with section display. We maintain a variable `$currentsection` and compare it against the `$foo->section` value to see if we have entered a new section. If we have, we print the new section:

```
$printsection = "";
if ($foo->section !== $currentsection) {
  if ($foo->section) {
    $printsection = $foo->section;
  }
  if ($currentsection !== "") {
    $table->data[] = 'hr';
  }
  $currentsection = $foo->section;
}
```

The standard Moodle convention is that each activity displayed in the table needs to have a hyperlink. This allows the user to click through to display it. Note the use of `$foo->visible` to determine whether the link should be assigned the dimmed CSS class:

```
if (!$foo->visible) {
  //Show dimmed if the mod is hidden
  $tt_href = "<a class=\"dimmed\" href=\"view.php?id=
    $foo->coursemodule\">".format_string($foo->name,true)."</a>";
} else {
  //Show normal if the mod is visible
  $tt_href = "<a href=\"view.php?id=
    $foo->coursemodule\">".format_string($foo->name,true)."</a>";
}
```

Here we assign sections if the format is weeks or topics:

```
if ($course->format == "weeks" || $course->format == "topics") {
  $table->data[] = array ($printsection, $tt_href, $fa);
} else {
  $table->data[] = array ($tt_href, $fa);
}
}
```

Committing output

Throughout this loop, we have not made any actual output; we have just been assigning values to the `$table->data` array. At the bottom of the file we output the display by using the following code:

```
print_heading($strfoos);
print_table($table);
print_footer($course);
```

The following screenshot shows an example of the resulting table, as rendered by Moodle:

Topic	Name	Did you learn?
1	Foo Activity Name	Yes
2	Foo2	No

Finishing view.php

The `view.php` file is responsible for displaying an individual activity and its interface. For our activity Foo! module, we have consolidated all of the functions into one page. In real world activities, it is common to see functions such as grading and reporting in separate PHP files.

Including submit_form.php

Around line 15 of the `view.php` template, we need to include our submit form. We define the new form in the file `submit_form.php`.

The form file works almost identically to the add instance form that we covered earlier. We use this to display our response submission form. To create the form, we extend the `moodleform` class. See *Chapter 13, Building Forms with formslib* for more information:

```
class foo_submit_form extends moodleform {
  function definition() {
    global $COURSE, $CFG;
```

Your code goes here

Starting around line 71 of the `view.php` file in the NEWMODULE template, there is an echo statement, `echo 'YOUR CODE GOES HERE'`. Most of the work we need to do to `view.php` will go after this line in this section of the code. This line also provides a simple way to test that the module is working at a basic level. We will comment out this line of code once we have created our own output. The first thing we need to do in a real world module is to determine if the user has access to see the data. We cover this in the next section.

Context control

We need to make sure that the user has access to the module. If not, we will skip all of the module output, including the input form. We accomplish this by wrapping the rest of this page's code in an `if` statement. You can see the initial conditional clause in the following lines:

```
$context = get_context_instance(CONTEXT_MODULE, $cm->id);
if (has_capability('mod/foo:submit', $context)) {
```

Although it can be a bit hard to read a large section of code wrapped in a large `if` statement, this is fairly common practice in Moodle core. There is a trade-off between the number of functions or files included and site performance. Next, we will discuss adding our input form.

Developing a form

To add our input form to the page, we first create an instance of the `foo_submit_form` class. Because we are using a single PHP file for all of the `view.php` functions, we pass this in as the parameter to the function call, along with the instance `id`:

```
$mform = new foo_submit_form("view.php?id=$cm->id");
```

The form processing is split into several major sections for the rest of the `view.php` file. These sections cover different types of submissions. First, we will cover the trivial 'cancel' option.

Cancel option

Our first section deals with the user clicking on 'cancel'. We don't take any special action on cancel, so the following section is empty:

```
if ($mform->is_cancelled()){
```

In the next section, we process submitted form data.

Submitted data

In this section, we validate any data submitted to the form by calling the form's `get_data()` member, and we add a log entry:

```
} else if ($fromform=$mform->get_data()){
  add_to_log($course->id, "foo", "add response",
          "view.php?id=$cm->id", $foo->name, $cm->id);
```

Next, we create an object to store the data and assign the response information:

```
$response = new object();
$response->response = $fromform->response;
$response->fooid = $foo->id;
$response->userid = $USER->id;
$response->timemodified = time();
```

These next lines will check to see if the user has already submitted a response, and if so, use the `update_record` function to change the value in the `foo_responses` table:

```
if ($old_response = get_record('foo_responses', 'fooid',
        $response->fooid, 'userid', $USER->id)) {
  $response->id = $old_response->id;
  if(! update_record('foo_responses', $response)) {
    echo get_string('errorupdateresponse','foo');
  }
}
```

Alternatively, we will insert a new value, and need to call `insert_record` instead:

```
else {
  if(!insert_record('foo_responses', $response))
    echo get_string('errorinsertresponse','foo');
}
```

In the next section, we deal with setting an appropriate grade value, based on what the learner submitted in the form.

Setting grades

Now that we have user data, we need to update the gradebook to reflect the learner's performance. We are going to reduce some of the complexity of the `view.php` file by creating a `foo_grade` function. We are placing the `foo_grade` function in the `lib.php` file, and the function is covered in detail towards the end of the `lib.php` section of the chapter. See the section on *Coding lib.php* for more details on this function. In the following code, we see an example of using the function:

```
foo_grade($foo, $USER->id, $response->response);
```

Next we will cover how to display the submission form. We should keep in mind that this is another section in our long main `if` block in `view.php`.

Displaying submission form

In this section of the code, we need to display our submission form. The first step is to see if there is an existing submission and preset the correct value:

```
$data = new stdClass();
$data->cmid = $cm->id;
// get response if already exists to preload in form
if ($old_response = get_record('foo_responses', 'fooid', $foo->id,
    'userid', $USER->id)) {
  $data->response = $old_response->response;
}// if
```

Now that we have the response preset, we can assign the data to the form object and call its display function, as follows:

```
$mform->set_data($data);
$mform->display();
```

Now that we have dealt with the form section of `view.php`, we can move on to our next major section, which will cover displaying our response data to the page.

Displaying submissions

The first thing that we need to do is check to see if the user has the mod/foo:viewall capability. If he or she does, we use the foo_get_participants function to get all of the participants. Then we loop through them, calling the foo_user_complete function to look up their responses:

```
echo('<br><strong>'.get_string('submissions',
    'foo').'</strong></br>');
if (has_capability('mod/foo:viewall', $context) && $participants =
        foo_get_participants($foo->id))   {
  foreach ($participants as $id => $participant) {
    $user = get_record( 'user', 'id', $id );
    echo( '<br>'.$user->firstname." ".$user->lastname.': ' );
    foo_user_complete( $user, $foo );
    echo( '</br>' );
  }// foreach participant
}// if has viewall capability
```

If the learner doesn't have the viewall capability, we just display the user's own submission results, again using foo_user_complete:

```
else {
  echo('<br>');
  foo_user_complete( $USER, $foo);
```

After the response data, we are going to build the group section of the view.php page. This will be covered in the next section.

Group support

Group support is one of the key features of Moodle. It allows instructors to create courses where sub-groups of learners can interact together, or where groups can be entirely hidden from each other. We use the groups_get_activity_groupmode function to see if groups are enabled for an activity. In the next several code sections, we will gather data into two distinct arrays, and then later will merge the results into a single data set for display on the screen. The following code section illustrates how we will use the function in activity Foo!:

```
$groupmode = groups_get_activity_groupmode($cm);
if ($groupmode) {
  groups_get_activity_group($cm, true);
  groups_print_activity_menu($cm, 'view.php?id='.$id);
}
```

If `$groupmode > 0`, then we know that groups are active for this activity and we need to look up the current group by using the `groups_get_activity_group` function:

```
if ($groupmode > 0) {
  $currentgroup = groups_get_activity_group($cm);
} else {
  $currentgroup = 0;
}
```

This line initializes a matrix in which we can store the response data for the group members:

```
$allresponses = array();
```

Now we use the `get_users_by_capability` function to get a list of all of the group participants and their user information:

```
$allresponses[0] = get_users_by_capability($context,
  'mod/foo:submit', 'u.id, u.picture, u.firstname, u.lastname,
  u.idnumber', 'u.firstname ASC', '', '', $currentgroup, '', false,
  true);
```

We call the `get_records` function to get a complete list of all responses for this activity instance, and save this list in `$rawresponses`. This code example is derived from the core 'choice' module, which has a similar structure to `foo`. Note that alternative methods of pulling data, such as the `recordsets()` function from the Moodle database, are covered in *Chapter 6, Developer's Guide to the Database*:

```
$rawresponses = get_records('foo_responses', 'fooid', $foo->id);
if ($rawresponses) {
```

In this loop, we merge the two results sets: 'responses' and 'users'. Again, we use `foo_user_complete` to display the response value. We loop through all of the responses and look up the user information for each responder:

```
foreach ($rawresponses as $response) {
  if (isset($allresponses[0][$response->userid])) {
    $userid = $response->userid;
    $user = get_record( 'user', 'id', $userid );
    echo( '<br>'.$user->firstname." ".$user->lastname.': ' );
    foo_user_complete( $user , $foo);
```

This completes the `view.php` page, which is the primary user interface for learners to interact with activity Foo!. In the next section, we cover the `lib.php` file, which is where all of the required and add-on library functions are defined for our activity module.

Coding lib.php

The `lib.php` file stores all of the basic functions used by the other files in the module. Most of the functions required by Moodle are included by the NEWMODULE template. Many of the functions defined in the template will work for activity Foo! without any changes. In this section, we will cover just the modifications necessary to make our activity function. This is also a good location in which to put our own additional functions. We might add functions, either for re-usability or for code clarity. An example of this is the `foo_grade` function, which will be covered at the end of this section. Note that you can optimize your code performance by placing these additional functions into the `locallib.php` file instead of `lib.php`. This improves performance because core Moodle functions will include the module's `lib.php` file, but they won't need the locally added functions. The Moodle core programming guidelines state that it is only necessary to create a separate file if you make significant additions.

Note that the example library code is derived from several Moodle activity modules including NEWMODULE, choice (from core), and groupselect (from the contributed module database), as well as from examples posted to `http://docs.moodle.org`. All of these have been released under the GPL.

In each of the following sections of the chapter, we will cover a single function in the `lib.php` file. The purpose of the function will be defined, and we will cover any changes to the template code necessary to implement activity Foo!. The first function that we will cover is `add_instance`.

Function add_instance

The `add_instance` function is called every time that we add a new activity instance to a course. The sample function provided by NEWMODULE is pretty complete, but it doesn't set the modification time. We add this line to set the modification time:

```
$foo->timemodified = time();
```

In the next section, we describe `foo_delete_instance`.

Function foo_delete_instance

`foo_delete_instance` is called each time that an instance of our module is deleted from a course. We just need to make one minor addition to the template. We need to delete any 'child' records stored in our `foo_responses` table that are related to this instance:

```
if (delete_records("foo_responses", "fooid", "$foo->id")) {
  $result = false;
}
```

Next, we will detail the `foo_user_outline` function.

Function foo_user_outline

The `foo_user_outline` function returns a summary of the user's activity in the `foo` instance passed to the function. This is used by the core system to display activity logs. However, it can also be useful in our `view.php` code in order to display information of our choosing to the user. First, we use the `get_record` function to query the `foo_reponses` table for a learner response:

```
function foo_user_outline($course, $user, $mod, $foo) {
if ($response = get_record('foo_responses', "fooid", $foo->id,
                           "userid", $user->id)) {
```

If we find a result, we assign it in the standard format for this function. `$result->info` gets assigned some informational value regarding the submission. In our case, this value will be a '1' if the learner responded that they learned and a '0' if they responded that they did not. The `$response->timemodified` value will be set to the time when the last response was submitted:

```
$result->info = "'".$response->response."'";
$result->time = $response->timemodified;
```

Now, we return either `$result` if we found a response record, or NULL if we did not:

```
    return $result;
} // if
else {
    return NULL;
} // else
```

This completes the changes that we need to make for `foo_user_outline`. Moving forward, we will cover the `foo_user_complete` function.

Function foo_user_complete

Function `foo_user_complete` prints the user's submission, if any, to the activity. This function is used by the core Moodle libraries, and also in activity Foo!'s `view.php` file. We use the `get_record` function to get any responses stored in the `foo_responses` table for this user and this instance:

```
function foo_user_complete($user, $foo) {
    if ($response - get_record('foo_responses', "fooid", $foo->id,
                               "userid", $user->id)) {
```

If we find a response, we check to see if it was 1 (yes) or 0 (no). We use the get_string function to look up a localized version of the value to display. We assign it to $result->info, and then we assign the modified time:

```
if($response->response) {
  $result->info = get_string('yes', 'foo');
}
else {
  $result->info = get_string('no', 'foo');
}
$result->time = $response->timemodified;
```

We use echo to output the response information:

```
echo get_string('responded', 'foo')." $result->info. "
  .get_string('updated', '', userdate($result->time));
```

If no response is found, we output the string notresponded from our language file:

```
} else {
  print_string('notresponded', 'foo');
```

We are now finished with all of the changes for foo_user_complete. In the next section, we tackle the function foo_get_participants.

Function foo_get_participants

This function returns a list of all of the users that have participated in the activity. It returns the raw result set of the query as an array of values. For activity Foo!, we just need to query the foo_responses table. We return all of the rows associated with the fooid that we passed into the function:

```
function foo_get_participants($fooid) {
  global $CFG;
  // create participants list
  $participants = get_records_sql("SELECT DISTINCT u.id, u.id

FROM {$CFG->prefix}user u,

{$CFG->prefix}foo_responses a

WHERE a.fooid = '$fooid' and

u.id = a.userid");
  return ($participants);
}
```

In our next section, we will revise the reset_course_form_definition function.

Function reset_course_form_definition

The `reset_course_form_definition` function is not a part of the NEWMODULE template. It is needed to implement the course reset. In this function, we modify the passed form, `mform`, to add a checkbox for resetting our module data. This is called by Moodle core to build the course reset form displayed to the user. This code section should look familiar, as it is based on the other forms that we have used in the chapter, which are also based on the Moodle form classes:

```
function foo_reset_course_form_definition(&$mform) {
  $mform->addElement('header', 'fooheader',
                     get_string('modulenameplural', 'foo'));
  $mform->addElement('advcheckbox', 'reset_foo',
                     get_string('removeresponses','foo'));
}
```

With this simple function added, we can move on to another function required for the course reset: `foo_reset_course_form_defaults`.

Function foo_reset_course_form_defaults

This function is not part of the NEWMODULE template. It is required to implement the course reset. It enables the display of our module in the course reset form:

```
function foo_reset_course_form_defaults($course) {
    return array('reset_foo'=>1);
}
```

This leaves us with one final function to complete the course reset feature: `foo_reset_userdata`.

Function foo_reset_userdata

`foo_reset_userdata` is not part of the NEWMODULE template. This function performs the actual user data reset for our module. It is called by Moodle core if a user selects the form value in the course reset:

```
function foo_reset_userdata($data) {
    global $CFG;
    $componentstr = get_string('modulenameplural', 'foo');
    $status = array();
```

First, we check to see if `reset_foo` was selected:

```
if (!empty($data->reset_foo)) {
```

Next, we search for all instances of 'foo' in the course. The course ID is passed as part of the data set as `$data->courseid`. We then pass the result set into the `delete_records_select` function in order to remove all of the records in the `foo_responses` table:

```
$foossql = "SELECT f.id
    FROM {$CFG->prefix}foo f
    WHERE f.course={$data->courseid}";

delete_records_select('foo_responses', "fooid IN ($foossql)");
    $status[] = array('component'=>$componentstr,
                    'item'=>get_string('removeresponses', 'foo'),
                    'error'=>false);
```

Finally, we wrap up by resetting the date values by using the `shift_course_mod_dates` function from the Moodle core:

```
/// updating dates - shift may be negative too
if ($data->timeshift) {
    shift_course_mod_dates('foo', array('timeopen', 'timeclose'),
                        $data->timeshift, $data->courseid);
    $status[] = array('component'=>$componentstr,
                    'item'=>get_string('datechanged'),
                    'error'=>false);
}

return $status;
```

This completes all of the changes for the functions called by Moodle core for activity Foo!. In our next section, we cover a local function `foo_grade`, which will illustrate how to connect to the Moodle gradebook.

Inserting grades into the gradebook

The `foo_grade` function is an example of adding an additional function to the `lib.php` file, which is not used or required by core Moodle. It was created by reviewing several core functions and how they interacted with the gradebook. Our grading mechanism for activity Foo! is very simple. If the learners respond that they learned, they get full credit. If they respond no, then they get zero points. The points awarded are the maximum points defined during the activity's creation. This can be set differently for each instance of activity Foo! that we create. Let's have a look at the code.

First, we define the function and the arguments to be passed into the function. We are passing in the `foo` instance, the `userid`, and the `response`:

```
function foo_grade($foo, $userid, $response) {
```

Next, we include the global $CFG variable and gradelib.php for access to Moodle's gradebook functions:

```
global $CFG;
require_once($CFG->libdir.'/gradelib.php');
```

Now that we have the basics in place, we need to check if there is a response. If the response is no, then we assign '0' to $grade. If yes, we assign $grade to the value of $foo->scale. $foo->scale gets set when we create the activity instance. When using quantitative scales, this variable is set to the maximum points allowed for an activity. To simplify grading for our module, if a learner gets credit, he or she will always get the maximum points allowed:

```
if($response == 0) {
   $grade = 0;
}// if
else {
   $grade = $foo->scale;
}// else
```

Using grade_update

Moodle's grading functions accept an array of grades. We are only assigning a single grade. However, we still need to assign it to the appropriate array structure accepted by the grade_update function. We have to assign both the userid and the rawgrade:

```
$grades = array('userid'=>$userid, 'rawgrade'=>$grade);
```

Next, we have to assign some grading parameters, including the itemname and the instance's idnumber:

```
$params = array('itemname'=>$foo->name, 'idnumber'=>$foo->id);
```

Setting the grade type

In this next section, we assign the grade type. These are standard boilerplate values from the forum activity—a core Moodle activity:

```
if ( $foo->scale == 0) {
    $params['gradetype'] = GRADE_TYPE_NONE;

} else if ($foo->scale > 0) {
    $params['gradetype'] = GRADE_TYPE_VALUE;
    $params['grademax'] = $foo->scale;
    $params['grademin'] = 0;
```

```
    } else if ($foo->scale < 0) {
        $params['gradetype'] = GRADE_TYPE_SCALE;
        $params['scaleid']   = -$foo->scale;
    }

    if ($grades  === 'reset') {
        $params['reset'] = true;
        $grades = NULL;
    }
```

Finally, we call the `grade_update` function with the variables that we have assigned through the rest of the function:

```
return grade_update('mod/foo', $foo->course, 'mod', 'foo', $foo->id,
                    0, $grades, $params);
```

We have now completed all of the updates necessary for the `lib.php` file to implement activity Foo!. At this point, we have an almost completely functioning activity module. In our next section, we will cover how to implement changes to our module's database configuration.

Upgrading our activity database

The `upgrade.php` file provides code to upgrade our module as we release new versions of Moodle. It is only necessary if we have deployed our module to users and subsequently make updates that require the database to be changed.

Using the XMLDB editor for database upgrades

The recommended method of updating an activity's database is to use the XMLDB editor. It provides a GUI that you can use to update the database, including adding new tables. The editor will output both a complete new `install.xml` file and the PHP code needed for our `upgrade.php` file.

Updating upgrade.php

This function is called by Moodle core when a new version of the module is detected. The version in Moodle's configuration database is compared to the value found in the module's `version.php` file. Following is a sample section of code generated from the XMLDB editor. It illustrates the code needed to add a scale field to the `foo` table.

Our `if` condition indicates that the upgrade should be run for any versions of the module older than '2009060103':

```
if ($result && $oldversion < 2009060103) {
/// Define field scale to be added to foo
$table = new XMLDBTable('foo');
$field = new XMLDBField('scale');
$field->setAttributes(XMLDB_TYPE_INTEGER, '10', XMLDB_UNSIGNED,
                      XMLDB_NOTNULL, null, null, null, '0',
                      'timemodified');
/// Launch add field scale
$result = $result && add_field($table, $field);
```

See `http://docs.moodle.org/en/Development:Installing_and_upgrading_plugin_database_tables` for more information.

Creating backup and restore support

The Moodle course backup system uses a simple XML file format to store activity data. Moodle core calls the functions in the `backuplib.php` file for all of the modules in a course. If `backuplib.php` is missing, the backup will execute without errors. However, none of our activities or learner results will be saved. This leads to lost user data! The user doesn't realize that the data is missing until they go to restore the course. The restore functions for an activity are stored in `restorelib.php`. Note that the backup and restore system is being completely re-written for Moodle 2.0, but the intention is to make it backward compatible. Activity Foo! uses a modified copy of the 'choice' module's restore code.

Here is an example of the XML for an instance of an activity:

```
<MOD>
            <ID>80</ID>
            <TYPE>foo</TYPE>
            <INSTANCE>1</INSTANCE>
            <ADDED>1250743636</ADDED>
            <SCORE>0</SCORE>
            <INDENT>0</INDENT>
            <VISIBLE>1</VISIBLE>
            <GROUPMODE>1</GROUPMODE>
            <GROUPINGID>0</GROUPINGID>
            <GROUPMEMBERSONLY>0</GROUPMEMBERSONLY>
            <IDNUMBER>$@NULL@$</IDNUMBER>
            <ROLES_OVERRIDES>
            </ROLES_OVERRIDES>
            <ROLES_ASSIGNMENTS>
            </ROLES_ASSIGNMENTS>
</MOD>
```

Here is an example of how a response is saved in the backup file:

```
<RESPONSE>
  <ID>1</ID>
  <USERID>2</USERID>
  <RESPONSE>1</RESPONSE>
  <TIMEMODIFIED>1250743885</TIMEMODIFIED>
</RESPONSE>
```

The activity Foo!'s `backuplib.php` file is based on the code from the core 'choice' module. It uses the exact code, with a search and replace on the module name and for database elements. The `foo_responses` structure is very similar to the `choice_answers` table. 'choice' actually has three tables, so a few items were removed.

Let's have a look at the required functions for each of these files types.

Exploring backuplib.php functions

The following section covers each function in activity Foo!'s `backuplib.php` file. These functions have been organized into two categories: those common to all activity modules, and those internal to a particular activity module.

Common backup functions

Common backup functions should be implemented for every activity module, in order to properly support the backup function. These are as follows:

- `foo_backup_mods()`: The main entry point for the backup process. Backs up one or more activities. Calls `foo_backup_one_mod()` for each instance of the activity in the course.

- `foo_backup_one_mod()`: Creates a backup for a single instance of the activity. Responsible for calling internal activity module-specific backup functions. In activity Foo!, this function calls `backup_foo_responses()`.

- `foo_check_backup_mods()`: Called from the core backup libraries found in `/backup`. This is used to generate information for the backup setting screens.

- `foo_check_backup_mods_instances()`: Called by `foo_check_backup_mods()` to generate instance information for each copy of the activity in a course. Calls the internal function `foo_response_ids_by_instance()`.

- `foo_encode_content_links()`: Necessary to support interactivity linking. Ensures that interactivity links stay intact between the backup and restore processes.

- `foo_ids()`: Returns an array of all of the Foo! IDs for a course. Used by `foo_check_backup_mods()`.

Internal backup functions

Internal backup functions should also be implemented for each activity module. However, they will vary depending on the internal structure of the module. Generally, you will need one of each of the following listed functions for each table that you implement for the activity:

- `backup_foo_responses()`: Creates the XML output to backup the `foo_responses` table. Executed from the `foo_backup_mods()` function.

- `foo_response_ids_by_course()`: Uses an SQL query to return an array of IDs from the table `foo_responses`. Called by `foo_check_backup_mods()`.

- `foo_response_ids_by_instance()`: Returns an array of IDs for a particular instance of `foo` from the `foo_responses` table. Called by `foo_check_backup_mods_instances()`.

Exploring restorelib.php functions

The following section covers each function in activity Foo!'s `restorelib.php` file. These functions have been organized into two categories: those common to all activity modules and those internal to a particular activity module.

Common restore functions

Common functions should be implemented for every activity module to properly support the restore function. These are as follows:

- `foo_restore_mods()`: This is the main entry point to the restore code for the module. It is called by core Moodle to perform restores. Calls the `foo_responses_restore_mods()` function to perform internal restore functions.

- `foo_decode_content_links_caller()`: Reverses the link encoding from the backup process in order to restore the interactivity links. Iterates through all module content and calls `foo_decode_content_links()` function where needed to perform the decode. It's called from the `restore_decode_content_links()` function.

- `foo_decode_content_links()`: Performs the actual decoding of content in the restore file. Required to support interactivity linking.

- `foo_restore_logs()`: Returns a log record. Called by `restore_log_module()`.

- `foo_restore_wiki2markdown()`: Converts instructions in FORMAT_WIKI to FORMAT_MARKDOWN.

Internal restore functions

Internal restore functions should also be implemented for each activity module. However, they will vary depending on the internal structure of the module. Generally, you will need one function for each table that you implement for the activity. It is as follows:

- `foo_responses_restore_mods()`: This function restores the `foo_responses` table entries and is called by the `foo_restore_mods()` function.

Summary

Well, that was a lot of work! But now we have a fully functioning, if simple, activity module. In this chapter, we covered a lot of ground. You learned how to create a new activity module by using the NEWMODULE template. You learned that activity modules are an order of magnitude more complex than the other plugin types that you have worked with in prior chapters. You have learned how to create various form elements for your module. You have added group support to your module. You have connected your code to the Moodle gradebook. And last but not the least, you have created working backup, restore, and course reset functions. These functions are often missed but are essential to a complete module. In the next chapter, we will cover various methods of tailoring Moodle's look and feel.

5
Customizing the Look and Feel

There are two primary ways to change the Moodle look and feel—themes and course formats.

Moodle themes provide a way for you to change the appearance of any Moodle page. Although this is primarily done through the appropriate use of CSS (Cascading Style Sheets) definitions, we will focus on methods of importance to programmers.

Course formats provide a way of changing how a course page is displayed. This allows you to completely change the way in which a course provides its main page information.

In this chapter, we will:

- Program a theme to display standard navigation links in both the header and footer
- Create a new course format to display a forum's discussions directly on the course page

Themes

Moodle themes provide a way of affecting the appearance of any page within Moodle. Through a mixture of CSS and PHP code, themes allow us to lay out our pages in creative ways.

How themes work

All themes require four files as a minimum: `config.php`, `styles.php`, `header.html`, and `footer.html`. They should also have one or more CSS files.

The `styles.php` file is standard and seldom needs to be changed. The `config.php` file defines all of the stylesheets used by the theme as well as other style options. The `header.html` and `footer.html` files define the opening and closing HTML respectively for all pages using the theme. The CSS files include all of the CSS styles defined by this theme. The standard themes break these out by function and include `styles_color.css` for color style definitions, `styles_fonts.css` for font style definitions, and `styles_layout.css` for layout style definitions. Breaking out your CSS into functional files is not required. However, it makes it simpler to replace only the styles that you need to when using a standard theme as the base for your own theme.

We won't go into details about how to configure your theme and create the styles that you want. That is best handled by the theme documentation. You can find more information on that in the online Moodle documentation at `http://docs.moodle.org/en/Make_your_own_theme`.

Instead, let's focus on the areas where programming will come in handy — the `header.html` and `footer.html` files.

Headers and footers

The `header.html` and `footer.html` files serve dual purposes. The primary purpose is to output the entire HTML, which will contain the page including the `<html>` container tags, the `<head>` container tags, and the `<body>` container tags. You should be familiar with the structure of an HTML document in order to understand this.

The actual content of a page is handled by the specific page being output; these files simply provide the containers necessary for the output to be displayed in a standard way.

The secondary purpose is to output dynamic HTML based on what is happening with the page being output. This is done through PHP statements, and may use variables defined elsewhere in the code. This also means that although these files have the `.html` extension, strictly speaking, they are not HTML files. They are actually PHP files whose primary responsibility is to output HTML sections.

Let's examine the structure of a standard `header.html` file from the Moodle standard theme.

header.html

Following is the complete code of the `header.html` file from a version of the Moodle `standard` theme. This file can be found in the `/theme/standard/` directory of your Moodle install, and may differ depending on the version:

```
<!DOCTYPE html PUBLIC "-//W3C//DTD XHTML 1.0 Strict//EN" "http://www.
w3.org/TR/xhtml1/DTD/xhtml1-strict.dtd">
<html<?php echo $direction ?>>
<head>
    <?php echo $meta ?>
    <meta name="keywords" content="moodle, <?php echo $title ?> " />
    <title><?php echo $title ?></title>
    <link rel="shortcut icon" href="<?php echo $CFG->themewww .'/'.
        current_theme() ?>/favicon.ico" />
    <?php include("$CFG->javascript"); ?>
</head>
<body<?php
    echo " $bodytags";
    if ($focus) {
        echo " onload=\"setfocus()\"";
    }
    ?>>
<div id="page">
<?php //Accessibility: 'headermain' is now H1, see
    theme/standard/styles_layout.css: .headermain
    if ($home) {  // This is what gets printed on the home page only
?>
    <?php print_container_start(true, '', 'header-home'); ?>
        <h1 class="headermain"><?php echo $heading ?></h1>
        <div class="headermenu"><?php echo $menu ?></div>
    <?php print_container_end(); ?>
<?php } else if ($heading) {  // This is what gets printed on any
    other page with a heading
?>
    <?php print_container_start(true, '', 'header'); ?>
        <h1 class="headermain"><?php echo $heading ?></h1>
        <div class="headermenu"><?php echo $menu ?></div>
    <?php print_container_end(); ?>
<?php } ?>
<?php //Accessibility: breadcrumb trail/navbar now a DIV, not a table.
      if ($navigation) { // This is the navigation bar with
breadcrumbs   ?>
    <div class="navbar clearfix">
        <div class="breadcrumb">
            <?php print_navigation($navigation); ?>
        </div>
        <div class="navbutton"><?php echo $button; ?></div>
```

```
     </div>
<?php } else if ($heading) { // If no navigation, but a heading, then
print a line
?>
        <hr />
<?php } ?>
     <!-- END OF HEADER -->
     <?php print_container_start(false, '', 'content'); ?>
```

You will notice that the file starts off looking pretty much like an HTML file, but then quickly you will see PHP tags and PHP statements.

Statements such as `<html<?php echo $direction ?>>` and `<?php echo $meta ?>` assume that variables have been initialized and set somewhere else; in these examples, the variables are `$direction` and `$meta`. These variables are set in the `print_header` function, which is also the function that includes this file and outputs it.

You'll also notice statements using the `print_container_start` and `print_container_end` functions. These are standard Moodle functions that help to structure a page in a known way so that it is easier to change the look of the page by using CSS. The `print_container_start` function allows you to pass it a list of classes and an ID to apply to the container used. In this way, you can have specific tag identifiers in your theme that can be utilized by CSS.

Also, the `header.html` file ends with a `print_container_start` statement that passes `content` as the `id` argument, but has no closing `print_container_end` function call. This container will be closed in the `footer.html` file.

When you get down to where the page actually starts, you begin to see more programming. You'll notice statements such as `if ($home) {` that separate out what is being displayed on the home page from any other page. Also you'll see the statements `if ($navigation) {` and `print_navigation($navigation);`. This is where the Moodle API is used to create standard breadcrumb navigation on a page.

footer.html

The `footer.html` file completes the page started by the `header.html` file. It will close the `body` and `html` section tags, close any other tags that were opened but not closed in `header.html`, and output any page display that should appear in a footer.

We won't analyze this page at this point. However, we will create our own in one of the coding examples that follow. For now, go ahead and open one of the footer files in a standard theme, just to familiarize yourself with its content.

Project 1: Changing the navigation breadcrumbs

Let's start our first *look and feel* project. For this project, our requirements are to change the navigation breadcrumbs on a Moodle page so that the category name and link are displayed before the course name, for a course page display.

To explain, if you look at a standard Moodle course page, you will see that the navigation breadcrumbs near the top of the page display the site short name and course short name, but not the category that the course belongs to. This situation is shown in the following screenshot:

We want to change the breadcrumbs such that the category name is inserted before the course name. We have several options to implement these changes. We can hack the `print_header` function, where the breadcrumb is received and assembled, or we can hack the page display functions for course pages and module pages. But, each one of these options involves modifying core code in Moodle, making it difficult to maintain the changes when we want to update our installation.

Instead, let's create our own theme and hijack the breadcrumb before it gets displayed. We can do this, because the breadcrumb gets displayed by a theme's `header.html` file. All we need to do is change what it is, before it gets displayed to the screen.

Creating our own theme

Let's begin by creating our own theme called `customnav`. The easiest way to do this is to copy an existing theme and give it a new name. Copy the files of the `standardlogo` theme directory to a new directory named `customnav` in the `theme` directory. You should now have a new directory called `customnav` that contains the same files as the `standardlogo` directory does.

The only file we are really going to concern ourselves with at this point is the `header.html` file.

Adding the category link

Next, we want to find a way to insert a category link with the category name before any course link. To do this, we will need to change the text in the $navigation variable before it gets written out by print_header.

The $navigation variable will be an array with two indexes: newnav and navlinks. The first index should only contain a '1', indicating it is using the 'new' navigation API. For this example, we will assume that all navigation will be using the 'new' navigation API.

The second index will contain the actual navigation string to be output. This is the one that we will have to change.

To change this, we will need to find the part of the navigation string that contains the course name and/or link. For a page with the course link, this is fairly easy. We just need to search for the string /course/view.php, which is part of the hyperlink to the course. For the course page itself, this is not so easy, as the link isn't there. It will be the second element of the navigation string. However, there are non-course pages that are the second element too.

The navigation string

The navigation string is structured as an unordered list, with all of the pieces surrounded by <li></li> tags. This means that we can find all of the pieces of the navigation by separating the string with the <li> tag. A good function for this is PHP's explode.

Execute the following code snippet:

```
/// If there are navigation pieces, separate them out.
if (!empty($navigation['navlinks'])) {
    $pieces = explode('<li>', $navigation['navlinks']);
} else {
    $pieces = array();
}
```

On executing the previous code snippet, we will get an array of all the parts that begin with <li>. If this result is empty, or contains less than two elements, then we need not do anything else, because the course piece would always be the second element.

If the result has two or more elements, then we need to check the second element to see if it has a course short name in it. The easiest way to do this is assume that it does, and extract it. This part will either be surrounded by a hyperlink or a list tag. We just need to extract the string between > and either </li> or </a></li>.

```
/// If its possible there is a course piece, find the short name.
$sname = '';
if (count($pieces) > 1) {
    $sname = $pieces[1];
    if (strpos($sname, '/course/view.php') !== false) {
        $sname = substr($sname, 0, strpos($sname, '</a></li>'));
    } else {
        $sname = substr($sname, 0, strpos($sname, '</li>'));
    }
    $sname = trim(substr($sname, strrpos($sname, '>')+1));
}
```

This code will get us a string that should be the course short name if that part of the navigation string is a course piece. We will use this string to search for the course and its category in the database. To do that, we add the following code:

```
/// If we think we have a short name, let's find the category.
if ($sname != '') {
    $select = 'SELECT c.id, cc.id as catid, cc.name ';
    $from   = 'FROM '.$CFG->prefix.'course c ';
    $join   = 'INNER JOIN '.$CFG->prefix.'course_categories cc ON
                cc.id = c.category ';
    $where  = 'WHERE c.shortname = \''.$sname.'\'';
    $sql    = $select.$from.$join.$where;
    $catinfo = get_record_sql($sql);
}
```

The code above gets a record from the course table with the determined short name, and joins in the category information for that course. After this code is executed, $catinfo will either contain an object containing the category information for the course, or nothing if this was not really a course. If we have the information, we can now reconstruct the navigation string and add the category component. The following code will run through and rebuild the navigation, inserting the category name and link in the appropriate place:

```
/// If we have category information, place it in the nav.
if (!empty($catinfo)) {
    $catlink = $CFG->wwwroot.'/course/category.php?id='.
                $catinfo->catid;
    $catpiece  = '<li>';
    $catpiece .= get_separator();
```

```
$catpiece .= '<a onclick="this.target=\''.$CFG->framename.'\'"
              href="'.$catlink.'">'.$catinfo->name.'</a>';
$catpiece .= '</li>';
$navigation['navlinks'] = $pieces[0];
foreach ($pieces as $i => $piece) {
    if ($i == 0) {
        continue;
    } else if ($i == 1) {
        $navigation['navlinks'] .= $catpiece;
    }
    $navigation['navlinks'] .= '<li>'.$piece;
    }
}
```

In the previous code block, the get_separator function returns a character that the navigation functions know to be a separator of the breadcrumb pieces. That way, they can process the breadcrumb pieces and render any graphical representation of a separator that is desired. The $CFG->framename is a configuration item that contains the name of any defined HTML frame that the site may sit in (typically none).

We now have a code that will find a course short name in the breadcrumbs, and insert the category name and link to the category page before the course short name. Make sure that you set your site to use your new theme. If we look at the same page (shown in the previous screenshot), we will notice it has been slightly modified as follows:

Note that we now see **Miscellaneous** in the breadcrumbs. This is the category to which the course that we are looking at belongs. Our theme change is a success!

Project 2: Adding a standard footer with site links

For this project, we want to add a footer that has a series of links to HTML pages with general information for our site. We want to add a **Terms of Use** page, a **Contact Us** page, and a **Privacy** page. We want these links to appear if we have defined a page for their use.

A page is defined if it exists in the Moodle data directory for the site. We will define static names for each file, and check if they exist, and if so, create links to them.

We'll use the same theme that we started previously. However, this time we will edit the `footer.html` file.

Before we make any changes, the footer should look similar to the following screenshot:

Creating the code

In the `footer.html` file, the following lines of code appear near the top:

```
print_container_end(); // content container
print_container_start(false, '', 'footer');
echo '<hr />';
```

The `print_container_start` function defines the beginning of the area where the footer is contained. We will insert our additions between this and the `<hr />` tag.

To begin, let's insert the following initialization lines, in order to define the strings that we will use:

```
/// Look for custom files for footer links:
$contactusn = '/'.SITEID.'/contactus.html';
$termsn = '/'.SITEID.'/termsofuse.html';
$privacyn = '/'.SITEID.'/privacy.html';
$footertext = '';
```

The first three lines define the filenames for the links that we will look for. The final line is the text that we will output; that is empty to start with.

The files that we will look for in the initialization lines are expected to be in the site directory of the Moodle data area for this site. In Moodle, this is a numeric value equal to the course ID of the specific course. The site directory is also a course numeric equal to the value stored in the SITEID constant (this is always '1', but it is safer to use the constant defined for this).

So, we will look for these three HTML files, and place a link to them in the footer if found.

Let's add the following lines of code to look for the first file, and add the results to the output string:

```
/// Look for contact us page
if (file_exists($CFG->dataroot.$contactusn)) {
    $link = get_file_url($contactusn, null, 'httpscoursefile');
    /// To use with pop-up... Must be a relative URL.
    $plink = str_replace($CFG->wwwroot, '', $link);
} else {
    $link = false;
}
if ($link) {
    $footertext .= '<a href="'.$link.'" target="_blank" '.
        'onClick="return openpopup(\''.$plink.'\',\'popup_'.SITEID.
        '\',\'directories=0,location=0,menubar=0,toolbar=0,statu=0,
            resizable=1,scrollbars=1,'.
            'height=450,width=620,top=250,left=250\');">Contact Us</a>
            | ';
} else {
    $footertext .= 'Contact Us | ';
}
```

First, we check to see if the file is present in the Moodle data directory. If it is, then we ask Moodle for a URL to the file, by using the `get_file_url` function. If we have a URL, we create a link tag to that file. For neatness, we have created that link as a small pop-up window so that we are not taken away from the site. The `openpopup` JavaScript function does this for us. We have created a new link called `$plink` for this, because `openpopup` expects a relative URL. If we don't find the file, we just create static text for the **Contact Us** part.

Here is the rest of the code, for the remaining two links:

```
/// Look for terms of use page
if (file_exists($CFG->dataroot.$termsn)) {
    $link = get_file_url($termsn, null, 'httpscoursefile');
    /// To use with pop-up... Must be a relative URL.
    $plink = str_replace($CFG->wwwroot, '', $link);
} else {
    $link = false;
}
if ($link) {
    $footertext .= '<a href="'.$link.'" target="_blank" '.
        'onClick="return openpopup(\''.$plink.'\',\'message_'.SITEID.
        '\',\'directories=0,location=0,menubar=0,toolbar=0,statu=0,
            resizable=1,scrollbars=1,'.
```

```
                'height=450,width=620,top=250,left=250\');">Terms of Use</a>
               | ';
    } else {
        $footertext .= 'Terms of Use | ';
    }
    /// Look for privacy page
    if (file_exists($CFG->dataroot.$privacyn)) {
        $link = get_file_url($privacyn, null, 'httpscoursefile');
        /// To use with pop-up... Must be a relative URL.
        $plink = str_replace($CFG->wwwroot, '', $link);
    } else {
        $link = false;
    }
    if ($link) {
        $footertext .= '<a href="'.$link.'" target="_blank" '.
            'onClick="return openpopup(\''.$plink.'\',\'message_'.SITEID.
            '\',\'directories=0,location=0,menubar=0,toolbar=0,statu=0,
             resizable=1,scrollbars=1,'.
            'height=450,width=620,top=250,left=250\');">Privacy</a> | ';
    } else {
        $footertext .= 'Privacy';
    }
```

As before, this creates links to the two files, or static text if the files could not be found.

Lastly, we write out what we have created, as follows:

```
echo '<div class="footerlinks">'.$footertext.'</div><br />';
```

We have enclosed the output in its own `<div>` tag with a defined class. This will allow any CSS developer to apply any other display characteristics to this area without, the need for programming.

Running the code

Now, with the code in place, the footer area of any page should look as shown in the following screenshot:

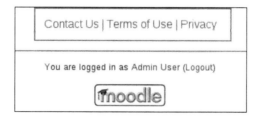

We now see the three textual parts of the files that we want, but no links. This is because we have not actually loaded any files into the Moodle site data area. If we upload files with the names that we used above, into the Moodle site area, our code would display links with the text.

To really see it work, let's create a file for each of the links. These are HTML files, so we will need HTML code, but the content doesn't matter for testing. We can always make it better, later.

Create a file with the following content on your local computer. You should call it `contactus.html`.

```
<!DOCTYPE HTML PUBLIC "-//W3C//DTD HTML 4.01 Transitional//EN">
<html>
<head>
  <title>Contact Us</title>
    <meta http-equiv="Content-Type" content="text/html;
      charset=iso-8859-1">
</head>
<body>
  <div id="content">
    <h2>General Inquiries</h2>
      <p>For general inquiries, please contact:</p>
      <blockquote>
        <p>
          Telephone: 555-555-5555<br />
          Fax: 555-555-5555</p>
      </blockquote>
  </div>
</body>
</html>
```

Navigate to your Moodle site and use the **Front Page | Site files** selection from the administration menu to access the site files area. Upload the file that you created previously to the root of the site file area.

Have a look at your footer. Now, **Contact Us** is a link to a file (as shown in the following screenshot), and if you click on it you will see the HTML file that you uploaded:

If you create a file for each of the other two text links, they will similarly be linked.

We have now used a theme to define a standard set of HTML links for our site, and have a method of maintaining those links and files. Further, because the files are stored in data storage they can be updated easily by any site administrator, thus avoiding the need for FTP access to the web server.

Course formats

Course formats provide a way of defining the way in which you want a main course page to be displayed. Moodle comes with six standard course formats: lams, scorm, social, topics, weeks, and weekscss. The last three are very similar and are most commonly used. These display a course in sections known as topics or weeks, depending on which format you are using. The Social format displays only one section. The LAMS and SCORM format are very specific formats that are used to display the specific types of learning activities associated with LAMS and SCORM, respectively.

You can play with each of these in order to familiarize yourself with the differences and what formats can do. We won't be describing these in any more detail here. You can learn more at http://docs.moodle.org/en/Course_formats.

How course formats work

All course formats require three files: format.php and config.php, located in a subdirectory with a unique name for the format in the /course/format/ directory, and a language file named format_yourformat.php in a standard language file structure under the course format directory.

The format.php file is the main file, and is responsible for handling all of the display logic for the course format. It writes out all of the content for the course, including any blocks. There are many standard functions in the /course/lib.php library to help perform this task. However, you may need to create your own library file depending on what you want to do with your course format.

The config.php file allows you to define the default blocks, and the location of the blocks, for a course using this course format.

The language file is primarily used to define a human readable name for the format, which is displayed in the format selector for the course settings.

Your format can also have a database directory (db) that contains files to create and upgrade specific data tables, access files for capabilities, a version file, backup and restore files, and a styles file. Read the README.txt file in your /course/format/ directory for detailed explanations of these files.

Creating our own course format

To best learn how we can change the way in which things work using a course format, let's create our own. To begin with, let's have a requirement.

We want to display a forum in a specific section of our course in an expanded way that shows all of the discussions and their recent statuses directly in that section. Essentially, we want to see a forum activity directly in the course section, as we would see if we clicked on it.

For now, we will assume that this happens for any forum displayed in section one of the course.

To begin with, let's create our own format by copying some of the files from the Topics format.

Create a subdirectory in the /course/format/ directory called extforum. Then, copy all of the files from the /course/format/topics/ directory into our new directory. We now have our own format that does exactly what the Topics format does.

Creating the course format language file

Create a new course, or edit an existing course. Look at the **Format** drop-down selector. You will see a format called **[[formatextforum]]**, as shown in the following screenshot:

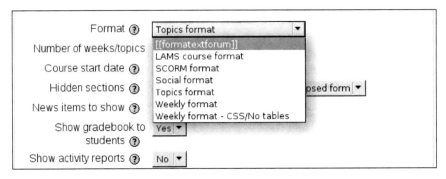

[[formatextforum]] is the course format that we just created. We need to create a language file to make the name a little more readable.

In our extforum course format directory, create the subdirectories /lang/en_utf8/. Then, create a file called format_extforum.php, and put the following code into it:

```php
<?php
$string['formatextforum'] = 'Extended forum section';
?>
```

This will provide a better looking name for our format in the drop-down selector. Load your course page, and you should see the following:

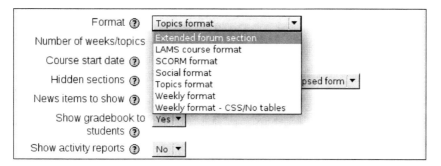

We now have a readable format name. Choose our format, and then save the course with that setting.

In this course, add a forum activity to section one. Add some discussions and posts to the forum; the actual content does not matter. Add another activity, such as an assignment, just for reference. Once you have completed these steps, you should have a course page that looks similar to the following:

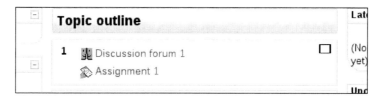

Modifying our course format function

Take a look in the `format.php` file. Around line 213, you will see the following statement:

```
print_section($course, $thissection, $mods, $modnamesused);
```

This is the function call to the standard library function `print_section` that displays all of the activities in the section. We need to change what this function does for our format, so that a forum in section one is displayed differently. The easiest way to do this without modifying the core is by copying the `print_section` function into our course format as a new function, and then using the new function instead.

Create a new file in your course format directory called `lib.php`. Open up the existing file `/course/lib.php`, and find the `print_section` function. Copy and paste that function into your `lib.php` file, and rename the function to `extforum_print_section`. After you have done this, your `lib.php` file should look similar to the following example:

```
<?php
function extforum_print_section($course, $section, $mods,
$modnamesused, $absolute=false, $width="100%") {
/// Prints a section full of activity modules
    global $CFG, $USER;
[rest of the code]
    if (!empty($section->sequence) || $ismoving) {
        echo "</ul><!--class='section'-->\n\n";
    }
}
}
?>
```

Next, we need to modify our `format.php` file to use this new function that we just created. In your `format.php` file, around line 213, where the `print_section` call is, change the call to `extforum_print_section`. Your line should now look as follows:

```
extforum_print_section($course, $thissection, $mods, $modnamesused);
```

We will need to include the library file that we just created to use our new function. At the top of the file, below the other `require_once` statements, add the following line of code:

```
require_once($CFG->dirroot.'/course/format/extforum/lib.php');
```

At this point, we haven't done anything to change the way in which the format functions, but we can now start to. If you use this format now, it will function exactly as the Topics format.

Changing the forum display

We want to change the section print code so that if a forum is being output in section one, we display the summary that we see when viewing a forum. We will also set it so that a normal activity display occurs if the course is being edited. In this way, all of the normal editing functions will still work as expected when editing.

In our new `lib.php` file, around line 110, just before the `Normal activity` comment, add the following lines:

```
} else if (!$isediting && ($mod->modname == 'forum') &&
        ($section->section == 1)) {
    $page = optional_param('page', 0, PARAM_INT);
    $forum = get_record("forum", "id", $mod->instance);
    forum_print_latest_discussions($course, $forum, -1, 'header', '',
    -1, -1, $page, $CFG->forum_manydiscussions);
} else { // Normal activity
```

This looks for a forum activity in section one, and if editing is not on, will call the forum library function to display the forum summary. Save your file.

When you look at the course now, you should see something similar to the following example:

Now, our forum is displayed in the course area, and shows the information for each discussion. Our new course format works!

Summary

In this chapter, you have learned how to programmatically change the look and feel of our Moodle site and courses by modifying functionality in a theme and a course format. You have become familiar with how a theme works, and how a course format works. You have also created functioning examples utilizing this knowledge.

In the next chapter, you will learn more about the database, and how it is structured, managed, and used.

6

Developer's Guide to the Database

Moodle supports a variety of SQL databases to store program information. To do that, Moodle provides powerful code libraries to let you write database-agnostic code. Moodle also enforces strict database layout design, allowing you to understand table structures easily. We will examine Moodle's database structures, policies, and libraries in order to better understand how to build our code.

This chapter covers the following topics:

- Overall structure of the Moodle database
- Coding methods and APIs for accessing databases
- Tools and programming tricks to help with your development projects

The database structure

Every data table in Moodle has one common element: the first field is an integer field called `id`. This field is a unique field that serves as the Primary Key for every table. It also serves as the Foreign Key to any other data table that contains a reference to that table.

Although this may seem excessive to some database programmers, as there are often other fields that can serve as unique references, this is a core rule to Moodle database programming that should never be broken; Moodle code depends on it! And if you use Moodle's database XML schema to validate your table, it is required.

The XML schema defines other requirements and restrictions—for example, naming conventions such as:

- A table name can be no longer than 28 characters
- Field names can be no longer than 30 characters

The remainder of the database structure requirements is maintained by agreement only. These can always be found at http://docs.moodle.org/en/ Development:Database.

Your table character set (collation) should be a UTF8 character set in order to support multi-language text. The first part of any plugin table name should contain the plugin name itself. Indices should be created for fields that are commonly used as search queries, and combination indices should be created when needed.

When you look at a database created by Moodle, you may notice that the tables you have created have characters at the beginning of their names that you didn't specify. This is shown in the following screenshot:

	Table							Rows	Type	Collation
☐	mdl_backup_log						✕	0	MyISAM	utf8_general_ci
☐	mdl_block						✕	35	MyISAM	utf8_general_ci
☐	mdl_block_instance						✕	24	MyISAM	utf8_general_ci
☐	mdl_block_pinned						✕	0	MyISAM	utf8_general_ci
☐	mdl_block_rss_client						✕	0	MyISAM	utf8_general_ci
☐	mdl_block_search_documents						✕	0	MyISAM	utf8_general_ci
☐	mdl_cache_filters						✕	0	MyISAM	utf8_general_ci
☐	mdl_cache_flags						✕	0	MyISAM	utf8_general_ci
☐	mdl_cache_text						✕	34	MyISAM	utf8_general_ci
☐	mdl_capabilities						✕	246	MyISAM	utf8_general_ci
☐	mdl_certificate						✕	2	MyISAM	utf8_general_ci
☐	mdl_certificate_issues						✕	484	MyISAM	utf8_general_ci
☐	mdl_certificate_linked_modules						✕	1	MyISAM	utf8_general_ci
☐	mdl_chat						✕	0	MyISAM	utf8_general_ci

This is the defined table prefix. It is configured in Moodle, and applied to table names when Moodle creates the tables. If you don't specify anything yourself, this will default to mdl_. The purpose of this is to allow a database to contain tables from more than one application (or more than one Moodle installation).

Maintaining Moodle tables

The easiest and most correct way to create and maintain Moodle data tables is through the database plugin mechanism. You will have noticed (as we used this in the previous chapters) that almost all plugins have an optional db subdirectory that contain files which manage data tables specific to the plugin. It is this subdirectory and the files within it that allow you to easily manage your data tables.

The db subdirectory can typically contains four files: `install.xml`, `upgrade.php`, `access.php`, and `events.php`. The first two are the ones we are concerned with here.

install.xml

The `install.xml` file contains XML that defines the tables required for your new plugin. It is a generic (database-agnostic) way to define data tables such that they can be created in just about any database technology (MySQL, PostgreSQL, and so on).

The following is a sample from the `label` module:

```
<?xml version="1.0" encoding="UTF-8" ?>
<XMLDB PATH="mod/label/db" VERSION="20060905" COMMENT="XMLDB file for
  Moodle mod/label"
  xmlns:xsi="http://www.w3.org/2001/XMLSchema-instance"
  xsi:noNamespaceSchemaLocation="../../../lib/xmldb/xmldb.xsd"
>
  <TABLES>
    <TABLE NAME="label" COMMENT="Defines labels">
      <FIELDS>
        <FIELD NAME="id" TYPE="int" LENGTH="10" NOTNULL="true"
          UNSIGNED="true" SEQUENCE="true" ENUM="false" NEXT="course"/>
        <FIELD NAME="course" TYPE="int" LENGTH="10" NOTNULL="true"
          UNSIGNED="true" DEFAULT="0" SEQUENCE="false" ENUM="false"
          PREVIOUS="id" NEXT="name"/>
        <FIELD NAME="name" TYPE="char" LENGTH="255" NOTNULL="true"
          SEQUENCE="false" ENUM="false" PREVIOUS="course"
          NEXT="content"/>
        <FIELD NAME="content" TYPE="text" LENGTH="small"
          NOTNULL="true" SEQUENCE="false" ENUM="false" PREVIOUS="name"
          NEXT="timemodified"/>
        <FIELD NAME="timemodified" TYPE="int" LENGTH="10"
          NOTNULL="true" UNSIGNED="true" DEFAULT="0" SEQUENCE="false"
          ENUM="false" PREVIOUS="content"/>
      </FIELDS>
      <KEYS>
```

```
        <KEY NAME="primary" TYPE="primary" FIELDS="id" />
      </KEYS>
      <INDEXES>
        <INDEX NAME="course" UNIQUE="false" FIELDS="course"/>
      </INDEXES>
    </TABLE>
  </TABLES>
  <STATEMENTS>
    <STATEMENT NAME="insert log_display" TYPE="insert"
      TABLE="log_display" COMMENT="Initial insert of records on table
    log_display">
      <SENTENCES>
        <SENTENCE TEXT="(module, action, mtable, field) VALUES
          ('label', 'add', 'label', 'name')"/>
        <SENTENCE TEXT="(module, action, mtable, field) VALUES
          ('label', 'update', 'label', 'name')"/>
      </SENTENCES>
    </STATEMENT>
  </STATEMENTS>
</XMLDB>
```

We have seen this before in the previous chapters, and have even created our own install.xml file, so we won't go into the details. What is important to understand is that this file should always completely define your database structure and any required values for an install. The plugin system sees this file when your plugin is first detected and installed.

upgrade.php

The upgrade.php file contains program instructions to update your data tables when new versions of your plugin are installed. Typically, this is used to add new tables, new fields to existing tables, change a field's format, or create new indices.

Plugins identify their version, and Moodle keeps track of this. If a plugin appears with a newer version than the one that Moodle knows about, Moodle will run any existing upgrade.php script. This file will usually have a separate section for each new version's upgrade code.

The following is an excerpt from the questionnaire module's upgrade.php script:

```
<?php //$Id: upgrade.php,v 1.1.2.14 2009/07/09 18:04:27 mchurch Exp $
function xmldb_questionnaire_upgrade($oldversion=0) {
    global $CFG;
    $result = true;
    if ($oldversion < 2008060402) {
```

```
            $table = new XMLDBTable('questionnaire_question_type');
            $field = new XMLDBField('response_table');
            $field->setAttributes(XMLDB_TYPE_CHAR, '32', null,
                    XMLDB_NOTNULL, null, null, null, null, 'has_choices');
            $field->setNotnull(false);
            $result &= change_field_notnull($table, $field);
        }
        if ($oldversion < 2008060403) {
            $table = new XMLDBTable('questionnaire_resp_multiple');
            $index = new XMLDBIndex('response_question');
            $index->setAttributes(XMLDB_INDEX_NOTUNIQUE,
                    array('response_id', 'question_id', 'choice_id'));
            $result = $result && add_index($table, $index);
        }
        return $result;
    }
?>
```

Because this is a module, Moodle expects to find a function with the name `xmldb_[module name]_upgrade` in the `upgrade.php` file. In this case, `module name` would be replaced by `questionnaire`.

This function gets passed an argument, which is the version number prior to the current upgrade. After an upgrade is successful, the final step is to record the current version. The code inside should check for the old version being less than the version that the upgrade is running for, and execute any code necessary for that version. The line `if ($oldversion < 2008060403)` will be placed in this file when the module is being upgraded to version 2008060403. All of the code after that condition will be data statements to perform whatever is necessary for this new version.

Actual version numbers are stored in different tables and fields depending on the plugin type:

- Module version numbers are in the module table
- Block version numbers are in the block table
- All others (assignment types, question types, and so on) are in the `config` table

The steps beneath that use the APIs defined in the XMLDB libraries (contained in `/lib/xmldb/*`) and the DDLIB libraries (contained in `/lib/ddllib.php`). The XMLDB libraries contain classes that define all aspects of the databases and data tables. The DDLIB (DD stands for Data Definition) contains functions that act on objects of these classes to actually make the structural changes within the database.

Take a look at the following example:

```
$table = new XMLDBTable('questionnaire_question_type');
$field = new XMLDBField('response_table');
$field->setAttributes(XMLDB_TYPE_CHAR, '32', null, XMLDB_NOTNULL,
        null, null, null, null, 'has_choices');
$field->setNotnull(false);
$result &= change_field_notnull($table, $field);
```

This code snippet defines a table and a field object, and then sets attributes for the field. The table and field class definitions are contained in the XMLDB, specifically in the `/lib/xmldb/classes/XMLDBTable.class.php` file and the `/lib/xmldb/classes/XMLDBField.class.php` file.

In this case, the table and field already exist, and the field definition is being changed; the field is being set to allow NULL values. Once the field has been set up with its new parameters, it is committed to the database by using the `change_field_notnull` function from the DDLIB.

Similarly, consider the following code snippet:

```
$table = new XMLDBTable('questionnaire_resp_multiple');
$index = new XMLDBIndex('response_question');
$index->setAttributes(XMLDB_INDEX_NOTUNIQUE, array('response_id',
        'question_id', 'choice_id'));
$result = $result && add_index($table, $index);
```

This code snippet defines a new index named `response_question` for the table `questionnaire_resp_multiple`, and adds that index to the database.

Maintaining local database customization

Sometimes, you may need to make changes to your database that don't involve any of Moodle's plugins. In this case, Moodle provides a mechanism for you to track and manage your local changes in one place. The `/local` directory can contain a `db` subdirectory that allows functions similar to the plugin functions.

One key difference in this structure is that `install.xml` is not used. Instead, all database maintenance is handled by an `upgrade.php` script. Inside the `/local` root, there needs to be a `version.php` file that defines the version information for the upgrade scripts. This file would contain a script similar to the following:

```
<?php
$local_version = 2009081600;
?>
```

As in the previous section, this defines the current version that Moodle tracks, and that can be compared against in an upgrade script. The upgrade.php file requires one function, called xmldb_local_upgrade. This will contain database code like the examples in the previous section.

The /local directory can hold many more site-specific customizations. For more information, see the documentation at: http://docs.moodle.org/en/Development:Local_customisation#local.2Fdb.2Finstall.xml

The XMLDB editor

One of the nicest secrets in Moodle is the interactive **XMLDB editor**, which is hidden in the **Site Administration** block's **Miscellaneous** menu (as shown in the following screenshot). This editor lets you interactively create and manage the XML code that goes into the install.xml files, by using online tools:

This cool little tool can create new files and edit existing ones (as shown in the following screenshot). It can also create the XML from already-existing data tables in your database. It will also tell you if there is anything wrong with your XML (if you happened to create it by hand):

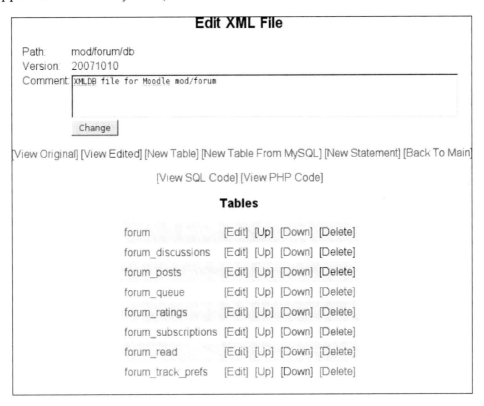

If you have the XML created, it can also generate the SQL that you need to execute for the database type that you are using. This is handy if you are developing the data tables and want to create these quickly. You can also generate PHP code suitable for the upgrade.php file by using the XMLDB and DDLIB functions. The following screenshot shows the table layout for an existing database table:

[View Original] [View Edited] [New Field] [New Key] [New Index] [Back]

[View SQL Code] [View PHP Code]

Fields

id	[Edit]	[Up]	[Down]	[Delete]	int (10) unsigned not null auto-numbered
course	[Edit]	[Up]	[Down]	[Delete]	int (10) unsigned not null default 0
forum	[Edit]	[Up]	[Down]	[Delete]	int (10) unsigned not null default 0
name	[Edit]	[Up]	[Down]	[Delete]	char (255) not null
firstpost	[Edit]	[Up]	[Down]	[Delete]	int (10) unsigned not null default 0
userid	[Edit]	[Up]	[Down]	[Delete]	int (10) unsigned not null default 0
groupid	[Edit]	[Up]	[Down]	[Delete]	int (10) signed not null default -1
assessed	[Edit]	[Up]	[Down]	[Delete]	int (1) signed not null default 1
timemodified	[Edit]	[Up]	[Down]	[Delete]	int (10) unsigned not null default 0
usermodified	[Edit]	[Up]	[Down]	[Delete]	int (10) unsigned not null default 0
timestart	[Edit]	[Up]	[Down]	[Delete]	int (10) unsigned not null default 0
timeend	[Edit]	[Up]	[Down]	[Delete]	int (10) unsigned not null default 0

Keys

primary	[Edit]	[Up]	[Down]	[Delete]	primary (id)
forum	[Edit]	[Up]	[Down]	[Delete]	foreign (forum) references forum (id)

Indexes

userid	[Edit]	[Up]	[Down]	[Delete]	not unique (userid)

This tool takes all of the drudgery out of hand-creating XML, and helps prevent the most common XML errors. Once you've started using it, you'll wonder how you ever got by without it.

Using the Moodle database in your code

Moodle has a well-defined API that can be used to perform almost any database function that you need. You would almost never need to access any SQL commands directly. The API is contained in the /lib/dmllib.php file (DM stands for Data Manipulation).

Retrieving data

There are three types of get functions for each of the three return types—fields, single records, and arrays of records. Each of these three types of functions specifies query information differently.

Query by parameters

The first type of function passes all of the query information through the parameter list for each of the three return types. All three types of functions take the table name as the first argument. This is always specified without the prefix (if there is one).

The first type is as follows:

```
get_field($table, $return, $field1, $value1, $field2='', $value2='',
        $field3='', $value3='')
```

This function returns a single field value, identified by the string `$return` parameter. If the field is not found, `false` is returned. It constructs a query from the field/value pairs specified as parameters. Each field/value pair becomes an equality comparison in the query. You must specify at least one pair; more than one are "and'ed" together.

This query is intended to find only one match, and will return only one match. If the query is ambiguous, you cannot be sure which record will be matched.

The following is an example:

```
$username = get_field('user', 'username', 'firstname', 'bob',
                    'lastname', 'roberts');
```

This will retrieve a single field, `username` that matches a `firstname` of 'bob' and a `lastname` of 'roberts' from the `user` table. If no match is found, `$username` will be `false`.

The second type is as follows:

```
get_record($table, $field1, $value1, $field2='', $value2='',
        $field3='', $value3='', $fields='*')
```

This function returns a single data record as an object. If the record is not found, `false` is returned. It constructs a query from the field/value pairs specified as parameters. Each field/value pair becomes an equality comparison in the query. You must specify at least one pair; more than one are "and'ed" together. You can specify the fields you want returned in the record or let it default to all.

As in the previous query, this one is intended to find only one match. If it finds more than one match, it will generate an error. So you should be using this in situations where you expect only one result.

The following is an example of this:

```
$userrec = get_record('user', 'firstname', 'bob', 'lastname',
'roberts', 'email', 'bob@email.com', 'username,firstname,lastname);
if ($userrec) {
    print_r($userrec);
}
```

This will retrieve a single data record called `$userrec`, with the items `username`, `firstname`, and `lastname`. If a record is found, the output will be as follows:

```
stdClass Object
(
    [username] => bobroberts
    [firstname] => Bob
    [lastname] => Roberts
)
```

The third type is as follows:

```
get_records($table, $field='', $value='', $sort='', $fields='*',
            $limitfrom='', $limitnum='')
```

This function returns an array of data records as objects, indexed by the first requested field, or the `id` field if a field is not specified. If no records are found, `false` is returned. This function constructs a query from the field/value pairs specified as parameters. If none are specified, then all records in the specified tables are returned. The `$sort` parameter lets you specify a field by which the returned array will be ordered. The `$fields` parameter lets you specify one or more fields to return. All fields should be separated by commas. If nothing is specified, then all fields are returned. The first field in the list will be used as the index for the array. If nothing is specified, the `id` field will be used as the index (remember, `id` is a required field in all Moodle tables). Lastly, you can limit the number of records returned by specifying a starting record (`$limitfrom`) and/or the maximum number of records (`$limitnum`).

The following is an example of this:

```
$userrecs = get_records('user', 'firstname', 'bob', 'lastname',
                        'id,firstname,lastname');
if ($userrecs) {
    print_r($userrecs);
}
```

This will retrieve all records matching the `firstname` condition, in an array indexed by the `id` parameter. If records are found, the output would be similar to the following:

```
Array
(
    [34] => stdClass Object
        (
            [id] => 34
            [firstname] => Bob
            [lastname] => Roberts
        )
    [123] => stdClass Object
        (
            [id] => 123
            [firstname] => Bob
            [lastname] => Williams
        )
)
```

Query by "where" string

The second type of function specifies the `where` part of the query as a single string parameter for each of the three return types. Each of these work exactly as their previous functions, except that the query is specified in the `$select` parameter. An example of a `$select` parameter would be: `name != 'bob'`, which would look for records where the name field does not equal the string `bob`. The advantage of these functions is that you can create more complex queries by using more than just equality and `'and'`.

These functions are as follows:

```
get_field_select($table, $return, $select)
get_record_select($table, $select='', $fields='*')
get_records_select($table, $select='', $sort='', $fields='*',
                $limitfrom='', $limitnum='')
```

An example using a query similar to the previous one would be as follows:

```
$select = "(firstname = 'bob' OR firstname = 'robert') AND lastname =
'roberts'";
$userrecs = get_records_select('user', $select);
```

Here, we are able to construct a more complex query by using two different possibilities for the `firstname`.

Query by full SQL

The third type of function requires a pre-constructed SQL string to be passed to the function. This SQL specifies all of the query handled by the parameters in the other functions, except for the $limitfrom and $limitnum parameters. For these functions, the table name must be constructed using the configured prefix. Care should be taken when constructing these so that the SQL works in all supported database technologies.

These functions are as follows:

```
get_field_sql($sql)
get_record_sql($sql)
get_records_sql($sql, $limitfrom='', $limitnum='')
```

An example using similar queries to the previous example would be as follows:

```
$sql = "SELECT u.id, u.firstname, u.lastname,
        MAX(ul.timeaccess) as lastaccess
    FROM {$CFG->prefix}user u
    INNER JOIN {$CFG->prefix}user_lastaccess ul
      ON ul.userid = u.id
      WHERE u.username = 'broberts'"
$userrec = get_record($sql);
```

This shows how more complex queries can be executed by using the standard APIs.

Storing data

There are really only two ways to store data using the Moodle API—by field and by record. The field functions allow you to use a query. The record functions expect a data structure to be provided that contains the data to be stored. In the case of an update to an existing record, this structure must contain the id field that identifies the record.

There are essentially four functions available, which are as follows:

- set_field
- set_field_select
- insert_record
- update_record

set_field and set_field_select

These functions allow you to set a specific field in a specific record to a provided value, using queries to identify the record. Their full specifications are as follows:

```
set_field($table, $newfield, $newvalue, $field1, $value1, $field2='',
          $value2='', $field3='', $value3='')
set_field_select($table, $newfield, $newvalue, $select, $localcall =
                 false)
```

Similar to the `get` functions, these functions allow you to specify a query either through the parameter list or through a constructed query string.

An example of this would be as follows:

```
$status = set_field('user', 'firstname', 'Robert', 'username',
                    'broberts');
```

This changes the `firstname` field of the record identified by the `username` 'broberts' to the string 'Robert' in the Moodle table `mdl_user` (assuming a prefix of `mdl_`).

insert_record and update_record

These functions allow you to create a new record or update an existing one with new data. Their full specifications are as follows:

```
insert_record($table, $dataobject, $returnid=true, $primarykey='id')
update_record($table, $dataobject)
```

If you don't specify otherwise, `insert_record` returns the `id` field of the newly-created data record to the caller. Both functions take a fully-defined data structure to insert the data. Each element of the structure that has a matching field name in the table is inserted into the record. It is important to note that, when inserting a new record, any fields in the table that cannot be NULL must have a corresponding element in the provided record.

An example of using these functions is as follows:

```
global $USER;
$newrec = new Object();
$newrec->id = $USER->id;
$newrec->firstname = 'Bill';
$newrec->lastname = 'Williams';
$newrec->username = 'bwilliams';
$newrec->password = hash_internal_user_password('secret');
$newrec->email = 'bwilliams@email.com';
$newid = insert_record('user', $newrec);
```

This will attempt to create a new record in the user table. The $newrec->id will be ignored (in fact it will be removed), because we are creating a new record and this will generate a new ID. If we called the update_record function with the same data object, the id field would define which record will be updated. In that case, all of the specified record elements would update their corresponding table fields.

There are many other functions available for accessing the Moodle databases. Familiarize yourself with the API in the /lib/dmllib.php file, and look at other code that is using data. You will find that you can do pretty much anything that you need to with these functions.

Common tables and relationships

Moodle has many tables, and plugins can add many more. There are a few tables that factor in to almost every task that you do. We will look at these, and their relationships to the other tables, in order to understand the data relationships in Moodle.

Course and module relationships

Let's take a look at course modules, and the tables that impact each one.

The following screenshot is a data relationship diagram showing the key relationships defined for the course_modules table. As you can see, this one table has links to five other Moodle tables. Every one of those links refers directly to an id field in another table.

The instance field links to the specific module table that the course_modules record is an instance of. In this case, it is a forum module, but it could be any valid Moodle module. In the following screenshot, the id field of the forum table is referenced by the instance field. The table to be referenced (for example, forum) is determined from the course_modules module field reference. The module field links to an id field in the modules table. The record it links to contains a name field, and this field defines the name used for the specific module table that the course_modules instance field refers to. In this example, the name field would contain the value forum.

You will also notice that three more tables have links to the course table (through a course or courseid field). This is quite common in the Moodle data structure, and was designed to make some queries easier.

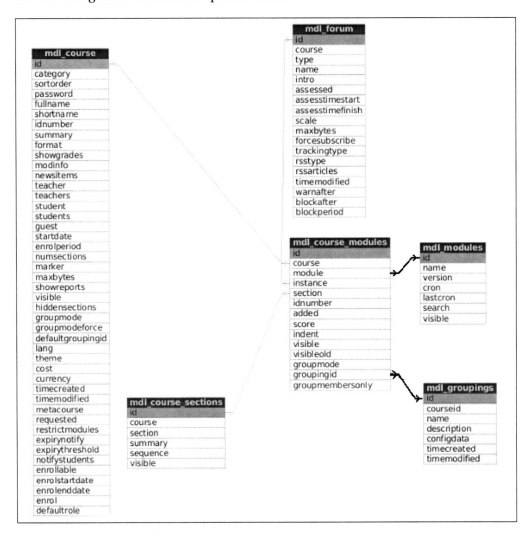

There are also some *hidden* relationships in the above diagram.

The sequence field in the course_sections table contains a comma separated list of course module id instances that defines the list and sequence of course modules installed in that section.

The modinfo field in the course table contains a serial encoded structure that contains information on all of the course modules installed in that course.

Hopefully, this helps you understand some of the complex relationships in the course and module structures, and why it is best to use the defined APIs where possible.

Programming best practices

When developing your database code, there are some best practices that you should adhere to. We will briefly discuss some of these.

Take only what you need

When extracting a large record from a data table, consider what information you actually need. Then, only get the field or fields that you need for processing. If it is one field you need, from one record, always use a get_field call. If you need more than one field, specify the ones you need in your get_record() call. Make sure that you include the id field as the first field if you are retrieving more than one record, so that there is a unique index for the returned array.

By retrieving only the data that you need, you can improve the speed of the database function and reduce the amount of memory needed for the program.

Limiting your returned data

When your code expects multiple records from a database call, it is always best to limit the number of records that you will get back. Use the $limitfrom and $limitnum parameters to do this. Using this method can control how much data gets returned at any one time, and can prevent the server from becoming overloaded.

The following is an example that uses the $limitfrom and $limitnum parameters:

```
$limitfrom = 0;
$limitnum = 100;
while ($records = get_records('user', 'deleted', 'n', 'id',
'id,firstname,lastname', $limitfrom, $limitnum) {
  foreach ($records as $uid => $userrec) {
    /// Do some processing ///
  }
$limitfrom += $limitnum;
}
```

This code gets all of the user records that aren't flagged as deleted, one hundred records at a time. This helps to control memory consumption and keeps your server from becoming overloaded.

Using recordsets

When you expect large datasets, it may be easier to use the `get_recordset` calls. These are called in the same way as the `get_records` functions. However, `get_recordset` uses internal recordset management to control memory use.

The full specification is as follows:

```
get_recordset($table, $field='', $value='', $sort='', $fields='*',
              $limitfrom='', $limitnum='')
```

The following is an example showing its usage (taken from the forum module):

```
$rs = get_recordset('course', '', '', '', 'id');
while ($course = rs_fetch_next_record($rs)) {
  $subcontext = get_context_instance(CONTEXT_COURSE, $course->id);
  forum_add_user_default_subscriptions($userid, $subcontext);
}
rs_close($rs);
```

Using a recordset consists of three steps:

1. Creating a recordset and saving it in a variable (`$rs = get_recordset`).

2. Fetching the next record from the set (`$course = rs_fetch_next_record($rs)`).

3. Closing the recordset when completed (`rs_close($rs)`). This frees up memory resources, which is important if you are doing any more processing in the same execution.

The internals of this manage the actual connections to the database, and are optimized to trade off query numbers and return data size for you.

Optimizing carefully with joins

When you have to get data that comes from multiple tables and does not already have an API defined for it, try to do as much of the work as you can through SQL JOINS instead of code. This requires knowledge of SQL: however, it can save a lot of processing resources if it is done properly. Remember, the database engine has been optimized to do its job—use it when you can. Just make sure that your SQL is database-agnostic.

Testing on more than one database engine

Always test your code using more than one database technology. You never know when something simple will break on one system, simply because of a database incompatibility. MySQL has been known for its fault tolerance, and can allow badly formed SQL to run when the same SQL would not run on another technology, such as PostgreSQL. Both MySQL and PostgreSQL are open-source products, so go ahead and install both in your test environment, and then test you code under both systems.

Summary

In this chapter, you have learned Moodle's database structure, its APIs, and how to manage its tables by creating and upgrading them. In addition, you have learned how to retrieve, add, and update data in tables. These skills will allow you to program in the most efficient way. Experiment with the database, play with it, and try out the different code functions so that you can become comfortable programming your applications with the database.

In the next chapter, we will explore several core Moodle modules.

7
Developing Pluggable Core Modules

Moodle can be extended by using a variety of plugins. Each of these plugin subsystems can be developed by using a variety of standard techniques and unique APIs.

In this chapter, we will look at several of these plugin systems, including:

- Assignment types
- Resource types
- Question types

We will also build our own assignment type.

Assignment types

An assignment is a Moodle activity module that allows specific tasks, which can be completed and tracked, to be assigned to students. The actual task is dependent upon the type of assignment that was selected when the activity is added to the course.

Assignments can be gradable, can be scheduled, and can be assigned due dates. Students complete an assignment through a specific submission action.

Types of tasks can include offline activities, uploading files, or composing content online by using a web-based editor. Assignment tasks are defined by a variety of assignment types.

What is an assignment type

Assignment types are a pluggable component in Moodle that allow specific tasks that can be carried out by students to be defined. Assignment types are selected directly from the **Add an activity...** drop-down menu, as shown in the following screenshot. The types available in that menu are defined by the presence of assignment type plugins:

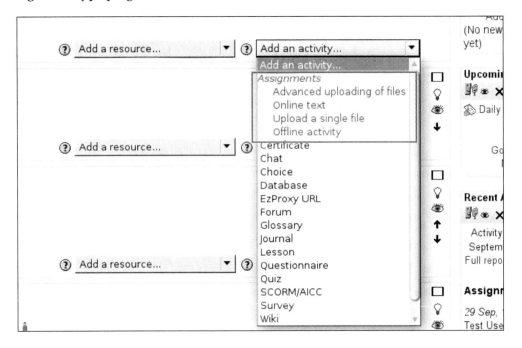

Standard Moodle comes with the following four assignment type plugins:

- **Offline activity**
- **Upload a single file**
- **Online text**
- **Advanced uploading of files**

Assignment types are all based on a similar architecture that includes a way to display the assignment instructions, provides a mechanism to submit the work performed, and provides a method of reviewing and grading the submission. They are created by extending the base assignment class in a new file.

Identifying assignment types

Assignment types are contained in a subdirectory of the `/mod/assignment/type/` directory, in a file named `assignment.class.php`. The subdirectory should be named something unique and descriptive of the specific type.

Like other plugins, database tables can be added and language strings can be defined through appropriate `db` and `lang/` subdirectories in the `type` subdirectory. Similarly, upgrades are defined through version definitions in a `version.php` file.

To load a new assignment type, move the entire assignment type subdirectory structure into the `/mod/assignment/type` directory and then visit the administration main page.

Assignment type basics

Let's examine the basic assignment elements that affect all plugins.

Standard assignments have two tables: `assignment` and `assignment_submissions`.

The `assignment` table keeps all of the data about the assignment. It contains five extra integer fields, `var1` through `var5`, which are available to any assignment type to use as it sees fit. For example, the `advanced upload` assignment type uses `var1` to store the number of files allowed to be uploaded, `var2` as a flag to indicate that notes are allowed, `var3` as a flag to indicate that the introduction text should be hidden before the assignment release date, and `var4` as a flag to indicate that users can let the instructors know when their files are ready. `var5` is not used.

The `assignment_submissions` table keeps all of the data about each user's submission. It contains three fields, which can be used by any assignment type the way they want. These are the text fields `data1`, `data2`, and `submissioncomment`. `submissioncomment` is intended to be used to contain the marker's comments. However, it is free to be used in other ways, if required by the assignment type.

These fields are there so that you can add new assignment types without having to create your own tables. You are still free to create your own tables, though.

For code, there is only one requirement. You need to create a file called `assignment.class.php` in a subdirectory in the `/mod/assignment/type/` directory, that contains a new class extended from the `assignment_base` class. The class must be named `assignment [your type]` and have a constructor with the same name. `[your type]` must be unique and should have a descriptive name. The constructor must set the object variable `type` to that same name.

In the next section, we will build our own assignment type, and demonstrate these requirements.

Building our own assignment type

We are going to build an assignment type that provides a daily journal between a student and a teacher. The assignment will provide the ability for a student to add entries daily, and each entry will be identified by the date on which it was entered. Additionally, we will plan for suitable privileged users to be able to comment on the entries. We will call our assignment type journal, and use it in place of the deprecated journal activity.

To make it simpler, we will assume there can only be one comment per entry and that the entire assignment can be graded, but not each entry.

Getting started

As described in the previous section, we need to create a new subdirectory in the assignment type directory. For our type, we will call it journal. Inside this subdirectory, create a new file called assignment.class.php, and enter the following code:

```php
<?php
/**
 * Extend the base assignment class for journal assignments
 *
 */
class assignment_journal extends assignment_base {
    function assignment_journal($cmid='staticonly', $assignment=NULL,
    $cm=NULL, $course=NULL) {
        parent::assignment_base($cmid, $assignment, $cm, $course);
        $this->type = 'journal';
    }
}
?>
```

This is all that we need, in order to have a valid assignment type. If you go to a course and add an assignment, you will be able to select this type. However, it won't do anything interesting until we finish coding it.

When you try to add this new type, you will notice that it is listed as [[typejournal]]. As always, this means that it is looking for a language string. We need to create a language file to define this.

In your new assignment type directory, create a new subdirectory called `lang/en_utf8/`. In this subfolder, create a file called `assignment_journal.php`. Put the following code in that file:

```php
<?php
$string['typejournal'] = 'Journal';
?>
```

 There is a bug in Moodle that actually prevents the language string created previously from working properly. It is scheduled to be fixed in version 1.9.6. See tracker issue MDL-16796 for more information.

Now that we have the absolute minimal basics done, let's plan out the rest.

Planning our data

As we described previously, student and reviewer comments are entered into this journal type. We also want to allow for more than one entry per student and reviewer. We could use the `data1` and `data2` fields in the `assignment_submissions` table for this. However, we would need to do some clever data manipulation to separate the different submissions. The `assignment_submissions` table only expects one entry per user per assignment.

To make our data easier to manage, we'll create new tables for the specific entries. The disadvantage of this is that we will have to create our own backup and restore procedures to save the data in our new tables.

We will continue to use the standard submissions table to identify each user's submission. However, we will add a new table that allows multiple entries per submission. This table will link to the submission number and contain one record for each entry. Each record will have a field for the user entry and the reviewer comment. We also want to track the creation and modification time for any entry. We won't worry about tracking changes to an entry.

To get our assignment type to create this table, add the file `install.xml` to our `type/journal/db/` directory as follows:

```xml
<?xml version="1.0" encoding="UTF-8" ?>
<XMLDB PATH="mod/assignment/type/journal/db" VERSION="20090928"
COMMENT="XMLDB file for Moodle mod/assignment/type/journal"
    xmlns:xsi="http://www.w3.org/2001/XMLSchema-instance"
    xsi:noNamespaceSchemaLocation="../../../../../lib/xmldb/xmldb.xsd"
>
  <TABLES>
```

```
    <TABLE NAME="assignment_journal_entries" COMMENT="Contains all
journal entries">
      <FIELDS>
        <FIELD NAME="id" TYPE="int" LENGTH="10" NOTNULL="true"
           UNSIGNED="true" SEQUENCE="true" ENUM="false"
           NEXT="submissionid"/>
        <FIELD NAME="submissionid" TYPE="int" LENGTH="10"
           NOTNULL="true" UNSIGNED="true" SEQUENCE="false"
           ENUM="false" COMMENT="Contains the submission id this
           entry pertains to" PREVIOUS="id" NEXT="entrytext"/>
        <FIELD NAME="entrytext" TYPE="text" LENGTH="big"
           NOTNULL="false" SEQUENCE="false" ENUM="false"
           COMMENT="The text of the entry"
           PREVIOUS="submissionid" NEXT="entrycreated"/>
        <FIELD NAME="entrycreated" TYPE="int" LENGTH="10"
           NOTNULL="false" UNSIGNED="true" DEFAULT="0"
           SEQUENCE="false" ENUM="false"
           COMMENT="Timestamp when created" PREVIOUS="entrytext"
           NEXT="entrymodified"/>
        <FIELD NAME="entrymodified" TYPE="int" LENGTH="10"
           NOTNULL="false" UNSIGNED="true" DEFAULT="0"
           SEQUENCE="false" ENUM="false"
           COMMENT="Timestamp when last modified"
           PREVIOUS="entrycreated" NEXT="commentuserid"/>
        <FIELD NAME="commentuserid" TYPE="int" LENGTH="10"
           NOTNULL="false" UNSIGNED="true" DEFAULT="0"
           SEQUENCE="false" ENUM="false"
           COMMENT="ID of the user who made the comment."
           PREVIOUS="entrymodified" NEXT="commenttext"/>
        <FIELD NAME="commenttext" TYPE="text" LENGTH="big"
           NOTNULL="false" SEQUENCE="false" ENUM="false"
           COMMENT="Text of any provided comment to this entry."
           PREVIOUS="commentuserid" NEXT="commentcreated"/>
        <FIELD NAME="commentcreated" TYPE="int" LENGTH="10"
           NOTNULL="false" UNSIGNED="true" DEFAULT="0"
           SEQUENCE="false" ENUM="false"
           COMMENT="Timestamp when created."
           PREVIOUS="commenttext" NEXT="commentmodified"/>
        <FIELD NAME="commentmodified" TYPE-"int" LENGTH-"10"
           NOTNULL="false" UNSIGNED="true" DEFAULT="0"
           SEQUENCE="false" ENUM="false"
           COMMENT="Timestamp of last modification."
           PREVIOUS="commentcreated"/>
      </FIELDS>
      <KEYS>
        <KEY NAME="primary" TYPE="primary" FIELDS="id"/>
      </KEYS>
      <INDEXES>
```

```
    <INDEX NAME="submissionididx" UNIQUE="false"
        FIELDS="submissionid" NEXT="commentuseridx"/>
    <INDEX NAME="commentuseridx" UNIQUE="false"
        FIELDS="commentuserid" PREVIOUS="submissionididx"/>
    </INDEXES>
    </TABLE>
    </TABLES>
</XMLDB>
```

In order to have the table created by Moodle, we need to create a `version.php` file in our `type/journal/` directory as follows:

```php
<?php
$plugin->version   = 2009090100;
$plugin->requires  = 2007101000;
?>
```

Now, visit the main administration page (notifications) and your table should be installed.

Adding custom settings

To start with, let's add some settings, to make the assignment more interesting. We will allow an option for resubmitting the assignment after it has been graded. With this on, the instructor can grade the journal iteratively as each new entry is added. If it's off, once the assignment has been graded, no more entries can be made. We will also add an option that enables or disables e-mail notifications when an entry is made, and one more option to define whether or not comments can be made on individual entries.

These settings are defined in the `setup_elements` function, as follows:

```php
function setup_elements(&$mform) {
    global $CFG, $COURSE;
    $ynoptions = array( 0 => get_string('no'), 1 =>
                get_string('yes'));
    $mform->addElement('select', 'resubmit',
            get_string('allowresubmit', 'assignment'), $ynoptions);
    $mform->setHelpButton('resubmit', array('resubmit',
                get_string('allowresubmit', 'assignment'),
            'assignment'));
    $mform->setDefault('resubmit', 0);
    $mform->addElement('select', 'emailteachers',
            get_string('emailteachers', 'assignment'), $ynoptions);
    $mform->setHelpButton('emailteachers', array('emailteachers',
                get_string('emailteachers', 'assignment'),
            'assignment'));
```

```
        $mform->setDefault('emailteachers', 0);
        $mform->addElement('select', 'var1',
                get_string('commentsallowed', 'assignment_journal'),
                $ynoptions);
        $mform->setHelpButton('var1', array('commentsallowed',
                get_string('commentsallowed', 'assignment_journal'),
                'assignment_journal'));
        $mform->setDefault('var1', 0);
    }
```

This form will now work, as-is. If you edit an instance of this assignment, you will see these new settings and can change and save them.

Making it do something useful

Although we now have a functioning assignment type, with the settings that we want, it doesn't do anything. Access it as a student and you'll see that it displays instructions and nothing else. It's time to add some function.

Viewing the journal

If you look at the standard view function in /mod/assignment/lib.php, you will see the following:

```
function view() {
    $context = get_context_instance(CONTEXT_MODULE,$this->cm->id);
    require_capability('mod/assignment:view', $context);
    add_to_log($this->course->id, "assignment", "view",
            "view.php?id={$this->cm->id}",
            $this->assignment->id, $this->cm->id);
    $this->view_header();
    $this->view_intro();
    $this->view_dates();
    $this->view_feedback();
    $this->view_footer();
}
```

The page is displayed by a set of view functions, each adding another layer to the page. What is missing is the display of any entries or the entry form. We need to replace this function with our own method, in order to display the student portion. Essentially, we need to insert another function in between the $this->view_dates() and $this->view_feedback functions.

We're going to borrow ideas (and code) from the standard online assignment type that comes with Moodle. Review the view method in /mod/assignment/type/online/assignment.class.php.

Getting the submission

First, we need to get a user's submission. In the standard assignment types, these are all stored in the `assignment_submissions` table and are retrieved through the `get_submission` function. In our example, part of the submission is in the standard table, and the rest is in our custom table. We could use the standard `get_submission` method and then add our own code to get the rest of the entries. Although this will work, it is more efficient to use the database to get the submission and other entries at once. Therefore, we will replace the `get_submission` function with our own function.

The code we will need for the SQL is as follows:

```
/// Construct the SQL to look for all entries to a submission.
/// Use the assignment_journal_entry.id as the first parameter for a
unique index.
$select = "SELECT je.id as jeid, s.*, je.entrytext, je.entrycreated,
          je.entrymodified, ".
         "je.commentuserid, je.commenttext, je.commentcreated,
          je.commentmodified ";
$from   = "FROM {$CFG->prefix}assignment_submissions s ";
$join   = "INNER JOIN {$CFG->prefix}assignment_journal_entries je ON
          je.submissionid = s.id ";
$where  = "WHERE (s.assignment = {$this->assignment->id}) AND
          (s.userid = {$userid}) ";
$order  = "ORDER BY je.entrycreated ASC ";
$sql    = $select . $from . $join . $where . $order;
$entries = get_records_sql($sql);
```

This will join the two tables that we care about, and return all of the information about all of the entries that the user has made. We use the journal entry ID as the first parameter, because the Moodle `get_records` functions return arrays of records indexed by the first parameter. The journal entry ID will be unique for all joined records.

We will return a standard submission record with a separate array element for the entries included. Refer to the provided code in the `get_submission` function for more information.

Adding an entry

The journal doesn't work very well if a user can't enter anything. We need to provide a mechanism for them to enter their daily entries.

To do this, we will add a new form to our file by using the Moodle formslib. This form will provide an HTML edit area that can be used to create an online entry.

The form code is a new class in our `assignment.class.php` file, and is as follows:

```
class mod_assignment_journal_edit_form extends moodleform {
    function definition() {
        $mform =& $this->_form;
      // visible elements
        $mform->addElement('htmleditor', 'text',
                get_string('todayssubmission', 'assignment_journal'),
                array('cols'=>60, 'rows'=>30));
        $mform->setType('text', PARAM_RAW); // to be cleaned before
                                            // display
        $mform->setHelpButton('text', array('reading', 'writing',
                'richtext'), false, 'editorhelpbutton');
        $mform->addRule('text', get_string('required'), 'required',
                null, 'client');
        $mform->addElement('format', 'format', get_string('format'));
        $mform->setHelpButton('format', array('textformat',
                get_string('helpformatting')));
      // hidden params
        $mform->addElement('hidden', 'id', 0);
        $mform->setType('id', PARAM_INT);
      // buttons
        $this->add_action_buttons();
    }
}
```

This code now allows us to display the form on the screen and retrieve any data that has been entered into it. We will use this in our main `view_submission` function. Note that we have used `get_string` with our assignment type in order to use language strings defined specifically for this assignment type.

Viewing a submission

We have inserted a new function called `view_submission` into our view function. This function will handle all aspects of viewing a user's submission, including the entry form. This function will also identify when submissions have not been made. It will allow a user to edit only the current day's entry. Other days' entries will be listed and can be selected for viewing.

If you look through this function in the provided code, you will see that we first create the new form, then set up its defaults, and then see if any data has been submitted through the form. If so, we handle that data and then update the submissions as appropriate. The data is updated through our new `update_submission` function.

If the form has been identified as being in use (the user clicked on the **Edit today's entry** button), the form is displayed. If not, we display all of the user's entries, including today's.

To separate the code out better, we have created a function for displaying the entries. The function `display_entries` does this. Review this function in the provided code.

We have separated our display into two sections. The top section displays today's entry and the button to edit today's entry. The bottom section lists all of the other days' entries as dates with links to view their content. Clicking on any of these links reloads the page and displays the content for that day in that section.

If you have been following along, go ahead and try out the assignment as a student.

Reviewing students' entries

We now have a functioning user interface that allows a user to create and review their daily entries. We need a way for instructors to be able to review and grade the entries.

When an instructor views the assignment, they will see a link at the top of the page that shows how many submitted assignments there are (as shown in the following screenshot). Clicking on this link takes them to a summary page for all of their students. This page is generated through the standard `submissions.php` file that calls the `submissions` function, which in turn calls the `display_submissions` function. These functions will work as-is for our purposes. However, we need to provide a function called `print_student_answer` in order for `display_submissions` to work:

The `print_student_answer` function provides a display of the requested user's submission in a way that can be linked to a more thorough display for grading. For our purposes, we'll provide a list showing the dates of all of the most recent entries. I've "borrowed" code from the `online` assignment type again, and modified it for our requirements. Review the `print_student_answer` function in the supplied code. Now, when we click on the submitted assignments link, we should see something similar to the following screenshot:

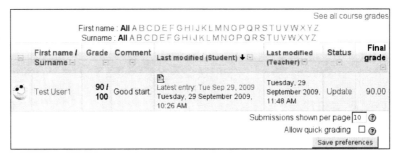

We need one more thing. In the journal example, when a teacher views the list of online assignment submissions, there is a link to a particular student's file. However, we want a link to a particular student's entry. By borrowing code from the `online` assignment type's `file.php` file, we can create a similarly-functioning file for the `journal` assignment type, called `entry.php`. Both `file.php` and `entry.php` ensure that the user viewing them has the necessary privileges (such as capabilities) to do so. In this case, we use the `mod/assignment:grade` capability.

Because the display that we want to show to the instructor is pretty much the same as the one that we show to the student, we just use the same `display_entries` function as before. However, here we provide the URL of the `journal` assignment type's `entry.php` script. This allows the instructor to review the submissions in the same pop-up window, as follows:

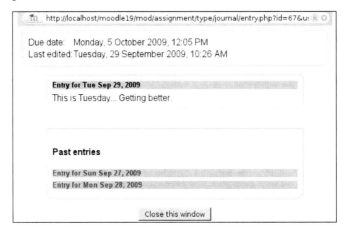

One special item that you may notice in the pop-up window is that the standard footer links are not present. This is due to a special coding function in the `print_footer` function that allows us to specify 'empty' as a parameter. This parameter will print the footer only with closing page tags, and leave the other links out. In a pop-up window such as this, it prevents navigation.

The rest of the functions now work. We can even grade the submission.

Backup and restore functions

As we've created our own table, we need to make sure that our assignment type can handle the backup and restore functions for that table. We can leave all other backup and restore functions to the main assignment function.

The main assignment class provides four functions: `backup_one_mod`, `backup_one_submission`, `restore_one_mod`, and `restore_one_submission`. Our type has an extra table for submissions, so we only need to worry about submission functions.

Review the functions `backup_one_submission` function and the `restore_one_submission` function in the provided code. You will see that all of the information from the `assignment_journal_entries` table is backed up and restored. To do this, we add a new "ENTRIES" section to the XML at the level it was left at, and a new "ENTRY" section for each of the user entries.

These functions will ensure that our user information can be restored safely.

Finishing up

There is one more function that we need to add in order to ensure complete operation of our assignment type. When an assignment is deleted, it calls the function `delete_instance`. This deletes all of the submission and assignment records. Unfortunately, it won't delete any of our `assignment_journal_entries` records.

To do that, we need to implement our own `delete_instance` function. Once we delete the records that we care about, we can just pass the rest of the function on to the parent function. If you look at the `delete_instance` function in the supplied code, you will notice that after we delete all of the `assignment_journal_entries` records we are concerned with, we finish the procedure with the following line of code:

```
return parent::delete_instance($assignment);
```

This passes the function to the parent function, which completes the deletions.

This completes our assignment type. If you feel experimental, try and complete the assignment by adding the ability for instructors to comment on the entries. Remember, we allowed for that possibility in the data structures.

Resource types

A resource is a Moodle module designed to present non-interactive information. The format of information is dependent upon the type of resource selected when it is added to a course.

Resource types include text pages, web pages, links to websites or files, directory listings, and IMS content packages.

What is a resource type?

Resource types are pluggable components in Moodle. They define the format and display of static information.

Similar to activity types, these are selected directly from an **Add a resource...** drop-down menu (as shown in the following screenshot). The options available in this menu are defined by the resource type plugins loaded in your Moodle system:

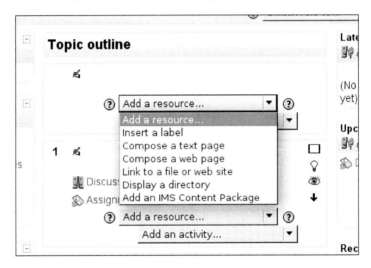

All resource types use the same base class and data table. Each resource type is responsible for what they display and how they display it. These are created by extending the base resource class in a new file.

Identifying resource types

Resource types are contained in a subdirectory of the /mod/resource/type/ directory, in a file named resource.class.php. The directory should be named something unique and descriptive of the specific type.

Language strings can be defined through appropriate `lang/` subdirectories in the `type` subdirectory. Unlike assignment type plugins, resource types cannot define their own data tables and thus do not contain `db` subdirectories or `version.php` files.

To load a new resource type, move the entire directory structure into the `type` subdirectory. There is no need to visit the administration page as resource types can perform no further installation.

Resource type basics

Let's examine the basic resource elements that affect all resource type plugins.

All resource types define themselves by using the same `resource` table. The table contains fields that are intended to be used in the same way by all types, and also the fields that can be used however the type needs them, as shown in the following screenshot:

Field	Type	Collation	Attributes	Null	Default	Extra
id	bigint(10)		UNSIGNED	No	*None*	auto_increment
course	bigint(10)		UNSIGNED	No	0	
name	varchar(255)	utf8_general_ci		No		
type	varchar(30)	utf8_general_ci		No		
reference	varchar(255)	utf8_general_ci		No		
summary	text	utf8_general_ci		Yes	*NULL*	
alltext	mediumtext	utf8_general_ci		No	*None*	
popup	text	utf8_general_ci		No	*None*	
options	varchar(255)	utf8_general_ci		No		
timemodified	bigint(10)		UNSIGNED	No	0	

The `reference` field is intended to contain a file, URL, or any other reference to an external resource. However, a resource type could use this for any necessary information as long as this information fits into the field's 255 character limit. Three other fields: `alltext`, `popup`, and `options`, are all intended to be used for whatever purpose the resource type needs.

A resource type needs to implement the `base` class, and requires the following code as a minimum:

```
class resource_new extends resource_base
{
    function resource_new($cmid=0)
    {
        parent::resource_base($cmid);
    }
```

```
function display()
{
    ///Display the resource
    global $CFG;
    parent::display();
}
function add_instance($resource)
{
    return parent::add_instance($resource);
}
function update_instance($resource)
{
    return parent::update_instance($resource);
}
function delete_instance($resource)
{
    return parent::delete_instance($resource);
}
function setup_elements(&$mform)
{
}
function setup_preprocessing(&$default_values)
{
}
}
```

For your type, you simply need to replace _new with the name of your type. So, if you created a new resource type called youtube, you would create a directory called /mod/resource/type/youtube/ with a resource.class.php file in it as done before, and having a class called resource_youtube.

Your new resource type only needs to provide two functions: the constructor, which only needs to call the parent constructor, and the display function. The display function is the function responsible for actually providing the screen output for the type.

Take a look at the provided resource types for examples of how to create your own.

Question types

Question types are part of the question engine and not actually a module. However, they are a core piece of the quiz module and are designed to be used by other activity modules.

A question, in Moodle speak, is the set of definitions that make up a reusable interactive element used for assessment. These definitions include the question text, its possible answers, any grading requirements, feedback to responses, and more.

What is a question type?

A question type is a pluggable unit in the question engine that provides all of the definition and functionality of an assessment. They can be managed from the **Questions** menu item on the front page and any course administration menu, or from the quiz activity editing screens.

The **Questions** menu (shown in the following screenshot) allows you to create, edit, view, and manage questions into categories. You can also import questions to and export questions from a variety of question formats.

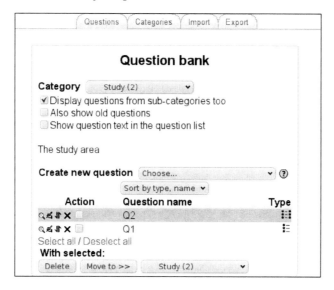

There are a number of standard question types that come with Moodle. These are as follows:

- Calculated
- Description
- Essay
- Matching
- Embedded Answers (Cloze Test/Gap Fill)
- Multiple Choice
- Short Answer
- Numerical
- Random Short-Answer Matching
- True/False

Each of these types defines its actions, views, and settings through an extended class.

Identifying question types

Question types are contained in the question directory structure under the `/question/type/` subdirectory, in a file named `questiontype.php`. The directory should be named something unique and descriptive of the specific question type.

Language strings can be defined through the appropriate `lang/...` subdirectories in the `type` subdirectory. Data tables and other database structures can be managed in a `db` subdirectory using appropriate `install.xml` and `upgrade.php` scripts.

To load a new question type, move the entire directory structure into the `type` subdirectory and then visit the main administration page.

Question type basics

Let's examine the basic question elements that affect every question type plugin.

As mentioned previously, a question type should have a subdirectory with a unique name describing your type. In that directory, you will need the following files:

- `questiontype.php`: The class file that extends the default question type class
- `edit_[yourtype]_form.php`: The editing form that defines the question settings and data
- `lang/en_utf8/qtype_[yourtype].php`: The language file that defines the necessary language strings that you will use
- `lang/en_utf8/help/[yourtype]/[yourtype].html`: Information on what your question is and how it works

You can also have the following files:

- `icon.gif`: An image file that is displayed as an icon to identify the question type
- `version.php`: The version file used to manage your question type; this is necessary if you have custom data tables
- `db/install.xml`: The definition of your database additions

There are other options available as well. See `http://docs.moodle.org/en/Development:Question_type_plugin_how_to` for more information.

Let's look at the important pieces in detail. Refer to the provided code, `/question/type/TEMPLATE`, taken from the new question template code provided in the Moodle `contrib` repository (`http://cvs.moodle.org/contrib/plugins/question/type/TEMPLATE/`).

The main class

Your `questiontype.php` file contains the extension of the `default_questiontype` class. The default class is located in the `/question/type/questiontype.php` file. The version is located in the `type` subdirectory.

There are two methods that you will have to define, which are as follows:

- `name()`: This returns the string name of your question type, and should be the same as the directory you defined.

- `print_question_formulation_and_controls(&$question, &$state, $cmoptions, $options)`: This is the main function that displays the question and all of its interactions to the user. The function receives the question object, the current state of this particular question instance, the `course` module record for the module, and options that can be used by the function to render the question in particular ways. Currently, the `$options` is only set by the quiz module in the `quiz_get_renderoptions` function in the `/mod/quiz/locallib.php` file. Review this function to see all of the options that the quiz might provide.

Many question types include an `html` file, such as `display.html`, as part of the display process. However, you can simply output all of the display code from this function, as well.

With these methods, you have everything that you need for a question type class.

There are many other methods that you may want to define. Review the template code provided, to determine which ones you may want to use.

The editing form

Your `edit_[yourtype]_form.php` file contains the extension of the `question_edit_form` class. This code generates the form that is used to define and modify a question of this question type. The `[yourtype]` portion should be replaced by the same name as that of the directory.

Your form only needs one function, the `qtype` function. This returns the name of your question type, just as the `name` function did in your question type class.

To add your own settings, extend the `definition_inner` function. With this function, you can add form elements specific to your question type. It receives the `mform` object as an argument so that you can continue adding form elements.

The following screenshot shows the form for the multiple choice question type, separating out the question-specific elements from the common elements. The common elements are the same for all question types. The specific elements are the ones that are specific to this question type.

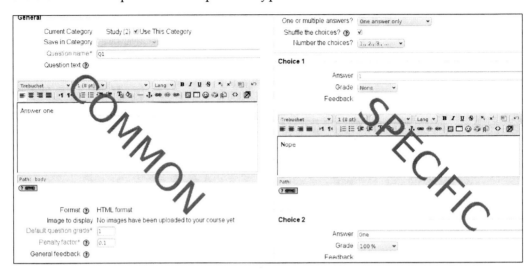

Two other functions that you will probably want to extend are the `set_data` and `validation` functions. The `set_data` function allows you to pre-process and load into the form extra data defined by your question type. The `validation` function allows you to process data that has been submitted, run validation rules on it, and return errors if it does not validate.

The main language file

The main language file, `lang/en_utf8/qtype_[yourtype].php`, defines the necessary language strings, and any extra strings that your question type needs.

As a minimum, your file needs to contain the following:

```
$string['[yourtype]'] = 'YOUR NAME';
$string['[yourtype]summary'] = 'One or two sentence summary of what
this question type does.';
$string['adding[yourtype]'] = 'Adding a [yourtype] question';
$string['editing[yourtype]'] = 'Editing a [yourtype] question';
```

As with the previous examples, replace the `[yourtype]` string with your question type name.

Examine the provided question types, and those provided in the Moodle `contrib` libraries (`http://cvs.moodle.org/contrib/plugins/question/type/`), for examples and ideas for building your own.

Other important question constructs

As you examine the question type code, you will notice that there are many other tasks that you can perform. Some of the most common ones are described in the following sections.

Grading

Questions such as multiple choice, matching, and true/false are graded automatically by the code. The class provides two functions that you should use if your question provides automatic answer checking and grading: `test_response` and `grade_responses`. The `test_response` function is intended to provide the code that verifies that the user has answered the question correctly, and return `true` or `false`. Most of the time, extending this will be all that you need to do, and you can let the default `grade_responses` function handle the rest. However, many question types completely override `grade_responses` and do all of their own work.

Other types of questions, such as the `essay` type, require manual grading. In these cases, you need to indicate that manual grading is required through the `is_manual_graded`, and optionally the `is_question_manual_graded` functions. These functions return `true` to indicate that the entire question type requires manual grading, or that a particular instance of a question requires manual grading, respectively.

Backup and restore functions

If you add your own data constructs, you will need to add your own backup and restore functions. This is done through the aptly-named `backup` and `restore` functions. If you examine a question type from the Moodle `contrib` repository (for example, `order`), you will see how to use these functions. They are called for any question providing them, from the `/question/backuplib.php` script.

Import and export function support

Question types have the ability to import and export their information in a variety of formats. The formats that are supported are limited, and currently only include Moodle XML, GIFT, and QTI2 formats. To give your question type the ability to import and/or export in any of these formats, you need to provide appropriate `import_from_[format]` and `export_to_[format]` functions. You need to provide one of these functions for each format that is supported, replacing `[format]` with the appropriate format name (for example, `export_to_gift`).

As an example, review a question type (for example, `order`) in the Moodle `contrib` repository.

CSS and JavaScript support

If your question needs some special layout information, or JavaScript enhancement, you can provide this through the inclusion of specific files. Add your CSS definitions to a file called `styles.css` in your question `type` subdirectory. Add any JavaScript that you need to a file called `script.js` in the same subdirectory. Both of these files will be loaded by the system when your question is accessed.

Where to get more help

The question system is a highly complex, evolving system. The API is still undergoing testing and modification, and may change (for the better). Fortunately, this particular system is fairly well documented.

You can find details of how to create a question type and a template question type in the Moodle `contrib` repository at `/plugins/question/type/TEMPLATE/`. This is further described in the document wiki at `http://docs.moodle.org/en/ Development:Question_type_plugin_how_to#Model_Question_Types`.

The main development documentation for the question component is located at `http://docs.moodle.org/en/Question_engine`. From there, you can find a large amount of documentation for all of the question component's functions.

Summary

In this chapter, you looked at the most common pluggable features of Moodle. We examined how each of the plugin types work and how each can be extended to provide new custom functionality for Moodle. You used these concepts to build your own assignment type (`journal`).

In the next chapter, you will learn how to create customized Moodle reports.

8
Creating Moodle Reports

Moodle's goal is learning. One of the key requirements of organizations that are delivering learning is to be able to measure that learning. One of Moodle's great strengths is its logging of user activity in courses. Just about every click within a course is logged, along with the time, date, username, user's IP address, module accessed, and the action performed by the user. Moodle also includes a large library of built-in reports. These reports compile and analyze the log tables and other data in the Moodle database into usable information for administrators, teachers, and students. Examples of these reports include grade reports, activity reports, sitewide statistics, and system health checks, amongst others. Administrators often find that they need a custom report to get the data in exactly the format that their organization desires. Because of Moodle's excellent logging system, we normally have all of the data that we need to provide new reports that meet these needs.

This chapter will cover a variety of methods for adding to Moodle's built-in reports. We will cover the following major topics:

- Creating course reports
- Creating gradebook reports
- Creating Admin reports
- Working with additional output formats: CSV, PDF, and Microsoft Excel

In our first section, we will create a course-level report. Let's get started.

Creating course reports

Moodle has a simple method of including new course reports. All that is required is a subfolder in the `./course/reports` folder and a file called `mod.php`. This file (`mod.php`) contains a fragment of HTML/PHP code that gets included in the course report list. Stay tuned! We will cover the specifics of how to do this in an upcoming section of this chapter. Typically the `mod.php` file will generate a link to another PHP file, normally `index.php`. We might also want to use some of our other tricks from past chapters. All of the common elements that we have studied in the past, such as language files, `version.php`, and `access.php` all apply to report modules. We will create a sample report, the non-participants report, which will use all of these elements. In the next section, we start to dig into this new report.

For the official developers' documentation for course reports, see `http://docs.moodle.org/en/Development:Course_Report_Plugins`.

Defining the non-participants report

Moodle has a useful report called the participants report. This allows an administrator or instructor to select an activity or resource, the time interval, the course role, and finally the action performed. The report then queries the Moodle log table creating a distinct list of users and their log counts meeting the criteria selected. It formats the results into a tidy table with a checkbox in each user's row. The report can then be used to send a message to one or more of the users. This is extremely valuable for an instructor; however, it is often important to know the opposite information: who did not participate. This is especially true of courses delivered online, where it is more challenging to make sure that learners stay engaged without face-to-face contact. To meet this need, we are going to create a non-participation report. Luckily, because Moodle is open source, we don't have to start from scratch! We can base our new report on the participation report, and we can just modify what we need to change. The new report will allow us to find students who haven't participated in a particular activity, and if so we choose to send them a message that they need to complete the activity.

In our office, I like to use a saying: "whether you are lazy or efficient depends on how much you get paid". I use this to reinforce the thinking that good programmers and system administrators should re-use as much work as possible, whenever possible. It might seem lazy to do this, but programmers and administrators should think of it as being efficient! The method that we are going to use in this chapter is very much in this philosophy. This highlights one of Moodle's greatest strengths: we can build on anything that exists in Moodle because we have the source code and the right to make use of it, as long as we follow the rules of the GPL. In the upcoming sections, we will borrow code from not just one location but two distinct parts of

Moodle. We could certainly spend some extra time and perhaps craft a solution that is a bit more efficient. However, for the purpose of learning, reusing code will give us an opportunity to explore this method in more detail. And we will also see a few more areas of Moodle code at the same time. This is common practice in the Moodle development community. Prior to the book you are reading now, many of these techniques were only documented in the code.

Getting started

There are two ways that we can get started. We can either create a new folder called `nonparticipation` in the `course/report` folder, or we can duplicate and rename the `participation` folder. I chose the former, in order to test each element individually as the sample for this chapter was developed. However, it is a bit faster to just duplicate the folder. We don't have to make that many modifications, but more than one might expect. We will have more on that later. For the most part, we just need to search any occurrence of `participation` or `participant` and replace it with `nonparticipation` or `nonparticipant`. Then later, we will add a query in order to gather a complete participants list for the course. Let's get into greater detail by looking at the `mod.php` file.

Updating mod.php

Remember that `mod.php` is the only requirement for this type of report. We need to copy `mod.php` from the participation report into the `nonparticipation` folder. Then, we need to make our first change around line 7. We just need to reference a new capability in this line so that we can control who can access the report:

```
if (has_capability('coursereport/nonparticipation:view', $context)) {
```

Notice that, as mentioned before, this file just uses the `echo` function to output some HTML that is included on the report list page:

```
echo '<p>';
```

Next, we need to replace the `get_string` referenced in order to change the label for our report. Keep in mind that we will later need to make an appropriate entry in our language file(s):

```
$myreport = get_string('nonparticipationreport',
                       'report_nonparticipation');
```

In this next line, we simply create a link to the report file. Note that we could have used any filename or URL in this reference. We could even link to an external site, passing some variables from Moodle as part of the URL or via a form action. Most of the time, we are going to just link to an index.php file inside our report folder. Another way that we might use this is to link to another report inside Moodle. In the following section of code, we link to the index.php file in our report folder:

```
echo "<a href=\"{$CFG->wwwroot}/course/report/nonparticipation/index.
php?id={$course->id}\">";
echo "$myreport</a>";
echo '</p>';
```

In the next section, we will define the capability referenced in the if statement seen previously.

Controlling access

As we have done with several other plugins, we need to create a capability to control access to the report. Let's create a db folder and copy the access.php file from the participation report. The format of this file is exactly what we need. We just need to rename the capability as follows:

```
$coursereport_nonparticipation_capabilities = array(
    'coursereport/nonparticipation:view' => array(
```

That's it. It's that simple. Now let's move on to some key points about how to work with language files for reports.

Language strings

Note that because the participation report is a core module, it doesn't define its language strings within its own folder. This is common for core modules. For the default language, English (**en_utf8**), most of these strings are defined in /lang/en_utf8/moodle.php file. There is a function defined in /lib/moodlelib.php file that defines a function called places_to_search_for_lang_strings(). It provides a nice reference for locations to search language strings and their formats. The function returns an array of paths keyed by module type. The relevant section of code is quoted as follows:

```
'__exceptions' => array('moodle', 'langconfig'),
'assignment_' => array('mod/assignment/type'),
'auth_' => array('auth'),
'block_' => array('blocks'),
'datafield_' => array('mod/data/field'),
'datapreset_' => array('mod/data/preset'),
```

```
'enrol_' => array('enrol'),
'filter_' => array('filter'),
'format_' => array('course/format'),
'qtype_' => array('question/type'),
'report_' => array($CFG->admin.'/report', 'course/report', 'mod/quiz/
                    report'),
'resource_' => array('mod/resource/type'),
'gradereport_' => array('grade/report'),
'gradeimport_' => array('grade/import'),
'gradeexport_' => array('grade/export'),
'qformat_' => array('question/format'),
'profilefield_' => array('user/profile/field'),
```

Although we have pretty thoroughly covered language files in other sections, there is one nuance with the naming of the language file for our non-participation report. Although the official developer documentation doesn't reference a specific naming scheme for language files for course reports, it does document a format for gradebook reports. The format is `report_<name>.php`, and to reference a string in the language file you use `get_string('my string', 'report_<name>')`. For our report, this translates to `report_nonparticipation.php`. Here is an example of using the language string:

```
get_string('nonparticipationreport','report_nonparticipation');
```

Note that this naming format is a convention, but not a requirement. Moodle's core libraries store the language strings with their file name. Generally, it's a good idea to follow Moodle's conventions, but there may be situations where we want to use some common strings across more than one module (for example, a series of related modules that use similar wording). In the next section, we will dig into the mechanics of gathering our report data.

Changes to Moodle's API

In early versions of Moodle, there was a series of `get_user` functions. These functions could be called to generate user lists. The `get_user` functions were all deprecated when 1.9 came out. This is the legacy of the roles system that was added with Moodle version 1.7. Prior to the current roles system, Moodle had a much simpler but less flexible access permission system. An unfortunate, side effect of adding flexibility was greater complexity. This caused some performance issues with the initial 1.7 release, for large sites. Each version since has improved on both the functionality and the performance of roles. However, the community is still wrestling with the best way to do this with the contexts, roles, and capabilities model. As a practical result of this, we have to apply a bit more elbow grease in certain areas in order to get the desired result. It leads to a better overall user experience at the cost of more development effort. Future versions of Moodle will continue to improve this area for both users and programmers.

Exploring the People block

To understand why we need to look at the People block next, we need to understand how the participant report works in a bit more detail. The key factor is that this report generates its data by querying the log table (`mdl_log`) for activity. If it finds a record for a user in our course, it then looks up the user's details in the `mdl_user` table. This information is then included in the report. In a sense, this is the exact opposite from what we need. However, to connect the dots, we need to generate a list of all course participants that have the selected role. Once we have this list, we can compare it against the log, and only display participants with no activity.

It so happens that the People block already does exactly what we need. We can simply find the segment of code that generates this list and put it into our report code. Now that we know we need to look at the People block, we need to find the specific source file to investigate. The easiest way to do this is to add an instance of the People block to a course and click on it. We can then examine the URL in our browser. As we can see in the following screenshot, the code that we need to look at is in the `./user/index.php` file:

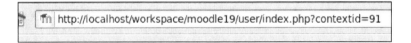

As we look through the file, we will find the start of the section that we need around line 387. One may be surprised to find how much work goes into getting a participants list, considering this is a Learning Management System; user lists are a pretty core function. We will have more information on this state of affairs later in this section. The overall structure is a series of if/then statements that assign query variables. We don't need all of the elements of the query for our report; we are only concerned with assigning `$select`, `$from`, and `$where` to our SQL query. Because we are always running our queries against a valid course, we can also ignore all but the first case in the if/then clauses. The other clauses are designed for special cases, such as the front page course, which does not have course reports.

Setting $select

In this first code section, we see the 'select' part of the query constructed. Note the use of the `DISTINCT` operator, which limits us to only one entry per user. There are several different select statements in this section of code. These are assigned depending on the context of the user list that is being generated. In our case, we need the select statement for non-front page courses: `if($context->id !=` `$frontpagectx->id)`. Then, we transplant the code from `/user/index.php` into `/course/report/nonparticipation/index.php` for our report. The appropriate section of code is as follows:

```
if ($context->id != $frontpagectx->id) {
  $select = 'SELECT DISTINCT u.id, u.username, u.firstname,
u.lastname, u.email, u.city, u.country, u.picture, u.lang, u.timezone,
u.emailstop, u.maildisplay, u.imagealt, COALESCE(ul.timeaccess, 0) AS
lastaccess, r.hidden, ctx.id AS ctxid, ctx.path AS ctxpath, ctx.depth
AS ctxdepth, ctx.contextlevel AS ctxlevel ';
```

Setting $from

In this section of the code, Moodle assigns the `$from` variable, which includes joins to the `context` and `role_assignment` tables (see *Chapter 1, Moodle Architecture* for coverage of Moodle's role system). This is where we limit the result set to both the appropriate course (as defined by the context ID) and the selected role assignment in the course. This is the section of the code where we really benefit from looking at how core Moodle accomplishes the task. Unless we were hand writing complex queries against the Moodle database every day, it would take us a significant amount of trial and error to come up with this set of joins. Keep in mind that any use of joins in queries should be carefully reviewed. This is especially true if you are querying fields that are not indexed. Joins on non-indexed fields can be very expensive in terms of server resources. This query comes from core, so we can have some confidence that it is safe:

```
if ($context->id != $frontpagectx->id or $roleid >= 0) {
$from    = "FROM {$CFG->prefix}user u
  LEFT OUTER JOIN {$CFG->prefix}context ctx
    ON (u.id=ctx.instanceid AND ctx.contextlevel =
    ".CONTEXT_USER.")
  JOIN {$CFG->prefix}role_assignments r
    ON u.id=r.userid
  LEFT OUTER JOIN {$CFG->prefix}user_lastaccess ul
    ON (r.userid=ul.userid and ul.courseid = $course->id) ";
```

Let's have a look at a representative assignment from viewing the participation list from a course:

```
FROM mdl_user u
  LEFT OUTER JOIN mdl_context ctx ON (u.id=ctx.instanceid AND
  ctx.contextlevel = 30)
  JOIN mdl_role_assignments r ON u.id=r.userid
  LEFT OUTER JOIN mdl_user_lastaccess ul ON (r.userid=ul.userid and
ul.courseid = 2)
```

Setting $where

We find the final section of what we need from the query at around line 424. Note that we are skipping some sections that we don't need, such as the sort order, because we will be using an array sort. This section assigns the query's where clause. Here, Moodle builds on the above joins, in order to limit our result set to just entries for our course and requested role assignment. Again, this is done by restricting the result set to the appropriate context ID (course) and role ID. We need to make a note of any variables used in this query. We will have to replace these with the appropriate ones in our reporting code.

For example, in the following section of code we need to find a suitable replacement for $selectrole:

```
if ($context->id != $frontpagectx->id) {
$where  = "WHERE (r.contextid = $context->id OR r.contextid in
                  $listofcontexts)
  AND u.deleted = 0 $selectrole
  AND (ul.courseid = $course->id OR ul.courseid IS NULL)
```

Note that in this section of the query we see some safety checks that remove certain roles and usernames. In our report, the role is going to be selected by a pull-down menu. Therefore, we won't need to do this in our report and will discard these sections:

```
  AND u.username != 'guest' $adminroles $hiddensql ";
$where .= get_course_lastaccess_sql($accesssince);
```

All that's left now is to put everything together.

Making the query call

We have analyzed the People block code, and isolated the components of the query that we will need. Let's look at a final line of code from the People block. In this line, we make the actual function call by using get_recordset_sql. This is found around line 487:

```
$userlist = get_recordset_sql($select.$from.$where.$wheresearch.$sort,
$table->get_page_start(),  $table->get_page_size());
```

As we mentioned earlier that's quite a bit of work just to create a participants list for a course. This is especially inefficient when we need to do this often in the course of programming an LMS. In the next section, we discuss how we reached this state of affairs.

Let's look at a few other options for generating participant lists. We can use the `get_users_by_capability` call from `accesslib.php`, and use a capability such as `moodle/course:view`. Or we can use `get_role_users` and specify a list of role IDs that we want to find. We can get a list of all valid roles for the course context to feed into this function call.

In the next section, we insert the code sections that we found in the People block into our report code.

Modifying index.php

We need to make several modifications to the `index.php` file in order to complete the creation of our new report. Let's start with some simple structural text substitutions.

Making text substitutions

Most of these substitutions require changing the text "participation" to "nonparticipation". When making changes of this type we can generally use our editor's search function to find all instances of the original text for replacement. It's a good idea to review this line by line to make sure that you are making the correct change.

At line 33 we need to change the log entry line to the following:

```
add_to_log($course->id, "course", "report nonparticipation", "report/
nonparticipation/index.php?id=$course->id", $course->id);
```

At line 35, we change the report's name by changing the `get_string` assigments as follows:

```
$strparticipation = get_string('nonparticipationreport','report_
nonparticipation');
```

We also need to update the `$baseurl` assignment for the report to reflect the report's new location. This is done at line 128. The code is displayed below:

```
$baseurl =  $CFG->wwwroot.'/course/report/nonparticipation/index.
php?id='.$course->id.'&amp;roleid='
```

Finally, there are two cases of a `<div>` tag being used for CSS that need to be updated at lines 215 and 221. The change is quoted below:

```
echo '<div id="nonparticipationreport">' . "\n";
```

In the next section, we start to change the logical structure of the report.

Changing the logical structure

Our first step in modifying the logical structure of the index.php file is to find the location in the code where the user list is output. By scanning the original file line-by-line, we find that at around line 286 there is a foreach loop that iterates through each user found to have a log entry. This is exactly the place where we need to insert our new code to modify the output of the report. Lines 287 to 310 of the new file cover the results of inserting the code from the People block. Only minor changes are needed from the original, most notably, $selectrole becomes r.roleid = $roleid. The final version of the code is listed below:

```
$select = 'SELECT DISTINCT u.id, u.username, u.firstname, u.lastname,
                u.email, u.city, u.country, u.picture,
                u.lang, u.timezone, u.emailstop, u.maildisplay,
                u.imagealt,
                COALESCE(ul.timeaccess, 0) AS lastaccess,
                r.hidden,
                ctx.id AS ctxid, ctx.path AS ctxpath,
                ctx.depth AS ctxdepth, ctx.contextlevel AS
                ctxlevel ';
$from    = "FROM {$CFG->prefix}user u
            LEFT OUTER JOIN {$CFG->prefix}context ctx
                ON (u.id=ctx.instanceid AND ctx.contextlevel =
                    ".CONTEXT_USER.")
            JOIN {$CFG->prefix}role_assignments r
                ON u.id=r.userid
            LEFT OUTER JOIN {$CFG->prefix}user_lastaccess ul
                ON (r.userid=ul.userid and ul.courseid =
                    $course->id) ";
$where   = "WHERE (r.contextid = $context->id OR r.contextid
                $relatedcontexts)
            AND u.deleted = 0  AND r.roleid = $roleid
            AND (ul.courseid = $course->id OR ul.courseid IS NULL)
            ";
$userlist = get_recordset_sql($select.$from.$where,
            $table->get_page_start(),  $table->get_page_size());
```

We can easily reproduce these results with any borrowed code segment, through a process of trial and error. We insert the code in the appropriate section, save the file, and execute the code in Moodle to see the results. We continue to iterate until all error messages are fixed and the output works as expected.

Tracking active users using a hash array

Now that we have generated our participants list, we need to create a hash array. We will use the array to merge and invert the list of active users from the original report. The array will be called `$active_users[ ]`, and it will have an entry for each participant in the course. The key of the array elements will be the `userid`. First, we will initialize the array with a value of 0 for each course participant. Our assumption at a coding level by doing this is that no users participated. Later in the code we will reset these values if we find log entries to indicate that a particular user did participate. The following section of code does this:

```
foreach ($userlist as $u) {
    $active_users[$u['id']]    = 0;
}
```

Next, we make a copy of the original `foreach` loop used to display the active users. We delete the lines that assign the values to the `$table` class and replace them with our variable assignment. We are going to assign a value of 1 to indicate that the user has participated. Once this loop completes, all of the participating users will have a value of 1. The remaining users, with 0 entries, are the non-participants. Here is the resulting section of code:

```
foreach ($users as $u) {
    $active_users[$u->userid] = 1;
}
```

We have to be careful when merging these sections of code together. We don't want to accidentally use the same variable name when we cut and paste. In our example, the list of course participants is stored in `$userslist`. The list of users with activity logs is stored in `$users`. Because we use different names for each group of users, there is no conflict or strange side-effects. Missing this check will lead to thorny and difficult-to-resolve bugs.

We modify the original `foreach` loop to iterate through the `$userslist` array instead of `$users`:

```
foreach ($userlist as $u) {
```

Here is where we invert the output. To do this, we just need to add an `if` statement, to make use of the hash array we created:

```
if ( ! $active_users[$u['id']] ) {
```

In the next section, we work on displaying the list of non-participants.

Displaying the report

The new `$userslist` array has a slightly different structure than the `$users` array from `/user/index.php`, so we need to make a few changes. In the original, we had `$u->userid` to reference a user ID, and in the new version we use `$u['id']`. Following are the modified lines of code:

```
$data = array('<a href="'.$CFG->wwwroot.'/user/view.php?id='.$u['id'].
'&amp;course='.$course->id.'">'.$u['firstname'].' '.$u['lastname'].
'</a>'."\n", '<input type="checkbox" name="user'.$u['id'].'"
value="'.'" />'."\n");
$table->add_data($data);
```

Note that the original report has three columns. One is reserved for a count of the log entries for each user. Because each of our non-participants will all have a count of 0, we can remove this column. Careful inspection of our array assignment will show only two values, instead of the original three. By using the built-in PHP function `var_dump()`, we can inspect what this new structure looks like, for a sample run of the report. In this case we see a two element array. The first value contains a URL with a direct link to the user view, for the Admin User, and the second array contains an input checkbox:

```
array(2) {
  [0]=>
  string(93) "<a href="http://localhost/workspace/moodle19/user/
view.php?id=2&amp;course=2">Admin User</a>
"
  [1]=>
  string(48) "<input type="checkbox" name="user2" value="" />
"
}
```

Finally, we display our table by using the `print_html` member function. This line performs all of the output for our table, based on the structure that we created in the lines above it.

```
$table->print_html();
```

Later, we will also clean up the table header so that it matches our new output format, and will discuss the `$table` class structure used in this example.

At this point, we have a working report that displays the correct values. However, we still have some small details to clean up, in the next section, before we are done. The following screenshot illustrates the current state of the report:

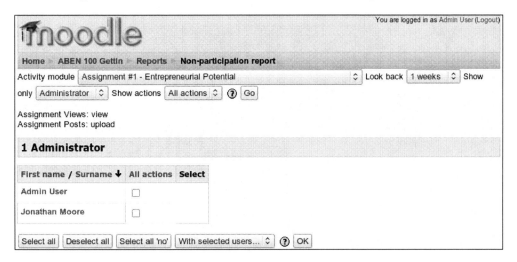

Cleaning up the final display

Let's clean up a few final items and put our report into production! The original participants report outputs a line before the results table, which displays the role and the number found. For our report, we will change this line to say **Non-participating Users**. Note that we have to add a line to the language file to do this correctly. The resulting line of code is at line 242:

```
echo '<h2>'.get_string('nonparticipating-users', 'report_
nonparticipation').'</h2>'."\n";
```

As mentioned previously, our new report table has only two columns. We need to remove the activity count column from the table header definition. This is the middle column on the original report. The column headers are defined at lines 151 and 152. Our new version looks as follows:

```
$table->define_columns(array('fullname','select'));
$table->define_headers(array(get_string('user'),
        get_string('select')));
```

Let's have a look at a sample run of our new report:

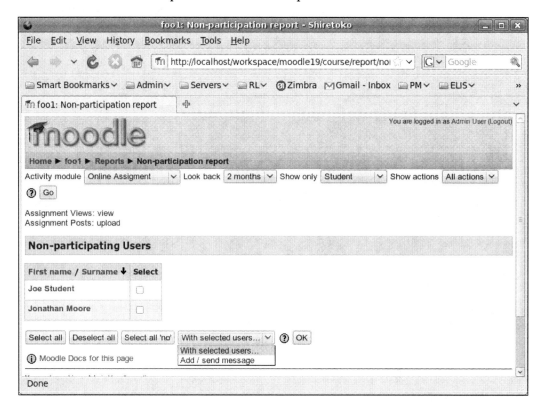

Let's reflect on what we have done so far in the chapter. We have created a highly-requested report, with a limited amount of coding. We accomplished this by modifying core components of Moodle. At the same time, we have done it in a clean and modular way. As with any other plugin, installation is as simple as copying the plugin folder to the correct location in our Moodle site.

Using flexible_table

You probably noticed the use of a new class, `flexible_table`, in our sample code. Around line 148 we define an instance of this class called `$table`:

```
$table = new flexible_table('course-nonparticipation-'.$course->id.
                            '-'.$cm->id.'-'.$roleid);
```

Throughout the rest of the `index.php` file, we use various member functions of `$table` to build our report output. It provides much functionality without having to manage all of the details by hand.

`flexible_table` is often used to provide tabular and paginated output in reports. Let's discuss a few of its elements. Lines 148 to 169 define various elements of `$table` in our report. These are worth reviewing if you wish to learn more about how to use this class. The general process for using `flexible_table` is to create the class, define the columns, and set the table options. Then we insert elements into the table in a loop structure as we iterate through our data set. The table is built by calling the `add_data()` function. It expects an array of values—one array element per column in the table.

An exercise for you

Although we now have a very usable course report, some instructors will often ask for a non-participation report that works across the entire course. Many administrators may ask for one that works across the entire site! As an exercise to sharpen your skills, create a new version of the non-participation report that adds all activities and all roles to the menu of options. Consider adding an option for the participation threshold: anyone with fewer log entries than the threshold should be listed in the report.

Creating gradebook reports

Gradebook reports use many of the same conventions as course reports. However, they do have a more standardized plugin structure. This eliminates the need for a `mod.php` file. The reason for this is that the gradebook was completely re-written for version 1.9. There are some additional requirements that come with this new structure. We will discuss these in the following sections. Another new component of the 1.9 gradebook is support for learning outcomes. Outcomes allow organizations to track the specific skills that are learned, separately from the scores on particular learning activities. This is a very powerful concept. Our sample report will fix a problem with one of the core gradebook reports and outcomes. In our next section, we will cover the requirements for a gradebook report.

The official documentation for gradebook reports can be found at `http://docs.moodle.org/en/Development:Gradebook_Report_Tutorial`.

Required components

There are just a few required components for the gradebook report: a folder in `./grade/report`, an `access.php` file, a `lang` folder, a `version.php` file, and an `index.php` file.

Creating our report folder

We must create a folder in `./grade/report`. The name of this folder, as with all Moodle plugins, should be related to the title and function of the report. Simply moving a properly written report into this folder is all that is needed to install it.

Creating access.php

The `db/access.php` file is a required component of gradebook reports, and needs to be named a certain way or the report will not work. We should be careful to get this right the first time. It can prove to be difficult to fix in testing, if done incorrectly the first time. The gradebook reporting system is hardcoded to assume that there will be a view capability when using a particular format. The format is `gradereport/report-<name>:view`, where `name` is the same as that of the report's folder.

If we make a mistake in creating the capability name of the folder, we have to manually delete a record from the `mdl_config` table. Typically, this will be the last entry in the table and it will be stored as the name of the capability.

Assigning language strings

We must create a language folder and file with the required elements. By default, we are only required to make two entries: `modulename` and `<name>:view`, where `name` is the report's folder name. By Moodle style convention, many components will reuse the name that we give to the folder. This enforces consistency throughout the module in its naming scheme.

index.php requirements

The `index.php` file contains all of the code required for generating our report. Typically, it will make use of the `flexible_table` class that we discussed in the course report section, and for grade reports a new class called `grade_report` will be used. We will briefly discuss `grade_report` in the next section.

Using version.php

As with prior modules, the `versions.php` file is used to track the current version of the module and the required version of Moodle. This is used to update any capabilities defined in the `access.php` file.

Using the grade_report class

The `grade_report` class is defined to provide access for reports that need to connect to the gradebook. `grade_report` is defined in the `/grade/report/lib.php` file. It provides a number of functions for formatting grade output. There is a great community tool for exploring the variables and member functions of any core Moodle class. This is called the PHP Cross Reference for Moodle, and is available at `http://xref.moodle.org`.

The `grade_report` class is designed to be extended as part of a new gradebook report. This is accomplished by creating a `lib.php` file in the new report's folder. The extended class should be named as `grade_report_<name>`, where `name` is the name of the report's folder. Let's see how we might use this in the `index.php` file. Here is an example of creating an instance of an extended class:

```
$report = new grade_report_myreport($userid, $gpr, $context);
```

Fixing the outcomes report

There is a significant shortcoming in the outcomes report included with Moodle. It assumes that you can average the results of measuring student performance on outcomes. This causes problems. The distance between each percentage point on a quantitative scale is equidistant. For example, 100 percent is twice as good as 50 percent. This allows quantitative results to be accurately averaged. However, outcomes performance is typically measured using a qualitative scale. Let's take the simplest form of an outcomes scale for an example: Satisfactory, and Not Satisfactory. What percentage of mastery equates to Satisfactory, which to Not Satisfactory? Although we can't average such results accurately, we can apply statistical analysis to these types of results. For example, we can count the number of students evaluated in each category. Often, these will be displayed as percentages of the learning population. Learning goals for a community will often be set based on the percentage of the population at each level of mastery. For example, this is the method used by the No Child Left Behind legislation, which is a United States Federal law detailing requirements for publicly-funded K12 schools. For this section's sample, we will modify the outcomes report to offer a disaggregation of values instead of an average. This report will be called Outcomes Disaggregated.

Note that the outcomes report doesn't use `flexible_table` to display its results. It is common to find components of the core that don't exactly follow the guidelines for development to the letter. `flexible_table` isn't strictly required for report making, but it does make things easier. In this report, we see more manual generation of HTML code because it doesn't use the `flexible_table` class.

Digging into the code

Because we have already covered one detailed example, we won't spend quite as much time on the outcomes example. Instead, we will cover the high points. Our basic process is to make a copy of the `outcomes` report folder and rename it to `outcomesdisaggregated`. Because the new report is not apart of core Moodle, we need to create a language folder. The full path to the language file for this example is `/grades/report/outcomesdisaggregated/lang/en_utf8/outcomesdisaggregated.php`. We also need to rename the capability defined in the `access.php` file to follow the required pattern. After that, we just need to make a few edits to the `index.php` file to change its output to our liking.

Note on line 27 that we include library files. These are typical for a grade report. In particular, the second line provides access to the `grade_report` class mentioned in the section above.

```
require_once($CFG->libdir . '/gradelib.php');
require_once $CFG->dirroot.'/grade/lib.php';
```

At around line 83, we have to modify the averaging function from the original report in order to create our disaggregated results. The first step is to change the loop control for this section. We will use the variable `$bucket` to store the individual outcome grades:

```
foreach( $info as $bucket) {
```

In this same section, we make use of the `grade_scale` class. This is another class that is included with the grade libraries. We will use it to translate our numerical scores into their qualitative descriptions. This line creates a new instance of the `grade_scale` class by passing in a scale ID for the outcome that we are processing:

```
$scale = new grade_scale( array('id' => $outcome->scaleid), false);
```

Now we need to make use of the `get_nearest_item` function. This is where the numerical value stored in the database gets converted to a human-readable form. Note that we are recycling the `$avg` variable from the original report, and renaming it to `$disaggregation` for clarity:

```
$disaggregation .= $scale->get_nearest_item($bucket->finalgrade)
.'('.$bucket->count.'), ';
$count += $bucket->count;
```

This completes the major changes to the report. We do have to comment out a few other code sections in order to remove an unneeded column. We also need to make some minor updates to the language file. All of this is documented in the included code samples. We are now ready to have a look at the results!

Reviewing our new report

In the following screenshot, we see the result of our code changes. In the next section we will dig into administrator reports:

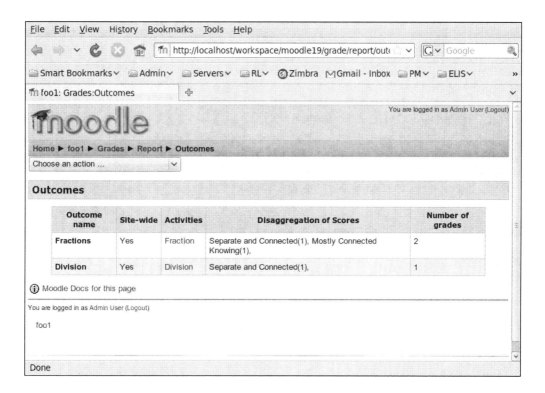

Creating administrator reports

Administrator, or sitewide, reports follow many of the same conventions that we have already discussed. However, there are minor differences versus the other types. The required elements are fairly simple. We need a folder within `/admin/report` that includes an `index.php` file. We also need a language file with one required string, `$string['<name>']` where `name` is the name of the report folder. Under this arrangement, the value of the language string will be displayed in the **Site Administration | Reports** menu list.

An example of this menu is displayed in the following screenshot:

The official documentation for Moodle administrator reports is available at `http://docs.moodle.org/en/Development:Admin_reports`.

Generating the Hello World administrator report

The sample for this section is a very simple "Hello World" report. It's a fully functional administrator report, but only displays "Hello World" for its output. It's a good starting template for creating a new report. Note that all of the techniques, functions, and classes that we have covered in the prior sections can be applied to an administrator report. These reports typically cover a sitewide data set.

Because our report folder is called `myreport`, we need a language file called `report_myreport.php`. This contains the following two lines of code, which create the report's menu name, and set the classic "Hello World" value:

```
$string['myreport'] = 'Helloworld Admin Report';
$string['helloworld'] = 'Hello World';
```

Tweaking index.php

Let's have a quick look at the `index.php` file. Note that we must include `adminlib.php` and we should require login for security. By default, the link only displays if the user has the `moodle/site:viewreports` capability.

```
require_once($CFG->libdir.'/adminlib.php');
require_login();
```

We can optionally define and use additional capabilities to control access further. Next we establish a few more administrator-specific details with `admin_externalpage_setup`, which displays our reports header.

```
admin_externalpage_setup('reportmyreport');
admin_externalpage_print_header();
print_heading(get_string('myreport', 'report_myreport'));
```

And finally, we output our Hello World text:

```
echo(get_string('helloworld','report_myreport'));
```

Viewing our administrator report

The administrator report can be seen in the following screenshot. Make a special note of where the report link displays as part of the **Site Administration** block. The link is visible in the lower left-hand corner of the screenshot, and the text reads **Helloworld Admin Report**.

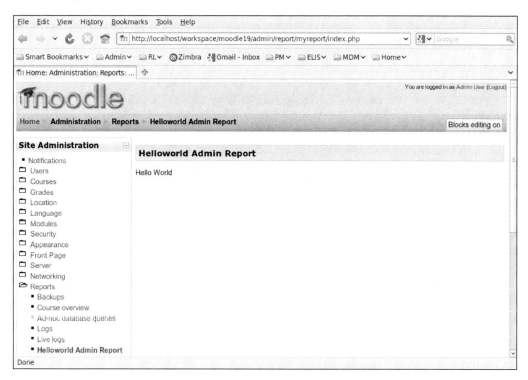

An exercise for you

Here are a couple of administrator report ideas that you can implement on your own. Take the outcomes disaggregated report and turn it into a sitewide report that shows students' performance on outcomes across the entire site. Create a sitewide report to show course completions for all students.

That concludes our look at administrator reports. In the next section, we will learn about a library that we can use to create output formats for our reports.

Other output formats

Reporting to the screen is not enough to satisfy most users. We also need to support CSV, PDF, and spreadsheet formats. Although space considerations won't allow us to go into great detail on this topic, a special reporting library is included with the source code for this book. This provides a reporting framework that includes built-in support for these additional output formats. This is the same coding library that we use in-house at Remote-Learner (http://www.remote-learner.net) for building reports within Moodle. Note that much of our new report development is now done with JasperSoft's business intelligence suite, another great open source project, which automatically supports multiple formats.

Summary

You now have a much better understanding of how reporting works in Moodle. You learned how to create course reports that are embedded into our Moodle courses. You created a new course report that shows non-participating users. This was created by modifying the participants report included with Moodle. You learned how to modify the gradebook to create new reports, and updated the outcomes report to include disaggregated results. You then looked at how to create sitewide administrator reports. You created a very simple "Hello World" administrator report to illustrate how all of the requirements fit together. Finally, we discussed briefly the Remote-Learner library that can be used to output reports in CSV, PDF, and Microsoft Excel formats. In the next chapter, we will learn about integrating Moodle with external systems.

9
Integrating Moodle with Other Systems

One of the most popular programming projects for Moodle is to integrate it with a third-party system. This chapter will cover the following topics:

- Overview of Moodle authentication and enrollment systems
- Creating user authentication plugins
- Implementing **Single Sign On (SSO)**
- Creating enrollment plugins

Before we dig into the programming, let's take a few minutes to better understand what Moodle provides out of the box. Often, we can use what's built-in to lessen or eliminate the need for new programming.

Built-in services and plugins

Moodle uses a plugin model for both its authentication and enrollment services. Authentication plugins are placed in the auth folder and are intended to control user management, authentication, and Single Sign On. Enrollment plugins are placed in the enrol folder and are intended to manage course enrollments or role assignments. Note that there is a gray area with both authentication and enrollment plugins. Each type can perform the work of the other. For example, the **LDAP (Lightweight Directory Access Protocol)** authentication plugin can create system-level role assignments for the course creator role. Conversely, the third-party Banner integration, an enrollment module, can perform user creations.

Although it's possible to blur the lines, there are certain advantages of using distinct plugins for each function. Plugins allow you to mix and match sources of users versus user enrollments. This is a powerful concept and one that is not always well understood. A simple example of this would be using the LDAP authentication module to create and maintain user credentials, but using the external database enrollment plugin to create course enrollments. This is a sensible combination, because many organizations centralize their authentication in an LDAP server, but store user enrollments in a database within a Student Information System (SIS) or Human Resource (HR) system.

Let's have a quick look at the most popular method of automating user creation—the batch upload.

Batch upload

Batch upload is not technically an authentication module. It allows an administrator to upload users for any of the installed authentication plugins. The batch upload function is found via the Moodle **Site Administration** menu, under **Users | Accounts | Upload users**.

This is currently the only built-in way to mass import custom profile fields. Other plugins can easily be modified to do this, but they require some customization to add this feature.

Batch upload handles passwords internally to Moodle. The password field can be left blank in the upload, in which case Moodle will create a random password and e-mail it to the address listed in the user's profile. Passwords can also be set to 'changeme' and this will force the user to change the password on his or her first login.

The historical weakness of this method has been that it didn't allow mass deletion of accounts. However, starting with version 1.9, you can delete accounts.

Batch upload also allows for the setting of user enrollments in courses. It is also the only built-in automation method that supports assigning course groups.

While this method is both powerful and popular, it does require the administrator to manually upload the file for each update. For many organizations, this feature provides the best balance between ease of use and time saving. It works particularly well in situations where the users or enrollments don't change very often. Another one of the challenges with batch upload is that it is subject to the Apache and PHP timeout and memory configuration. Some larger organizations find that they have to split their files into several chunks in order to get them to load.

Built-in authentication plugins

As mentioned earlier, authentication plugins are primarily intended for user management and authentication. Let's have a quick look at some of the built-in authentication plugins.

Manual/Internal authentication

This is the default authentication method. It is used for any accounts created by the administrator using the built-in administrative interface. It is also the default authentication type set for batch upload of users. Note that both of these methods of user creation allow for the authentication type to be set to a different value. Moodle stores all user information in its internal database, including an MD5 hash of the password.

LDAP/Active directory authentication

This module is recommended as a best practice for user management. LDAP is an industry standard for authentication management and is supported by most enterprise software applications. It allows an organization to manage all of the user credentials in a single repository, while connecting multiple front-end applications. This allows users to have just a single username and password to remember.

With the Moodle LDAP integration, user accounts are created and user data, including passwords, are synced from the remote LDAP server.

There is an optional batch sync script that can be run to pre-create users in the Moodle system prior to their first login. Users not created by batch sync may still log in into Moodle; their accounts will be created on first login. Batch syncing is useful for enrolling users into courses prior to their first login. If a user disappears from the remote source, Moodle can optionally disallow them from having Moodle access.

Enough user profile data can be mapped so that the edit profile screen will not load on the first login. This prevents double re-entry, thus providing a better and more efficient user experience. The LDAP authentication module also supports automatic assignment of the course creator role to an LDAP group. Later in the chapter, we will modify the LDAP module to take this to the next level!

External database authentication

The external database plugin is modeled on the LDAP plugin. The external database authentication plugin uses PHP's ADOdb library to connect to the most popular SQL database systems. This is the Swiss army knife of integration plugins. It can be used to connect most systems that use an SQL database to Moodle for authentication or user profile information. If the remote database supports database views, one can be very creative in the use of this module.

The external database authentication plugin has the same features as described for the LDAP authentication plugin. There is a sync script for mass syncing of user accounts and profile information, and the external database is also checked at login.

A common technique to work around the shortcoming in the batch upload feature is to develop a CSV to external database converter script. This allows you to have Moodle update the user list automatically by using the external database plugin, but doesn't require a manual file upload via the Moodle GUI.

The external database can be directly connected to most common SQL database types. The recommended configuration is to set up a read-only view on the remote database with a username and password specific to the integration. The view should provide one user per row for user authentication.

E-mail account based authentication plugins

There are also several built-in plugins that can use login credentials from e-mail systems in order to manage logins. These include: IMAP, POP3, and FirstClass. These can be useful, as most e-mail servers are not locked behind a firewall. They do not provide any passing of user profile information—just username and password.

Let's have a look at some of the built-in enrollment plugins.

Built-in enrollment plugins

Enrollment plugins are primarily intended for managing user enrollments in courses. More generally, they are used to control user role assignments. Let's have a quick look at some of the built-in plugins.

LDAP enrollment plugin

The enrollment module is less popular than the authentication module because most LDAP databases are not organized to have a user group for each course in Moodle. This plugin supports course enrollments based on LDAP group membership. If a course is referenced in an enrollment but does not exist in Moodle, then the plugin can be set to create an empty course shell for this course. The plugin also supports the specification of an optional template course to use when creating course shells. The module also supports auto-removal of dropped students. A sync script is provided that works similarly to the one for the authentication module.

External database enrollment plugin

The external database enrollment plugin is recommended as a best practice because most student management, HR, or e-commerce systems store enrollment data in an SQL database. External enrollment can also be used to automatically create courses. Any course referenced in an enrollment, but that doesn't already exist in Moodle, can be created automatically either as an empty course shell or by using a master course template. Note that there are several useful patches to this module available in the Moodle community. These extensions provide expanded capabilities, such as connecting to a database of course descriptions and templates. These extensions can be found by searching the `http://moodle.org/` forums, and the modules and plugin databases.

E-commerce based enrollment plugins

Moodle has built-in support for selling courses via either PayPal or Authorize.Net. These are available as enrollment plugins. Once enabled, a new setting is displayed in the course setup. The course can be assigned to the e-commerce enrollment plugin, and a dollar value can be set either globally or per course. The built-in plugins have a few weaknesses. Firstly, they only work on a one-course-per-purchase basis. Also, these plugins don't have any provisions for a purchasing agent buying multiple courses on behalf of someone else. They also do not support seat limits or subscriptions. Meeting these objectives requires custom development.

This completes our look at the built-in authentication and enrollment plugins. Let's have a look at some other integration options.

Web services

There are several web service libraries available for Moodle. We have made available to the community the R-L web service library. This library is based on **Simple Object Access Protocol (SOAP)**, which makes it easy to use in many common development platforms outside of PHP, including .NET, Flash, and Java amongst others. It can be used to create and update users, courses, course enrollments, and grades. It also provides a Single Sign On mechanism. Moodle also provides services via the Moodle Networking protocol, or MNet. Moodle Networking provides an XML-RPC based web service when implemented. Moodle 2.0 will provide an entirely new and pluggable system for providing web services. *Chapter 14, Development for the Adventuresome: Web Services*, digs into more detail on using web services with Moodle. Web services are particularly strong for providing real-time integrations with third-party systems.

Activity plugin as an integration bridge

A Moodle activity module can also be used to integrate with an external system. Good examples of contributed modules of this type of integration are the several synchronous conferencing tool integrations available for Moodle, including Adobe Connect Pro, Elluminate, Wimba, and Dimdim integrations.

Now that we have a better understanding of the overall possibilities, let's dig into the coding. In the next section, we cover how to create authentication plugins for Moodle.

Creating user authentication plugins

Authentication plugins are placed inside Moodle's `auth` folder. They have two major requirements: an `auth.php` file and a language file. In this section, we will cover the minimal requirements of creating as basic a module as we can. This module will be called `simple`.

Exploring authentication requirements

Authentication plugins are of medium complexity. They don't require many files to be defined. However, there are several functions that can be defined in the plugin classes. Let's have a look at the primary file.

Looking at auth.php

The `auth.php` file needs to include `/lib/authlib.php`. This library defines the `auth_plugin_base` class that is the basis for any new authentication module. Within the `auth.php` file, we need to extend class `auth_plugin_base` as `auth_plugin_<name>`, where `name` is the name of the module's folder. For the `simple` authentication module this looks similar to the following:

```
class auth_plugin_simple extends auth_plugin_base {
```

As a minimum, we need to define two member functions for the class: the constructor and `user_login`. The constructor must assign `$this->authtype ='myauth'`, or the language files will not work properly. Here is an example:

```
function auth_plugin_simple() {
   $this->authtype = 'simple';
}
```

Let's have a look at a simple `user_login()` function. This is derived from the manual login module. It will behave in much the same way as a standard account made by the Moodle administrator. In this example, note that we are passing in both the username and the password as entered in the login page:

```
function user_login ($username, $password) {
   global $CFG;
```

Also, note the use of `get_record` to look up the user's information from the database:

```
if ($user = get_record('user', 'username', $username, 'mnethostid',
   $CFG->mnet_localhost_id)) {
```

We make use of the `validate_internal_user_password` to compare the password entered by the user with the one on record in the database. By default, passwords are stored as one-way MD5 hashes in the database encoded with a recommended password salt set in the sites `config.php` file. If a valid password was entered, this function returns a user object:

```
return validate_internal_user_password($user, $password);
```

If any one of the conditions fail, it returns false:

```
return false;
```

Making the language file

The language file convention for authentication plugins is `auth_<name>.php`. In the case of our `simple` module the filename is `auth_simple.php`. There are two required strings for our module: `auth_<name>title` and `auth_<name>description`. An example from the `simple` module is quoted as follows:

```
$string['auth_simpletitle'] = 'Simple Authentication';
$string['auth_simpledescription'] = 'A simple but functional
                                     authentication module';
```

Note that while testing, versions of Moodle 1.9.4+ were found to have a bug. Hence, this method didn't work across the entire Moodle interface. The language string would not display properly in the user profile screen with Advanced Options visible. Additional testing under version 1.9.6 did not exhibit this problem. This shows the benefits of regular updates based on the latest weekly stable version of Moodle.

Testing simple authentication

Now that we have completed our first authentication module, let's talk a bit about how to test it. In the **Site Administration** menu of your Moodle site, click on the **Users | Authentication | Manage authentication** option. This displays a list of all of the authentication plugins installed in the system. We need to click on the closed eye icon next to the **Simple Authentication** entry. This should change the icon to an open eye, indicating that the plugin is now active. Next, we need to create a new account. In the **Add a new user** page, click on the **Show Advanced** button to bring up the extra settings, and in the **Choose an authentication method** drop-down menu select **Simple Authentication** and then save the new account. Log out and log back in with the new account. To confirm that the new account is indeed using our new module, we log back in as an administrator and disable the module. We can then repeat the log in process with the new account, which should fail.

Adding optional functionality to authentication

There are other optional functions we can define in our extended class. Moodle will use these to provide additional functionality. Some of the more commonly-used functions are defined as follows. The `manual` plugin is a fairly simple module that defines many of these:

- `user_update_password()`: Called when the user's password is reset.
- `is_internal()`: Will return true or false depending on whether this is a core Moodle plugin. All user contributed plugins should return false.

- `can_change_password()`: Returns true if this module allows user password resets.

- `change_password_url()`: Returns a URL to the user password reset page. Returns null if default should be used.

- `can_reset_password()`: Returns true if password resets are allowed. Note that this is different than just changing the password. Resets are typically used to automatically allow a user to reset their password if they forgot it.

- `config_form()`: Function responsible for displaying a configuration screen, if any.

- `process_config()`: Processes the results of the configuration form.

- `user_confirm()`: Some authentication plugins support self-registration. Moodle provides account confirmation tracking for self-registration. This function is generally only called when changing from one authentication type to another for a user.

- `sync_roles()`: Called by core when the user logs into the system. Can be used to sync role assignments for the user. See the chapter source code for a special version of the `simple` authentication module that uses this. With the modified `sync_roles` plugin, any user with this authentication module is assigned site wide administrator access on login. Use this with caution.

In the next section, we will tackle a more real world use case for an authentication module.

Creating the RLLDAP authentication plugin

Remote-Learner both hosts and provides support for hundreds of organizations' Moodle installations. Managing support access for such a large number of sites, each running their own Moodle code and database, can be challenging. One way to reduce the burden of such a massive undertaking is through the use of LDAP. R-L maintains an internal staff LDAP server, and has developed a customized version of the LDAP module that provides certain staff members with administrator rights on login. This supports best practices in security and user management by each user having an individual login credential that provides the appropriate access.

One of the challenges of such an undertaking is deciding how much maintenance to take on with a fork of a core module. The more core code that is changed, the more that has to be merged with each update of Moodle or the module. In our example case, we are going to take a minimalist approach, in order to reduce maintenance costs. We can do this because the LDAP module already has almost all of the functionality that we need. It already supports the assignment of a group of users to the course creator role at the site level. In our modification, we will change enough of the module so that it can be installed alongside the core LDAP module without conflicts, and we will change the course creator role assignment and labeling to that of the site administrator.

Coding RLLDAP

In the following sections, we take a look at the code changes needed to make the RLLDAP module a reality.

Changing LDAP string to RLLDAP

We need to make sure that the copy of the first module doesn't store any of its configuration information using the same values and names as the original. One might be tempted to perform a mass search and replace on the term LDAP. However, this will create some problems with calls being made to the php-ldap library.

While we can't safely replace all references to the text 'ldap', there are some global replacements that we can make.

Mass change auth/ldap to auth/rlldap

In all files in the module, let's replace the path `auth/ldap` with `auth/rlldap`. This will make many of the updates required to remove conflicts between the original core module and our new version. This updates both the relative path links between files and also configuration values stored in the `mdl_config_plugins` table.

Mass change 'ldap' to 'rlldap'

On inspection of the code, we can determine that all instances of `ldap` in single quotes in the code need to be changed to `rlldap`. This will generally be the case for every other plugin. However, it's a good idea to inspect each change as they are made to confirm that they don't break anything. We need to do this across all files in the module. When used like this, in single quotes, it is making a reference to Moodle's name for the module. When not referenced in quotes, the string `ldap` may be referring to function names, configuration values, or php-ldap library calls. Here are some examples of changes made as a result of this search-and-replace:

- `config.html` (around line 481): `print_auth_lock_options('rlldap', $user_fields, $help, true, true);`

- `auth.php` around lines: 474, 677, 724,765,794, 792,839,862,1049,1931, and 1934
- `auth_ldap_sync_users.php` around lines: 38, and 43

Mass change role assignment

The original code looks up the course creator role by using the following function call:

```
get_roles_with_capability('moodle/legacy:coursecreator', CAP_ALLOW))
```

We need to mass change all instances of `moodle/legacy:coursecreator` to `moodle/legacy:admin`. This change will cause the existing role assignment mechanism to assign the Administrator role instead of the Course creator role.

Updating and renaming the auth_plugin class

If we try to install and run the module in its present state, we would immediately get an error that the class is already defined. We need to change the class name around line 36 of the `auth.php` file. Our updated code looks similar to the following:

```
class auth_plugin_rlldap extends auth_plugin_base
```

We also need to update the constructor name to match the new class name around line 41, and change the `authtype` to `rlldap`:

```
function auth_plugin_rlldap() {'
  $this->authtype = 'rlldap';
```

Creating our language file

Our language file for the new module will be called `auth_rlldap.php`. Making the least changes needed, we are going to leave most of the strings pointing to the original module strings. LDAP is a core module, so we can be pretty confident that the strings will be in place on any Moodle site. However, we are making this a new module and we require the following two strings:

```
$string['auth_rlldaptitle'] = 'RL LDAP';
$string['auth_rlldapdescription'] = 'A modified version ....
```

We also need to add two new strings for our administrator role feature. These will be used to update the user interface in the plugin configuration screen:

```
$string['auth_rlldap administrators'] = 'Group for admins',
$string['auth_rlldap_administrators_key'] = 'Administrator\'s
                                            context';
```

In the next section, we look at changes to the `config.html` file.

Modifying config.html

We need to make a few changes to the `config.html` file in order to update the user interface for our administrator role assignment. We are going to take over, rename, and slightly modify the functionality of the course creator auto-assignment. Again, our purpose is to keep our changes as minimal as possible in order to reduce ongoing maintenance costs.

Around line 410 is the section that displays the configuration for the course creator group. We are going to change it to record the configuration for our administrator's group. Let's have a look at the code. Note that the `print_string` functions now use the new language strings that we created earlier. The following is a condensed display using the new strings. The original code follows:

```
print_string('coursecreators')
```

This code is modified as follows:

```
print_string('administrators')
```

Note that we are still using a core language string for the title of `'administrators'`, which is a default role.

In the next sections, we have to also reference our new language file explicitly. The original looks like the following:

```
print_string('auth_ldap_creators_key','auth')
```

In the new module, this gets modified to the following:

```
print_string('auth_rlldap_administrators_key','auth_rlldap')
```

We follow this same pattern through the rest of this section, which ends around line 422.

Storing administrator group

The course creator auto-assignment has only one stored configuration value: `$config->creator`. We need to do a search-and-replace across all files in the module. An example of the change can be seen around lines 32 and 33 of the `config.html` file:

```
if (!isset($config->administrators))
  {$config->administrators = ''; }
```

Note that on testing with an OpenLDAP server, we find special settings are needed to get the group mapping to work. The group mapping only works if the member attribute is set and group override is set to 1 in the module's configuration. Also note that administrator roles are mapped at the time of login rather than when using the user sync script.

The following screenshot displays the results of our configuration changes:

```
Administrators

Administrator's   [                              ]   Group for admins
     context
```

Let's have a look at how to create a Single Sign On mechanism for Moodle.

Implementing Single Sign On

Any authentication module can implement **Single Sign On** (**SSO**) by adding a `loginpage_hook` member function. The Moodle core system will call this function, for each registered authentication plugin, prior to displaying the login page. By hooking in front of the login page, we can perform identity verification using information from a third-party application. Examples from core Moodle include the LDAP module's support for SSO from the user's Windows login and the CAS module. Both of these plugins implement the `loginpage_hook()` function to accomplish this.

Let's take a look at a simple example of SSO.

Creating a URL-based SSO

In this section, we will expand the `simple` authentication module in order to support a basic SSO. The method used will be a specially-formatted URL. The format of our URL for SSO will be as follows:

```
http://my_site/login/index.php?username=myaccount&secret=mysecret
```

The URL includes two parameters: `username` and `secret`. The `username` will be used to indicate which user account we want to log in into the system using. The `secret` parameter will be set to a pre-determined secret code, which is used to confirm that the URL was created by a trusted source. In our sample code, we will set the secret value to 'mysecret'.

It's important to note this is a simple example to illustrate the required components of the SSO process. The method implemented here is not secure and is not appropriate for most production environments. The only way that it can be secure is if the SSO URL is hidden from the end user via URL redirection. Even with these caveats, it does provide a very simple and easy-to-test method that fully implements a Single Sign On integration.

Digging into the code

First, we define the function and our required global variables:

```
function loginpage_hook() {
  global $CFG, $USER, $SESSION;
  $site = get_site();
```

Next, we need to obtain the parameters sent in the URL for 'username' and 'secret':

```
$username = optional_param("username",0,PARAM_TEXT);
$secret = optional_param("secret",0,PARAM_TEXT);
```

Finding the user's account

Now that we have the username, we need to confirm that the user exists and if so, obtain their details. We do this by using the get_record function:

```
$user = get_record('user', 'username', $username, 'mnethostid',
                   $CFG->mnet_localhost_id);
```

Confirming that the login criteria have been met

In this section, we verify that all of the necessary conditions are met for our SSO. These include confirming that the user is not logged in or if they are logged in, they are logged in as a guest user. We also check that the correct secret code was passed with the URL. Finally, we confirm that the user account does exist:

```
if ( (isguestuser() || !isloggedin()) && $secret == 'mysecret' &&
    $user) {
```

Completing login

Now that we have verified that all of the requirements have been met, we need to actually log in the user. We will use the complete_user_login function from Moodle core. Let's look at some code adapted from the LDAP SSO. It has been simplified for clarity and this context. First, we need to create a log entry verifying the user login:

```
add_to_log(SITEID, 'user', 'login', "view.php?id=
          $USER->id&course=".SITEID, $user->id, 0, $user->id);
```

Then we call the `complete_user_login()` function. At this point, the user is logged in to the system:

```
$USER = complete_user_login($user);
```

Redirecting the user to the correct location

This leaves us with just a few wrap-up steps before we can provide a polished user experience. We need to determine the correct URL to link the user to, by calling the `redirect()` function with the correct URL. This is necessary in order to implement one of Moodle's usability features. Moodle will remember which URL you originally requested while it verifies your identity. With our URL based SSO, this allows us to deep link into any course, activity, or resource from the remote system while still triggering the SSO. We just have to append the required parameters:

```
if (user_not_fully_set_up($USER)) {
  $urltogo = $CFG->wwwroot.'/user/edit.php';
  // We don't delete $SESSION->wantsurl yet, so we get there later
} else if (isset($SESSION->wantsurl) and (strpos($SESSION->wantsurl,
          $CFG->wwwroot) === 0)) {
  $urltogo = $SESSION->wantsurl;    /// Because it's an address in
                                    /// this site
  unset($SESSION->wantsurl);
} else {
  // no wantsurl stored or external - go to homepage
  $urltogo = $CFG->wwwroot.'/';
  unset($SESSION->wantsurl);
}
redirect($urltogo);
```

Testing the URL SSO

The SSO can be tested simply by entering the correct URL into your web browser. We need to make sure that we are not already logged into the system. Then, we need to enter our Moodle site URL followed by the parameters for the username and our 'secret' value. The username must be for a valid user in the Moodle system. Because we are not checking for the authentication type of the user, this SSO will work for any valid user in the system. To fully test this, we need to try using the URL when already logged in to the system, with an invalid user and with the wrong 'secret' value. The login should fail in any of these conditions and result in the login page being displayed.

In the next section of this chapter, we will learn how to program enrollment plugins.

Creating user enrollment plugins

Enrollment plugins have a similar structure to authentication plugins. However, Moodle does not provide an extensible base class for creating enrollment plugins. Instead, it relies on a consistent naming convention for the class names and member functions. The end result is similar, but not quite as clean from an object-oriented design perspective.

Reviewing plugin requirements

As with all of the other plugins that we have covered, our module needs its own folder. Enrollment plugins go into the `/enrol` folder.

Creating enrol.php

Each enrollment plugin needs an `enrol.php` file. Each enrollment plugin needs to include the required base library:

```
require_once($CFG->dirroot.'/enrol/enrol.class.php');
```

Within this file, there must be an enrollment class defined. The naming convention for this class is: `enrolment_plugin_<name>`. Here is an example from the external database enrollment plugin from the Moodle core:

```
class enrolment_plugin_database {
```

Creating the setup_enrolments function

The meat of any enrollment module is the `setup_enrolments` function. This is where the majority of the functionality happens:

```
function setup_enrolments(&$user) {
```

Moodle core will call this function for each user logging into the system. This ensures that external enrollments integrated through this mechanism are always updated when the user logs into the system. This also provides a simple optimization mechanism for data exchanges that might otherwise be very expensive to perform if these were called with each page build. Note that the practical implication of this is that a user must log out and then back in order to receive new enrollments from the external system. This is generally not a problem in production environments, but does come into play for developers as they test new plugins.

Making the language file

The naming convention for language files is `enrol_<name>.php`. An example would be the `enrol_simple.php` file for the plugin called `simple`. There are two required values for this file: `enrolname`, and `description`. An example from the simple enrollment plugin is shown below:

```
$string['enrolname'] = 'Simple';
$string['description'] = 'A simple enrollment plugin that assigns
   any user the course creator role at the system context';
```

Other requirements

Both `config_form` and the `process_config` member functions must be defined, otherwise users will receive an error message after clicking on the **Settings** link for your module. These function identically to the functions for authentication plugins. Although they need to be defined, the functions themselves do not have to contain any working code. In our 'simple' example, the functions are just defined as stub functions.

Making the 'simple' enrollment plugin

We can easily make a simple enrollment plugin in order to confirm our understanding of the basic requirements. In addition to the requirements specified previously, we need to implement some actual role assignments in our `setup_enrolments` function. For the following code snippet, we have implemented the function by taking the exact code from the 'simple' authentication module's `sync_roles` function. The only change is that we are now applying the 'coursecreator' role, instead of the 'administrator' role in order to make it easier to test:

```
global $CFG;
if ($roles = get_roles_with_capability('moodle/legacy:coursecreator',
           CAP_ALLOW)) {
  $adminrole = array_shift($roles);
  $systemcontext = get_context_instance(CONTEXT_SYSTEM);
role_assign($adminrole->id, $user->id, 0, $systemcontext->id, 0, 0,
           0, 'simple');
}
```

Note that most enrollment plugins implement course-level enrollments. However, for the purpose of making the example simpler, we have implemented a global-level role.

In the next section, we cover some optional functions for our enrollment plugins.

Using optional enrollment functions

The following are optional enrollment functions:

function print_entry($course)

This function displays a course entry dialog. This can be as simple as the internal enrollment prompt, "Do you want to enter this course?". It can also be complex, as in the case of an e-commerce integration like the PayPal module.

function cron()

This function hooks into the `cron.php` script, in order to run periodic updates. For example, this might be used to automatically update enrollments even without a new login. It could also be used to send notifications to users about enrollments.

function sync_enrolments()

This function is typically used by integrations that provide a synchronization script, in order to allow pre-enrollments across an entire site. Both the LDAP and Database enrollment plugins implement this function.

function create_course()

Many enrollment plugins will implement automated course shell creation, often from a template or template library. This is the function that is used to implement this feature. Both the LDAP and Database enrollment plugins implement this function.

Now that we have completed the creation of our enrollment plugin, let's have a look at how to use it within Moodle.

Assigning enrollment plugins to courses

The 'simple' enrollment module works at the user-level, on login. Enrollment plugins have an alternative mode of operation: they can be assigned to specific courses. This is implemented through the `print_entry` function. This allows use cases, where a site might want to have one set of rules for one course and another set of rules for another. The enrollment plugin to use for a course can be set from the course settings page. A specific example is allowing some courses to be free on a site and others to be paid for.

Grade or completion passing

Prior to Moodle 1.9, Moodle did not have well-established grade import and export APIs. This made it much more difficult to write reusable and module grade passing integrations. Doing so generally involved directly accessing the database in order to pull grades from Moodle via a separate cron process. This is still a popular method, but with the new gradebook we also have a standardized approach using gradebook import and export plugins.

Working with the built-in import/export plugins

It is not well known, but Moodle 1.9 actually has built-in import and export plugins. Import and export plugins are included for both flat files and XML. The feature must first be enabled at the site-level and then individual courses can be set up to publish their grades to a URL or to import grades from a URL. Access is restricted via a secure key, but storage of the secure URLs need to be carefully managed to prevent their theft. These are enabled under **Site Administration | Grades | General settings**. The following screenshot shows these settings:

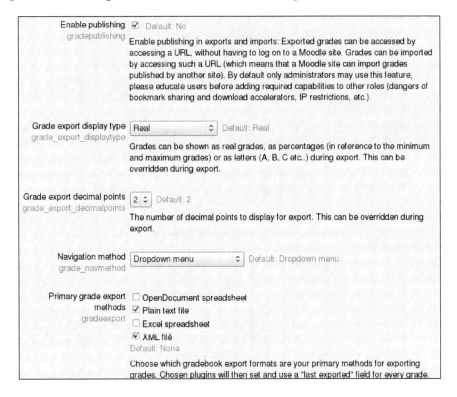

Additional information on grade importing can be found at `http://docs.moodle.org/en/Grade_import`.

In the next section, we will take a brief look at adding new plugins.

Creating grade import/export plugins

As mentioned previously, the Moodle 1.9 gradebook supports import and export plugins. These plugins are installed under `/grade/import` and `/grade/export` respectively. Each module is stored in its own folder. Both the XML and CSV plugins provide good examples of the correct structure for these plugins. The main weakness of what is provided in the core is that per course setup is required. This can be labor intensive and subject to human error. However, there is a hook function that developers can use in order to automate importing or exporting of the entire gradebook. Grade import and export plugins can implement a cron function, just like any other module. The naming convention is `grade_import_<name>_cron()`. This function must be created in the `lib.php` file for your plugin. For example, if our plugin is for importing grades and is named `auto_xml`, then the function should be called `grade_import_auto_xml_cron()`. The function would be placed in the `/grade/import/auto_xml/lib.php` file.

An exercise for you

There are a couple of exercises that you can carry out in order to learn more about import/export plugins:

- Modify the existing XML export function to implement the `cron` function so that the entire site's grades can be exported via a secure URL

- Create a new set of import/export plugins modeled on the external database authentication and enrollment plugins

Summary

In this chapter, you started out learning about the significant built-in functionality of Moodle that can be used to integrate with external systems. You have also learned how to create authentication plugins. You have learned how to implement Single Sign On between two systems. You have also learned how to create enrollment and role assignment plugins. And finally, we discussed methods for grade passing integrations between Moodle and other systems.

In the next chapter, we cover how to implement good security practices in our Moodle coding.

10
Writing Secure Code

The Moodle development team is very concerned about security. Making sure that Moodle protects its user data is one of the most important considerations to them. As a developer of Moodle code, you also need to treat security as being important, and must write secure code.

This chapter will cover the most common security concerns and best practices when developing code for Moodle. Moodle security policies are set up to deal with:

- User access protection
- SQL injection attacks
- Cross Site Scripting (XSS)
- Sanitizing user input

User access issues

User access is the first line of protection that Moodle has. Content and functionality can be protected so that anyone has to first log in using a valid account before they can access the content or functions of the site. Beyond that, specific functions within the site can be controlled by allowing or preventing capabilities for roles (see the section on access controls in *Chapter 1, Moodle Architecture*).

Any main script in Moodle must verify a user's identity and their ability to access the script's function.

 A main script is one that is called from the browser and executed directly, as opposed to a library function that is called somewhere from within another script

We will examine the common scripts that you need to use in order to make your user code secure.

Making sure that a user has logged in

Moodle sets a number of session variables that track the duration of a user's session. These can all be left for Moodle to manage as long as the user has been logged in and identified. Your script must make sure this has happened.

Moodle makes this easy. You just have to call the `require_login` function with the required parameters. You can do this with a statement such as:

```
require_login($course);
```

Here, `$course` is a pre-loaded course object or an integer identifier of a course.

The `require_login` function has the following specifications:

```
function require_login($courseorid=0, $autologinguest=true, $cm=null,
                       $setwantsurltome=true) {
```

Generally speaking, you will only be passing the course and/or the course module parameters. These allow you to have the system check to see if the user is allowed to access those contexts without being logged in (if they are not logged in).

The obvious purpose of this function is to see if the user is logged in. If they are not logged in, the function will see if they can access the identified context without logging in. If they can, then it will identify them as being able to be logged in as a guest. In either case, they will be redirected to the login function.

The less obvious purpose of this function is to check and make sure the logged in user has the ability to access the course and/or course module context that was passed in as an argument. This is different than checking capabilities; this is checking whether users need to be logged in to access the requested item.

Also, note that if the user is not logged in, they will be redirected to the `require_login` script again once they do log in.

Making sure that the user's session is the current one

With web access, there can be many opportunities for a URL to be re-executed when it should not be. This can happen with bookmarked URLs, browser history URLs, URL posts, or reports.

What this means is that if an appropriately-privileged user accessed a URL that executed an unexpected or unintended command, they could inadvertently perform an action they did not expect. This type of activity could happen accidentally, or maliciously.

To prevent this, Moodle requires you to include a `sesskey` parameter that identifies the session the URL was executed with, in forms or action URLs, and checks this identifier in scripts that perform the action, through the `confirm_sesskey` function.

For example, deleting a forum post is performed by executing the command:

```
http://[yoursite]/mod/forum/post.php?delete=3
```

This is then confirmed, as follows, by the form script:

```
http://[yoursite]/mod/forum/post.php?delete=3&confirm=3&sesskey=Ap
j5BqT4eO
```

The first URL is not all that dangerous, as it generates a confirmation form that requires a user to verify that the action should be taken. The second URL is the confirmation form. This one, if executed, would delete the post identified by the numeric identifier in the `delete` and `confirm` parameters.

You will notice there is another parameter, called `sesskey`, which contains a ten-character string. This string identifies the particular session that the user is running under, and is unique to that session.

Now, what if you accidentally posted the second link in a forum post that you were creating (you wouldn't do that on purpose, would you?), making it available for anyone reading the post to click on? Most regular users would simply be refused from executing the command. But, what if someone with sufficient privileges clicked on it? They would end up unintentionally deleting that post. I'm sure you can now imagine worse events than this!

That's where the `sesskey` comes in. The code that handles the actual deletion should call `confirm_sesskey()`, and only perform the action if the result is 'true'. `confirm_sesskey` will only return 'true' if the `sesskey` argument is the same as the current user's `sesskey` value.

The second form of the script referenced above (the confirmation form) contains the lines:

```
if (!empty($confirm) && confirm_sesskey()) {    // User has confirmed
the delete
```

This code prevents the delete confirmation action from taking place if the `sesskey` is not the same.

In this way, if the privileged user that we mentioned before clicks on the link, the action will not take place, because the user who posted the link could not have known a future user's `sesskey` value.

When you write your code, make sure that you consider these types of actions and provide appropriate `sesskey` protection. Incidentally, you get the `sesskey` value for the current session by a call to `sesskey()`.

Making sure that the user has appropriate capabilities

So we now know the user has logged in, and that he or she is, indeed, the user in the current session. Next we need to make sure that the user actually has privileges to perform the action he or she is attempting.

In the previous chapters, we've discussed the role and capability features of Moodle; so we won't go into too much detail about that system here. However, we will discuss the two important functions to control access to a script and its functions: `require_capability` and `has_capability`.

Both of these functions check that a user has the requested capability in the requested context. The difference between them is that `has_capability` returns a Boolean and allows your script to decide what to do based on the result, whereas `require_capability` prints an error and stops execution immediately if the user does not have the requested capability.

`require_capability` is best used in a script that should not be accessed by users, except in controlled situations. That is, a user would not be expected to access the script, except through a link or action that would have only been displayed to them if they were suitably privileged. Failing this test implies, "you should not be here, so we are closing the script". Examples of this would be any script displayed to administrator level users.

`has_capability` is used in a script to see what options the user should have. In other words, you expect users of varying capability levels to be using the script, and you want to tailor the actions to the specific capabilities of the current user.

For our previous example, we would want to use `has_capability` to verify that the user is allowed to delete the post. We can use this function in our code as follows:

```
if ( !(($post->userid == $USER->id &&
        has_capability('mod/forum:deleteownpost', $modcontext))
            || has_capability('mod/forum:deleteanypost', $modcontext)) )
{
    error("You can't delete this post!");
}
```

This code uses `has_capability` to allow the action only if the post belongs to the user and they can delete their own posts, or if they can delete any post.

Your code should always check to make sure that the user has appropriate capabilities before performing any actions.

SQL issues

The biggest worry you have when dealing with SQL and your database queries is the risk of SQL injection.

SQL injection is an attack technique that tries to take advantage of an SQL query by inserting other unexpected queries into it. Typically, this is done by taking advantage of incorrectly-filtered string literals in a PHP, or other programming language, script.

Let's consider what this would mean if our code was insecure.

Taking a look at vulnerable code

Let's say we have a fictitious script that takes an integer value (representing a user ID value in a user data table) from a form or direct URL parameter, and uses it. For example:

```
http://[oursite]/processuser.php?userid=4
```

Now, let's say our script looked similar to the following (remember this is fictional; don't really do this! This is a big security hole!):

```php
<?php
require_once('config.php');
$username = $_GET['username'];
$sql = "SELECT * FROM {$CFG->prefix}user WHERE username = $username";
$user = get_record_sql($sql);
print_object($user);
?>
```

Looks pretty harmless, right? All it's going to do is print out the user record it finds with the username value of the one passed into the script, isn't it?

Well, this is true as long as the value passed in is simply an expected username value.

Now, what if some malicious user executed this instead?

```
http://[oursite]/processuser.php?userid=admin%27;%20DROP%20TABLE%2
0mdl_user;%20SELECT%20*%20FROM%20mdl_user%20WHERE%20username=%27xxx
xjjj
```

This tries to stretch the SQL out to more statements by closing the first query and starting others. After being created, this query would end up looking as follows (if the code worked as our attacker thinks it does):

```
SELECT * FROM mdl_user WHERE username = 'admin'; DROP TABLE mdl_user;
SELECT * FROM mdl_user WHERE username='xxxjjj';
```

As you can see, what has been attempted is to inject two completely unexpected queries—one that drops an entire table!

The good news is this won't happen if you run the previous script. Moodle has several security elements built into its use that prevent these things from happening. We'll look at these next.

Incidentally, if you want to learn more about the type of attacks you are trying to prevent, look at the Wikipedia listing for SQL injections at `http://en.wikipedia. org/wiki/SQL_injection`.

Quote protection

Moodle processes all `$_POST`, `$_GET`, `$_COOKIE`, and `$_REQUEST` global arrays, and escapes any quotes it finds. What this means to our security is that unexpected quote closures cannot sneak in through parameters passed in from these global arrays.

In the previous example, what would have actually been rendered as SQL would be:

```
SELECT * FROM mdl_user WHERE username = 'admin\'; DROP TABLE
mdl_delme; SELECT * FROM mdl_user WHERE username=\'xxxjjj'
```

Note that the quotes we tried to inject now have a backslash character in front of them, effectively making the extra statements we tried to inject a part of the value being queried. Adding a backslash in front of a quote is known as "escaping".

This also means that when you are passing in data that needs to contain quotes, when it is stored in the database, they will already be correctly escaped.

Database API

Moodle's database API and the underlying database libraries that it uses (XMLDB and ADOdb) have many protections built in to help defend against these types of attacks.

That's why you should always use the minimal function call available when you can (see the *Retrieving data* section in *Chapter 6, Developer's Guide to the Database*). In the previous example, there was no reason for us to construct a complete SQL statement for such a simple query. Instead, we should have used:

```
$user = get_record('user', 'username', $userid);
```

This would, by its very nature, prevent more complicated SQL from getting into the system. And further, it limits the expected results to one record.

Another thing about using the standard Moodle database APIs is that it will not allow multiple SQL statements to be executed at one time. In the previous example, we tried to close off the initial select and start a "DROP" command. This will be prevented by the Moodle database libraries.

Because there are other SQL injections that do not involve multiple SQL queries, you should still be diligent when creating your own SQL statements. In particular, make sure that there are no missing quotes that could be taken advantage of.

Use of addslashes

Data that goes into a database needs to have its quote characters escaped with backslashes. In PHP, this is done with calls to addslashes().

Escaping embedded quote characters guarantees that the string data will be inserted correctly, prevents database errors, and prevents SQL injections. However, you should only do it in specific circumstances.

As described previously, this is done for you for all data coming from web input. You should not add extra slashes for this data. However, if you read data from the database, and write it back to the database, you must use addslashes. Moodle also provides an extra function called addslashes_object that allows you to process all fields in a data record at once.

Keep all of these issues in mind when you create code that involves SQL.

Form issues

Getting data from web forms is the single riskiest action in a web application. Unfortunately, it's also the single most useful function in a web application.

We've already seen that Moodle helps with form data by escaping quoted strings that come in through the form `$_GET` and `$_POST` constructs. However, you don't ever need to access these constructs directly in Moodle and, in fact, shouldn't. Instead, either build all of your data input forms using the Moodle formslib library or use the `required_param` and `optional_param` functions.

Both formslib and the `param` functions use defined parameters to help control and limit what is entered to what you expect. We will explain how these are used in subsequent paragraphs. However, for reference, the following are some of the most used parameters (all constants are defined in `moodlelib.php`):

- `PARAM_INT`, `PARAM_INTEGER`: Integers only, use when expecting only numbers.
- `PARAM_NUMBER`: A real/floating point number.
- `PARAM_ALPHA`: Contains only English letters.
- `PARAM_ACTION`: An alias for `PARAM_ALPHA`, used for various actions in formats and URLs.
- `PARAM_FORMAT`: An alias for `PARAM_ALPHA`, used for names of plugins, formats, and so on.
- `PARAM_NOTAGS`: All HTML tags are stripped from the text. Do not misuse this type.
- `PARAM_TEXT`: General plain text compatible with `multilang` filter, no other HTML tags.
- `PARAM_MULTILANG`: Alias of `PARAM_TEXT`.
- `PARAM_FILE`: Safe file name, all dangerous characters are stripped, protects against XSS, SQL injections, and directory traversals.
- `PARAM_PATH`: Safe relative path name, all dangerous characters are stripped, protects against XSS, SQL injections, and directory traversals.
- `PARAM_HOST`: Expected **Fully Qualified Domain Name** (FQDN) or an IPv4 dotted quad (IP address).
- `PARAM_URL`: Expected properly formatted URL. Please note that domain part is required; just `http://localhost/` is not accepted but `http://localhost.localdomain/` is OK.

- PARAM_CLEANFILE: Safe file name, all dangerous or regional characters are removed; use when you want to store a new file submitted by students.

- PARAM_ALPHANUM: Only numbers and letters.

- PARAM_BOOL: Converts input into 0 or 1; use for switches in forms and URLs.

- PARAM_CLEANHTML: Cleans submitted HTML code and removes slashes. Do not forget to use addslashes() before storing into database!

- PARAM_ALPHAEXT: Has the same contents as PARAM_ALPHA, plus the characters in quotes "/-_" are allowed, suitable for include() and require().

- PARAM_SAFEDIR: Safe directory name, suitable for include() and require().

The Moodle formslib library

The Moodle formslib library provides a couple of vital functions: it provides a standard and easy way to create forms and common Moodle input functions, and provides some standard ways to secure the input received. For this section, we'll focus on the security issues.

Specifying a type

When you define an element by using the formslib library, you can also specify its type. The various types are all defined as parameter constants in the moodlelib.php file. Some of the most useful ones are listed in the previous section, *Form issues*. Specifying a type for a form element limits the input that can be provided to that element. This helps make the input more secure.

For example, if you specify a text input box as a PARAM_INT type then a user cannot enter anything but a valid number.

Following is an example of specifying a form element and its type, taken from the forum editing form (/mod/forum/mod_form.php):

```
$mform->addElement('text', 'warnafter', get_string('warnafter',
                    'forum'));
$mform->setType('warnafter', PARAM_INT);
```

By specifying this form element as a PARAM_INT, only integer values will be allowed as an entry.

Validation rules

Validation rules work best in conjunction with parameter types. Specifying a parameter type will guarantee that no incorrect data will be returned from the form. Specifying a rule will allow the user to be notified that the values have been specified incorrectly.

Specifying a rule has several components. The parameter specification is as follows:

```
* @param    string    $element     :Form element name
* @param    string    $message     :Message to display for invalid data
* @param    string    $type        :Rule type, use getRegisteredRules()
                                     to get types
* @param    string    $format      :(optional)Required for extra rule
                                     data
* @param    string    $validation  :(optional)Where to perform
                                     validation: "server", "client"
* @param    boolean   $reset       :Client-side validation: reset
                                     the form element to its original
                                     value if there is an error?
* @param    boolean   $force       :Force the rule to be applied,
                                     even if the target form element
                                     does not exist
function addRule($element, $message, $type, $format=null,
$validation='server', $reset = false, $force = false)
```

The key elements are the first three: the name of the element to apply the rule to, the message to display if the data is invalid, and the name for the rule type.

Extending the code from the previous example, we see:

```
$mform->addElement('text', 'warnafter', get_string('warnafter',
                'forum'));
$mform->setType('warnafter', PARAM_INT);
$mform->setDefault('warnafter', '0');
$mform->addRule('warnafter', null, 'numeric', null, 'client');
```

Next, we added the 'numeric' rule to the 'warnafter' form element. Because we haven't specified an error message, the default one for that rule will be used. Now, not only will non-numeric data not be allowed, but a message will be displayed to the user telling them they must enter numeric data into that field (if they try to enter any other type of data).

The default rule types available are required, maxlength, minlength, rangelength, email, regex, lettersonly, alphanumeric, numeric, nopunctuation, nonzero, callback, and compare. It is also possible to define and create your own rules.

'param' functions

There are two param functions: `optional_param` and `required_param`. These functions allow you to get parameters that are passed into your script via the `$_GET` and `$_POST` global variables in a safe, controlled way.

The function specifications are:

```
function optional_param($parname, $default=NULL, $type=PARAM_CLEAN)
function required_param($parname, $type=PARAM_CLEAN)
```

The difference between the two functions is how they handle non-provided variables. `required_param` throws an error and stops execution if the requested variable has not been provided. `optional_param` substitutes the specified default value if the requested variable has not been provided.

Both functions do perform validation on the data according to the parameter type specified. The parameter types are the same as the ones specified previously, and the ones used to define element types in forms.

As an example of how these are used, following is some code from the `/mod/forum/report.php` file:

```
$id   = required_param('id', PARAM_INT);
$sort = optional_param('sort', '', PARAM_ALPHA);
```

The first example assigns the `'id'` parameter received to the `$id` variable, and forces it to be an integer. If no `'id'` parameter is found, the script throws an error and stops execution. The second example assigns the `'sort'` parameter received to the `$sort` variable, and forces it to be an alphabetic string. If no `'sort'` parameter is received, `$sort` is set to an empty string.

These parameters are all processed by the `clean_param` function, which returns whatever was entered, in the specified parameter format, no matter what was entered. This provides the necessary security for parameters passed in from web scripts.

Use these coding methods in your scripts to secure your programs from form-based exploitation.

File system issues

Files uploaded and used in Moodle are stored in Moodle's file system. The file system is the directory set up and configured as `$CFG->dataroot`. Administratively, this should *always be set up outside of the browsable web space* in order to ensure that the files can only be accessed programmatically through Moodle's PHP scripts.

The Moodle data directory (often referred to as 'moodledata') is structured such that the root of the directory contains only subdirectories. Each of these subdirectories is responsible for holding data files for different purposes. We will look at several of the common areas found at the root of this directory.

Course file areas

You will notice a number of subdirectories that have numbers for names. These are the course file areas, and are named according to the data ID of the course that they belong to. There will be one directory for every course on your system.

Inside each of these numbered directories, there can be two system-created directories, called `backupdata` and `moddata`. The `backupdata` directory contains any backup files created within the course it is associated with. The `moddata` directory contains files associated with activities in the course. Any other files and/or directories that you see there have usually been created by the course `files` function (as seen in the following screenshot):

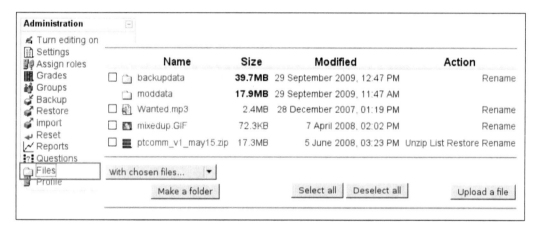

Inside the `moddata` directory will be a named subdirectory for any module that contains files. The directories are named for the module name (for example, 'forum'). The structure within each module directory is managed by the module.

User file areas

At the same level as the course file areas, you will see a subdirectory called `user`. This contains files specific to users. Inside it, you will see a number of subdirectories starting with '0', and possibly other subdirectories starting with '1000' and increasing by 1000 thereafter. Each of these subdirectories contains other numeric directories starting with one more than the parent directory name, and containing as many as 1000. This is because Moodle separates the user directories into groups of one thousand for efficiency and to avoid directory number limitations in some file systems. The groups of one thousand contain numeric directories named by the user data ID.

The user directories contain any profile images uploaded by the user in their profile. At this point, that's all they are used for.

Other file areas

There are a number of other file areas used only by the system, such as `cache`, `sessions`, `temp`, and `upgradelogs`. There is a `blog` directory which, like the forum module directories, contains attachments per blog post ID. There is a `groups` directory which, like the `user` directory, contains only profile images for the group. The `lang` directory contains any installed language packs other than the standard `en_utf8` one, and any local versions that have been modified. All of these should be accessed through standard Moodle means.

Getting a file URL

When files are added to modules, a URL is generated that allows access to files. This URL is controlled by a Moodle PHP script so that access can be controlled. To get the full URL used to access the file, call the `get_file_url` function with the path, any parameters you wish to include, and the file type. The function will then return the full URL to that file.

For example, if there is an attachment uploaded to a forum post, it will be located in the `moddata/forum` directory in the specific course's directory in the `moodledata` structure. Inside that directory will be a numbered directory corresponding to the forum's data ID, and below that, there will be numbered directories corresponding to the data ID of any post that has an attachment.

You would get a URL to that attachment by issuing the following code:

```
$courseid = 4;
$forumid = 10;
$postid = 7;
$attachmentid = 'mypic.jpg;
$ffilename = "$courseid/$CGF->moddata/forum
            /$forumid/$postid/$attachmentname";
$fileurl = get_file_url($ffilename, NULL, 'coursefile');
```

At the end of this, we would get a file URL called: `http://[oursite]/file.php/4/moddata/forum/10/7/mypic.jpg`. This URL allows Moodle to display a file that is not actually located in the browsable web space, and can apply Moodle protection controls to that access.

When you create code that requires access to files in the `moodledata` area, be sure to use the naming techniques and access methods described here.

Screen output issues

At some point, as you create your code, you will need to output information to the screen. Because you can't always be sure what you are writing is safe, you need to make sure that you process it before writing it out. This is especially true for output that has been created dynamically by others, such as forum posts.

One of the main reasons to do this is to prevent Cross Site Scripting (XSS) attacks. These techniques inject client-side scripts into a displayed web page in order to try to bypass security measures and gain information that they should otherwise not have. These types of attacks can be very dangerous. For more information, see the Moodle Docs page: `http://docs.moodle.org/en/Development:Security:Cross-site_scripting#Cleaning_input`.

Moodle provides four main functions for this purpose: `p()`, `s()`, `format_text()`, and `format_string()`.

The p() and s() functions

These functions are used to strip everything but text out of the passed in strings, and convert HTML tags to their harmless equivalents. Use these when you are outputting strictly text and need no HTML formatting.

The `p()` function prints directly to the screen; the `s()` function returns a string. In fact, the `p()` function just echoes the output of the `s()` function; so all of the work is done in the `s()` function.

The entire specification and code of these functions is as follows:

```
/**
 * Add quotes to HTML characters
 *
 * Returns $var with HTML characters (like "<", ">", etc.) properly
   quoted.
 * This function is very similar to {@link p()}
 *
```

```
 * @param string $var the string potentially containing HTML
   characters
 * @param boolean $strip to decide if we want to strip slashes or no.
   Default to false.
 * true should be used to print data from forms and false for data
   from DB.
 * @return string
 */
function s($var, $strip=false) {
    if ($var == '0') {  // for integer 0, boolean false, string '0'
        return '0';
    }
    if ($strip) {
        return preg_replace("/&amp;(#\d+);/i", "&$1;",
                        htmlspecialchars(stripslashes_safe($var)));
    } else {
        return preg_replace("/&amp;(#\d+);/i", "&$1;",
                        htmlspecialchars($var));
    }
}
```

From this, you can see that by passing in your text, you will be returned text that will have all of its HTML (and any other scripting language) tags removed. This makes it safe to output in areas that require only text.

This could be used for values displayed inside of HTML tags, such as:

```
<input type="text" name="name" size="60"
  value="<?php p($post->subject) ?>" />
```

In this bit of an HTML form, the value that will be displayed is run through the `p()` function to make sure that nothing is there that would break the form input element.

The format_text() and format_string() functions

Just like the `p()` and `s()` functions, these two functions are related. However, the `format_string` function is again intended to be used on non-HTML text while the `format_text` function is intended to process HTML text.

The `format_text` function is a heavy duty function that cleans dangerous content and also applies filtering, supports the different text formats (HTML, Markdown, Moodle), performs automatic conversions for smileys and links, and provides caching of text to help improve performance.

The part that we are concerned with here is the cleaning function. The specification for the function is:

```
function format_text($text, $format=FORMAT_MOODLE, $options=NULL,
                     $courseid=NULL )
```

The first parameter is the text to process. The second specifies the format that the text should be processed as. Currently, there are four supported formats:

- `FORMAT_HTML`: Most common format
- `FORMAT_PLAIN`: Text only, like `s()`
- `FORMAT_MARKDOWN`: Simple formatting rules to create HTML
- `FORMAT_MOODLE`: Mostly plain text with some auto-conversion

The third parameter specifies options that can be used in the formatting. The `$options` parameter, if specified, is an object that contains variables specifying a variety of formatting options, namely:

- `$options->trusttext` (default = false): If enabled, does not clean the provided text—ONLY USE IF YOU ARE REALLY SURE!
- `$options->noclean` (default = false): If enabled, does not clean the provided text—overridden by `trusttext` and should be used the same way
- `$options->nocache` (default = false): If enabled, will not cache the provided text
- `$options->filter` (default = true): If enabled, text will be run through active filters
- `$options->smiley` (default = true): If enabled, will convert smiley code to pictures
- `$options->para` (default = true): If enabled, will enclose paragraphs between `<p></p>` tags in `FORMAT_MOODLE` mode
- `$options->newline` (default = true): If enabled, will add `<br/>` tags to lines with linefeeds in them in `FORMAT_MOODLE` mode

The last parameter is the course data ID for the course applicable to the output. This allows for any course specific filter settings to be taken into account.

The meat of the work, from a security standpoint, is done by the `clean_text` function, which is called from within `format_text`. This function replaces HTML entities, removes tags and scripts, and cleans other potentially dangerous strings that could lead to Cross Site Scripting (XSS) exploitation.

When creating code that outputs to the screen, make sure that your output is filtered, by using these functions.

Logging your actions

Although not strictly a way to secure your site, logging your actions will enable you to determine what was done and who did it. Moodle provides a function, add_to_log, which allows you to create log entries that identify what was done in your code.

The specification of the add_to_log function is as follows:

```
/**
 * Add an entry to the log table.  These are "action" focussed rather
 * than web server hits, and provide a way to easily reconstruct what
 * any particular student has been doing.
 *
 * @param    int      $courseid  The course id
 * @param    string   $module    The module name - e.g. forum, journal,
 *                               resource, course, user etc
 * @param    string   $action    'view', 'update', 'add' or 'delete',
 *                               possibly followed by another word to
 *                               clarify.
 * @param    string   $url       The file and parameters used to see
 *                               the results of the action
 * @param    string   $info      Additional description information
 * @param    string   $cm        The course_module->id if there is one
 * @param    string   $user      If log regards $user other than $USER
 */
function add_to_log($courseid, $module, $action, $url='', $info='',
               $cm=0, $user=0) {
```

Its usage is straightforward, and allows you to track any action that someone may want to investigate some time after it has been done.

For example, using our delete post action from before, the code logs the activity with the line:

```
add_to_log($discussion->course, "forum", "delete post",
        $discussionurl, "$post->id", $cm->id);
```

This function will log the actual deletion event so that if we ever want to know what happened to it, we can take a look. The log record contains the specific details about the course, module, and specific post, as well as a human-readable description of the action ("delete post") and the actual URL of the post when it was present. The user who performed the action will also be logged with the record, by default.

In some cases, a log record may not have a viewable interface in Moodle. But, no matter what, you can always find the logs in the database log table.

Summary

In this chapter, we looked at how Moodle provides us with tools to create more secure code. You learned how to make sure that your users have the correct access privileges, how to make your database code more secure, how to protect yourself from malicious form input, and how to make sure that you don't output dangerous HTML.

In the next chapter, you will learn how to use Moodle's notification system.

11
Sending Notifications to Users

As you write applications, you will occasionally want to notify users other than the current one of events that have happened or will happen. This is different than displaying it on the screen as it happens.

This chapter will cover methods of communicating with users via various notification methods. To do this, Moodle provides many methods, including:

- E-mail
- Sending Moodle messages
- RSS Feeds

Requirements

Let's set up some reasons to notify users, so we can try out the different methods. We'll bring back the journal assignment type from *Chapter 7, Developing Pluggable Core Modules*.

What if you could set up each day's journal to notify certain people and allow them to read it, once a user posts an entry.

So, we need a system that grants users the ability to receive notification of any journal entry posted. And, we want to be able to select the way that the notification is generated: e-mail, Moodle messaging, or RSS feed.

We can start by adding another setting to our assignment type that allows us to define if and how entry notifications will be sent. We will use the current `mod/assignment:grade` capability to define who can receive the notifications.

It's time to start programming again.

Setup

Let's start with the easy pieces.

We need to add a new setting that defines whether the assignment will send entry notifications and how it will send them. We will use the var2 field of the assignment table to store this setting (recall from *Chapter 7, Developing Pluggable Core Modules* that var2 is a field set aside, along with var1 and var3 to var5, for custom types). As var2 is an integer type, we will use numeric code to represent the various methods: 0 for no notification, 1 for e-mail, 2 for messaging, and 3 for RSS.

Let's open up our assignment.class.php file.

First, let's use good coding practices and set up some constants for the settings. Near the top of the file, enter:

```
/*
 * Define some constants for entry notification settings.
 */
define ('ASSIGNMENT_JOURNAL_EN_NONE', 0);
define ('ASSIGNMENT_JOURNAL_EN_EMAIL', 1);
define ('ASSIGNMENT_JOURNAL_EN_MESSAGING', 2);
define ('ASSIGNMENT_JOURNAL_EN_RSS', 3);
```

This will allow us to use the named constants in place of the numeric values wherever we refer to the settings.

Next, let's add our extra setting to the assignment settings form. In the setup_elements function, append the following code:

```
$mform->addElement('select', 'var2', get_string('entrynotify',
                   'assignment_journal'), $enoptions);
$mform->setHelpButton('var2', array('entrynotify',
        get_string('entrynotify', 'assignment_journal'),
        'assignment_journal'));
$mform->setDefault('var2', 0);
```

We will also need to define the language strings and the help file that we use in our language files. Review the included language files in the code package for these strings.

With this in place, we can now specify a type of notification to use on our assignment settings screen. Go ahead and try it; it should look similar to the following screenshot:

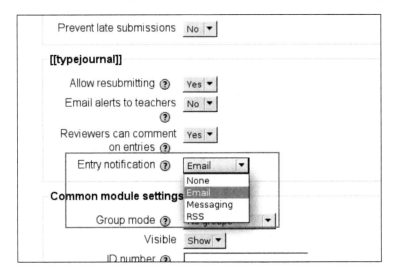

Now that we have the settings, we need to start using them. We'll start simple.

In our `view_submission` function, there is a section that handles the newly-entered journal entry. In that same section, you can see a standard call to `email_teachers`. This function is one that notifies teachers that a submission has been provided. Below that, we'll add our new function call to handle entry notifications. Enter:

```
/// Handle any entry notifications.
$this->entry_notification();
```

We will create this function to handle the notifications. It will do two things: determine who should receive the notifications, and send them. Create this function with the following code:

```
/**
 * Handle any necessary entry notifications and dispatch to right
handler.
 *
 * @return boolean
 */
function entry_notification() {
    /// Determine who should receive this notification:
    if (empty($this->context)) {
        $this->context = get_context_instance(CONTEXT_MODULE,
                         $this->cm->id);
    }
```

```
$currentgroup = groups_get_activity_group($this->cm);
if (!$users = get_users_by_capability($this->context, 'mod/
    assignment:grade', 'u.*', '', '', '', $currentgroup, '',
    false)) {
    return true;
}
/// Get the from user record.
$fromuser = get_record('user', 'id', $this->submission->userid);
/// Handle notifications based on the setting.
/// If setting is 'none' or undefined, do nothing.
switch ($this->assignment->var2) {
    case ASSIGNMENT_JOURNAL_EN_EMAIL:
        return $this->entry_notify_email($users, $fromuser);
        break;
    case ASSIGNMENT_JOURNAL_EN_MESSAGING:
        return $this->entry_notify_messaging($users, $fromuser);
        break;
    case ASSIGNMENT_JOURNAL_EN_RSS:
        return $this->entry_notify_rss($users, $fromuser);
        break;
    default:
        return true;
}
}
```

Add stubs for the missing functions, and we're done with the general part:

```
/**
 * Handle email based notification.
 *
 * @param $users
 * @param $fromuser
 * @return boolean
 */
function entry_notify_email($users, $fromuser) {
    return true;
}
/**
 * Handle Moodle messaging based notification.
 *
 * @param $users
 * @param $fromuser
 * @return boolean
 */
function entry_notify_messaging($users, $fromuser) {
    return true;
```

```
}
/**
 * Handle RSS based notification.
 *
 * @param $users
 * @param $fromuser
 * @return boolean
 */
function entry_notify_rss($users, $fromuser) {
    return true;
}
```

Your assignment type should now run. Now we need to add the actual notification function.

Using e-mail

E-mail is probably the simplest and most common way of notifying users about information in Moodle. Forum subscriptions, activity submissions, and course welcome messages, all use this method.

In Moodle, there are also various reasons why specific users should not receive e-mails. Users can specify in their profile that they do not want to receive e-mails. Moodle may have determined that a user's e-mail address is bouncing. Or, a user may have their account suspended or terminated. In these cases, you want to make sure you are obeying the settings and not send e-mail to those users.

Also, users may want to receive text-only e-mail or prefer to receive HTML e-mail (as seen in the following screenshot). You would want to make sure you sent the message in the appropriate format:

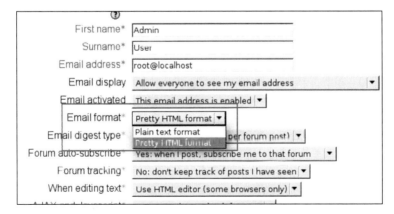

Fortunately, Moodle makes this easy for you. You just need to use its `email_to_user` API function, and let the function worry about whether the e-mail should be sent and in what format it should be sent.

Send e-mail API

Let's flesh out our `entry_notify_email` function. First, let's examine the `email_to_user` API function in `moodlelib.php`.

The specification of `email_to_user` is as follows:

```
function email_to_user($user, $from, $subject, $messagetext,
    $messagehtml='', $attachment='', $attachname='',
    $usetrueaddress=true, $replyto='', $replytoname='',
    $wordwrapwidth=79)
```

The key parameters we will concern ourselves with are:

- `$user`: The Moodle user object that the e-mail is being sent to
- `$from`: The Moodle user object that the e-mail should be from
- `$subject`: Text to display in the e-mail subject line
- `$messagetext`: Text-only version of the e-mail message
- `$messagehtml`: HTML formatted version of the e-mail message

So, to use this function, we need to define who we are sending it to, who it is from, what the subject text is, and what the message text and HTML are. The users we are sending it to and the user it's from, we know from the parameters passed in from `entry_notification`. We need to create the subject and the message. Let's add these to our function.

Creating the subject text

Because the message that we are sending is about a new post to a journal assignment, it's probably best to identify the assignment it's from in the subject. Some text such as "New post to, journal [assignment name]" should suffice. We will substitute "[assignment name]" with the actual name of the assignment. We could hardcode this but its best to use a language string. That way, other language pack developers can substitute their translations easily.

In our `lang/en_utf8/assignment_journal.php` file, add the following line:

```
$string['notifyemailsubject'] = 'New post to journal $a';
```

We will pass the $a portion to the string function when we call it, and this will contain the assignment's name.

Now, in our entry_notify_email function, add the lines:

```
$a = $this->assignment->name;
$subject = get_string('notifyemailsubject', 'assignment_journal', $a);
```

Using the language string function, we have now defined our subject text for the e-mail.

Creating the message text

The message text only needs to be the journal posting itself. Our e-mail function allows us to specify both HTML formatted and plain text formatted versions of the message, so we will provide both.

The HTML version of the message is already there. The user will have entered their post by using the assignment's HTML editor and we have that in our assignment object. We need to derive the plain text version from the HTML version. Moodle provides a simple function format_text_email for this, which we will use.

In our function, add the lines:

```
$messagehtml = $this->submission->current_entry->entrytext;
$messagetext = format_text_email($this->submission->
                   current_entry->entrytext, FORMAT_HTML);
```

We now have all of the arguments that we need in order to send the e-mail.

Sending the e-mail

Now that we have everything ready, we can add the code to send the e-mail notifications to the identified users. Because the users we are sending to are contained in an array, we will loop through it and send one message at a time.

Let's add the following lines, to complete our function:

```
foreach ($users as $user) {
  email_to_user($user, $fromuser, $subject, $messagetext,
                $messagehtml);
}
```

We have now sent notification messages to all of the identified users, via e-mail. The users will receive the e-mail in the format of their choice—text or HTML. In the following screenshot, you can see a sample of what an e-mail notification would look like:

You can see the complete function listing in the code provided for this chapter.

Using Moodle messaging

Moodle provides an instant messaging type of communication that allows you to send messages to any Moodle user. If a user is online when a message is sent, they will receive it in their message box and can view it in a pop-up window. If the user is not online within a configured timeframe, the message will be sent to them via e-mail.

This mechanism can therefore be a more effective communication tool than just e-mail. It can alert a user in the Moodle environment and fall back to e-mail.

Let's complete our `entry_notification_messaging` function to use Moodle messaging.

Moodle messaging internals

Moodle messaging uses two data tables to handle message delivery: `message` and `message_read`. When a message is sent to a user, it is inserted into the `message` table. Its existence indicates an unread message to that user, and will trigger the message indicators when that user is online. Once the user has viewed that message, the record is moved to the `message_read` table. This allows all messages to be retained, while tracking whether they have been delivered.

The Moodle messaging API is primarily located in `/message/lib.php`. We will need to include this in our function, with the lines:

```
global $CFG;
require_once($CFG->dirroot.'/message/lib.php');
```

The function that we are concerned with is the `message_post_message` function. Its specification is as follows:

```
function message_post_message($userfrom, $userto, $message, $format,
                              $messagetype)
```

As you can see, this is very similar to the e-mail function that we used previously. The parameters are:

- `$userfrom`: The Moodle user object that the message is from
- `$userto`: The Moodle user object that the message is being sent to
- `$message`: The message text to be sent
- `$format`: The format code of the message
- `$messagetype`: Currently unused; only valid value is 'direct'

So, for our purposes, we need the users we are sending it to, the user it is coming from, and the actual message we are sending. We have the user information; we just need to create the message.

Creating the message

Our message text is in HTML, so we will send it to the messaging system that way. At present, the messaging system doesn't provide an HTML interface. However, it will still honor the format, especially if the message is immediately sent by e-mail.

We're going to basically copy what we did for e-mail and re-construct it to work a little differently. Although Moodle messaging doesn't have a subject line like e-mail, if the message is eventually sent by e-mail, a subject is constructed from the first 30 characters of the message text. We'll construct a subject and add it to the beginning of the message.

So, our message construction code is as follows:

```
$a = $this->assignment->name;
$subject = get_string('notifyemailsubject', 'assignment_journal', $a);
$message = $subject .
           "<br />\n" .
           (addslashes($this->submission->current_entry->entrytext));
```

Note that we have created the same subject that we had for e-mail, and inserted it into the beginning of the message text with line breaks for formatting. This will help both with the message display in the message interface, and with an e-mail if it is sent.

Sending the message

The rest is simple. Send the message to all of the users. Insert the following code:

```
foreach ($users as $user) {
  message_post_message($fromuser, $user, $message, FORMAT_HTML,
                       'direct');
}
```

This function will now send the constructed message to each of the identified users, from the posting user. Each receiving user will receive a notification and a message, as shown in the following screenshot:

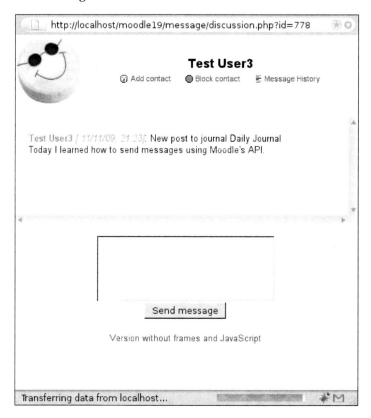

You can see the complete function listing in the `assignment.class.php` file for this chapter.

Using RSS feeds

RSS is a method of publishing web information in a way that can be picked up by subscribers. This allows specialized readers to summarize web content for reading.

The way that this works is that an XML-formatted file is identified and provided, which contains the content and its description. RSS readers can then look for that file and load it when necessary, such as when it has been modified.

In Moodle, the common way to distribute content via RSS is by providing a `[module name]_rss_feeds` function in a `/mod/rsslib.php` file. This gets called by the main cron job on a regular basis in order to distribute what the module identifies.

The assignment module does not currently provide a way to do this however, and so assignment types cannot automatically publish their own feeds. Instead, we will publish a new feed when a posting has been made.

Setup

For our purposes, RSS is probably not the best way to distribute journal posts, as it allows anyone to subscribe and does not care about Moodle privileges. However, to show off its functions, we'll do it anyway. We'll add a layer of protection to it by using links to the full journal text, in place of the entire message.

Because the assignment module does not provide a mechanism to feed the RSS cron job, we'll just post a new RSS file when a journal is posted. The functions that we will need are all contained in the `/lib/rsslib.php` file. Include this in our `entry_notify_rss` function with the following lines:

```
global $CFG;
require_once($CFG->libdir.'/rsslib.php');
```

The functions that we will be using are:

- `rss_file_name`: Returns a properly constructed filename for the native file system, based on the module type and instance to contain the RSS XML

- `rss_standard_header`: Returns the RSS XML header for the information provided

- `rss_add_items`: Returns the RSS XML for all of the content items provided

- `rss_standard_footer`: Returns the RSS XML footer for the information provided

- `rss_save_file`: Saves the RSS file to the required location

Now, let's go about creating this RSS file.

Creating the RSS XML file

We'll use the `entry_notify_rss` function that we created, in order to do this. It is called when the assignment has been configured to use RSS and when a user posts to their journal. For our purposes, we will retrieve the last ten journal posts from all users when this event happens, and add these to the RSS XML file.

So, let's add the code to get the data that we will want to post to the RSS file:

```
/// Number of articles to post in RSS feed. Ideally this should be
///settable.
$numarticles = 10;
/// Construct the SQL to get the posts to display in the feed.
$select = "SELECT aje.*, u.id as userid, u.firstname, u.lastname ";
$from = "FROM {$CFG->prefix}assignment_journal_entries aje " .
        "INNER JOIN {$CFG->prefix}assignment_submissions asb ON asb.id
        = aje.submissionid " .
        "INNER JOIN {$CFG->prefix}user u ON u.id = asb.userid ";
$where = "WHERE asb.assignment = {$this->assignment->id} ";
$order = "ORDER BY aje.entrymodified DESC";
$sql = $select . $from . $where . $order;
if (!$records = get_records_sql($sql, 0, $numarticles)) {
    return '';
}
```

What we are doing here is getting one record for each journal entry of the last ten posted for the current assignment. The record contains the entry itself and the information about the user. If there are none, we're done and we can move on. We have set the number of entries that we retrieve to ten, inside the code. A better method would be to make this number configurable for the assignment. Make a note to improve this at a later date.

Next, we need to construct each entry into an RSS item:

```
/// We have the posts, let's process them.
$items = array();
foreach ($records as $record) {
    $item = new Object();
    $item->title       = get_string('notifyemailsubject',
                        'assignment_journal', $this->assignment->name);
    $item->author      = fullname($record);
    $item->pubdate     = $record->entrymodified;
    $item->link        = $CFG->wwwroot.'/mod/assignment/type/journal/
                        entry.php?id=' . $this->assignment->id .
```

```
                            '&userid=' . $record->userid;
        $item->description = format_text($record->entrytext, FORMAT_HTML,
                            NULL, $this->course->id);

        $items[] = $item;
    }
```

Each item in an RSS list is a record containing a title, author, publication date, a link to the entire post, and the post itself. The entire list of items is stored in an array. We build each item from the records that we retrieved, and load these one by one into an array. This provides us with the data that we need to create the RSS file.

Lastly, we construct the RSS file using the API:

```
/// First get the rss feeds common headers.
$header = rss_standard_header($this->course->shortname.': '.format_
        string($this->assignment->name, true),
        $CFG->wwwroot."/mod/assignment/view.php?id=". $this->cm->id,
        format_string($this->assignment->description, true));
/// Get all the items into a formatted structure.
$articles = rss_add_items($items);
/// Now all rss feeds common footers.
$footer = rss_standard_footer();
/// Now, if everything is ok, concatenate it.
if (!empty($header) && !empty($articles) && !empty($footer)) {
    $rss = $header.$articles.$footer;
    ///Save the XML contents to file.
    $status = rss_save_file('assignment', $this->assignment, $rss);
}
else {
    $status = false;
}
return $status;
```

Looking through this code, we first construct an RSS header using the course and assignment information, a link to the assignment, and the assignment's description. Then, we add all of the items that we created as the content of the RSS feed. Then, we create a footer. Lastly, we create the file from the RSS XML that we built and the assignment information. The location of the file is controlled by the rsslib API. So, as long as we use the API, we can always find it.

We now have all of the code we need in order to create and update an RSS XML feed whenever a new entry is posted to the journal. If we run the assignment now, and add a new entry, we will see that a new file has been created in the RSS file area (located in your moodledata directory in the rss subdirectory). Following is an excerpt from our test run:

```xml
<?xml version="1.0" encoding="UTF-8"?>
<rss version="2.0">
  <channel>
    <title>CF101: Daily Journal</title>
    <link>http://localhost/moodle19/mod/assignment/view.php?id=67
    </link>
    <description> This is my journal </description>
    <generator>Moodle</generator>
    <language>en</language>
    <copyright>&amp;#169; 2009 Moodle 19 Test Site</copyright>
    <image>
      <url>http://localhost/moodle19/pix/i/rsssitelogo.gif</url>
      <title>moodle</title>
      <link>http://localhost/moodle19</link>
      <width>140</width>
      <height>35</height>
    </image>
    <item>
      <title>New post to journal Daily Journal</title>
      <link>http://localhost/moodle19/mod/assignment/type/journal/
            entry.php ?id=3&amp;userid=2</link>
      <pubDate>Fri, 13 Nov 2009 17:05:40 GMT</pubDate>
      <description>by Admin User.  &lt;p&gt; Today is Friday
        the 13th. &lt;/p&gt;</description>
      <guid isPermaLink="true">
        http://localhost/moodle19/mod/assignment/type/journal/
        entry.php?id=3&amp;userid=2
      </guid>
    </item>
  </channel>
</rss>
```

This proves that we can create the RSS file as needed. Now, let's make it viewable.

Viewing the RSS feed

Although we have the RSS file created, RSS is not intended to be viewed directly from its XML. Internet users expect to be provided with a link option that allows them to tell their RSS reader program to subscribe to the feed. This is often provided through an RSS icon somewhere on the page.

Fortunately, Moodle makes this easy for us, too. The RSS API has a function to return an icon and a link to display the RSS feed information. Your browser will usually give you options to load it into a configured RSS reader, or you can copy the link into your reader.

To put this in our assignment, let's place the icon next to where the "submitted assignments" information is located. To do this, we will need to add some code to the `submittedlink` function. Copy the following `submittedlink` function into your journal class:

```
function submittedlink($allgroups=false) {
    global $CFG, $USER;
    $submitted = parent::submittedlink($allgroups);
    if (empty($this->context)) {
        $this->context = get_context_instance(CONTEXT_MODULE,
                         $this->cm->id);
    }
    /// If user is allowed and rss is activated at site and this
        activity is using rss, show link.
    if (!empty($CFG->enablerssfeeds) &&
        ($this->assignment->var2 == ASSIGNMENT_JOURNAL_EN_RSS) &&
        has_capability('mod/assignment:grade', $this->context)) {
        require_once($CFG->libdir.'/rsslib.php');
        $tooltiptext = get_string('rsssubscribers',
                       'assignment_journal');
        if (empty($USER->id)) {
            $userid = 0;
        } else {
            $userid = $USER->id;
        }
        $submitted .= '<span class="wrap rsslink">';
        ob_start();
        rss_print_link($this->course->id, $userid, "assignment",
                       $this->assignment->id, $tooltiptext);
        $submitted .= ob_get_contents();
        ob_end_clean();
        $submitted .= '</span>';
    }
    return $submitted;
}
```

We also added the following statement to the language file:

```
$string['rsssubscribers'] = 'Display the RSS feed.';
```

This code will check to see if RSS is enabled and being used. If it is, it will use the `rss_print_link` function to capture the output of an RSS icon that displays the RSS subscriber information for our RSS feed. It captures the output from the print function by using PHP's output buffer commands, `ob_start` and `ob_end_clean`. These functions allow us to grab output headed for the screen before it gets there, and use it in our code.

Now, when we look at our assignment screen, we should see the following:

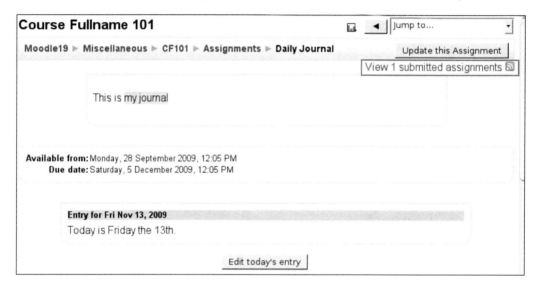

Notice the orange RSS icon beside the **View 1 submitted assignments** message. Clicking on this will give us the RSS subscription information. This information allows users to include this feed as a subscription option in the RSS reader of their choice.

In Firefox, with a certain configuration, clicking on the icon shows a page similar to the following screenshot:

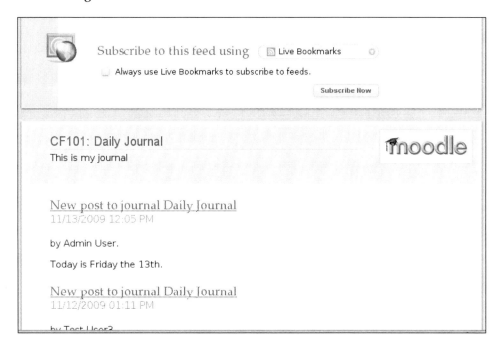

The full source listing for this function is available in the code provided for this chapter.

Summary

In this chapter, you looked at the most common ways of notifying users of specific information by using the provided Moodle functions. You looked at using e-mail, Moodle messaging, and RSS feeds notification methods. Additionally, you extended your journal assignment code to use these notification methods, and looked at real working examples.

In the next chapter, we will look at Moodle's page library and how to use it in your code.

12

Constructing and Displaying Pages by Using the pagelib Library

The pagelib library is used for constructing and displaying pages in Moodle. This chapter will cover the basic concepts of using pagelib. pagelib is an important core library, but has little, if any, official documentation. Although the source code includes comments, most of the functions are not documented in PHP Doc format and so are not visible from the Moodle Xref site. They can only be viewed by direct inspection of the `/lib/pagelib.php` file. This chapter covers the following major topics:

- Page classes
- Core modules that use pagelib
- pagelib core functions
- Requirements for using pagelib
- Updating activity Foo! to use pagelib
- Related libraries

Note that the ultimate goal of this chapter is to show you how to use pagelib in your development projects. Because there is little reference material available in the Moodle community on pagelib, we have included it in this chapter. If you want to see the practical application, feel free to skip ahead to the section on updating activity Foo!.

Introduction to pagelib

pagelib describes itself as the library that contains the parent class for Moodle pages, `page_base`, as well as the `page_course` subclass. A page is defined by its page type (that is, course, blog, or activity) and its page ID (courseid, blogid, activity ID, and so on).

pagelib defines three classes: `page_base`, `page_course`, and `page_generic_activity`. Let's have a quick look at each of these types.

Class page_base

All other page types are ultimately derived from this base class. Most Moodle extensions will extend from one of the other two page types that are derived from this base class.

Class page_course

`page_course` is the page type that is used to build course pages. We can extend this base type when creating new course formats.

Class page_generic_activity

`page_generic_activity` is for use with activity modules. This is the base class used by most of the core activity modules to create their page displays.

In the next section, we will take a brief look at the areas of Moodle core that make use of pagelib.

Core modules that use pagelib

Although pagelib is used throughout core and should be the basis for all page displays, it is not used by all areas of core. For example, not all of the core activity modules use pagelib. Many of the core activity modules use manual embedded HTML tags to build their pages. As a result, these modules do not support blocks. Here is a list of the major areas of Moodle that do use pagelib. Inspecting the code of these modules can provide valuable insight into the appropriate usage of a minimally-documented library such as pagelib:

- Admin (`admin/pagelib.php`)
- Blog (`blog/lib.php`)
- Course (`course/rest.php`)

- My Moodle (`my/pagelib.php`)
- Tag (`tag/pagelib.php`)
- Lib (`/lib/blocklib.php`, `/lib/adminlib.php`, `/lib/moodlelib.php`)
- Modules (`/mod/resource/lib.php`, `/mod/data/pagelib.php`, `/mod/lesson/pagelib.php`, `/mod/chat/pagelib.php`, `/mod/quiz/pagelib.php`)

In the next section, we will look at the functions responsible for creating page objects. These are called factory functions.

Additional reference material on this topic can be found at the following wiki pages:

- `http://docs.moodle.org/en/Development:Notes_about_legacy_page_classes`
- `http://docs.moodle.org/en/Development:Navigation_2.0_implementation_plan#.E2.9C.94_Page_object`

Using pagelib factory functions

Factory functions can be used by modules working with pagelib. Factory functions are used to aggregate functionality that is provided by a series of related object classes. They are used in the creation of objects in order to provide loose coupling of classes and functions for large, complex systems. The function `page_create_instance` is the primary function called by outside code. The function `page_import_types` can also be useful in external code.

See the IBM Developer Works article at `http://www.ibm.com/developerworks/library/os-php-designptrns/#N10076` for more information about the factory design pattern.

Let's have a look at pagelib's factory functions. These functions are listed in the same order as they are defined in the source code.

page_import_types

`page_import_types` finds all of the page types defined for a particular module. This is done by looking for a `pagelib.php` file within the passed `$path`. This file is then included, and the `$DEFINEDPAGES` array is returned if set. Otherwise, an error is returned.

page_create_instance

Any code that creates a page object by using pagelib passes its instance identifier into the `page_create_instance` function. The function then determines the correct page class and page ID with the help of the function `page_create_object`. It finally creates an instance of the correct pagelib class, which is then returned. Note that this function relies on a **weblib** library function to help determine the create type and page identifier. This may all seem confusing at the moment, but we will get into some practical examples later in the chapter.

page_create_object

The `page_create_object` function is called by the `page_create_instance` function. This function is a key part of the process to instantiate page instances. Given the page type and page ID, this function creates an instance of the correct page class, and returns it.

page_map_class

The `page_map_class` function accepts the string name for a page class and converts it to the appropriate data structure to be used in creating a page class instance. It is called by the `page_create_object` function.

Let's have a look at the member functions defined by the class `page_base`.

page_base member functions

`page_base` member functions define our basic tools for page creation and manipulation. Because pagelib is object oriented, we can extend from this base and override any of the functions in order to add new capabilities for our extensions and their pages. Following is a list of the member functions and a description of their purpose. Because both `page_course` and `page_generic_activity` are derived from `page_base`, each of the three page class types defines these functions. In most cases, we can use the parent function. However, we can also override any of these functions as we develop our own page types. Note that later in the chapter we will dig into code examples in order to help fill in the gaps of these brief descriptions.

page_base() and construct()

page_base() and construct() are constructor functions for the class. The dual function definitions are needed to work with all of the versions of PHP currently supported by Moodle. Typically, one function calls the other, in order to make maintenance simpler. For example, see the following code snippet:

```
function page_base() {
   $this->construct();

}
```

get_id()

get_id() is a simple wrapper function to abstract and return the internal variable $this->id. It returns the instance ID of the page. Normally, this doesn't need to be overridden when extending the class.

get_body_class()

get_body_class() is a simple wrapper function to abstract and return the internal variable $this->body_class. Normally, this doesn't need to be overridden when extending the class. Note that we are referring to PHP class objects rather than Moodle courses and classes. Also note that this function is rarely overridden. There are no examples in the Moodle core of this happening.

get_body_id()

get_body_id() is a simple wrapper function to abstract and return the internal variable $this-> body_id. Normally, this doesn't need to be overridden when extending the class.

edit_always()

The edit_always() member function returns true if this page is always editable.

init_quick()

The init_quick() function is for light-weight initialization. We should keep heavy SQL out of these functions. This function should include only basic validation and required decisions for startup.

init_full()

The `init_full()` function is for full initialization. Any heavy SQL or other heavy processes need to be checked against `$this->full_init_done`. Anything not needed for basic setup goes here. Any expensive setup steps should be cached so they only need to be performed once.

user_allowed_editing()

The `user_allowed_editing()` member function checks to see whether the user has permission to edit. It is mainly used for user activities, but also has to account for blocks.

user_is_editing()

The `user_is_editing()` function returns true if editing is enabled.

print_header()

`print_header()` prints the page's header, including the navigation breadcrumbs.

get_type()

The `get_type()` function returns the class's page type. This is primarily used to confirm that the class type was correctly assigned in `page_create_object()`. It can also be called publicly by other code in order to confirm type. Example types from core include: `PAGE_ADMIN`, `PAGE_MY_MOODLE`, and `PAGE_COURSE_VIEW`.

get_format_name()

The `get_format_name()` function returns the format name, which is the equivalent of a page category. Examples are course format types for course pages, or activity names. This provides a secondary mechanism for categorizing the page type beyond what is returned by the `get_type()` function. Think of this as a sub-type for the page type. Note that this function is rarely overridden. No core page classes override this function.

url_get_path()

`url_get_path()` returns a full URL for the page to display this object. This is useful for building relative links for page tabs or other relative links within your page.

url_get_parameters()

The `url_get_parameters()` member returns an array of parameters that are needed by the page class in order to display the page. If no parameters are required, it should return an empty array.

blocks_get_positions()

`blocks_get_positions()` returns all of the valid block positions for this page type. In core Moodle, these are typically defined as BLOCK_POS_LEFT, and BLOCK_POS_RIGHT. However, additional positions can be defined in our own page classes.

blocks_default_position()

The `blocks_default_position()` member function returns the default position to assign a new block for this page. It should be one of the positions defined above.

blocks_get_default()

`blocks_get_default()` returns a list of default block names. Any new pages created using this page type will automatically have these blocks enabled. Note that the course type base class assigns default blocks by course format type and by pulling the values from the configuration database.

blocks_move_position()

`blocks_move_position` takes a block instance and direction to move the block. Note that this function does not control vertical or relative positioning of blocks within the defined position. It only controls the defined positions—namely moving between the right-hand and left-hand side columns.

In the next section, we discuss the required elements to make use of pagelib in a module.

Meeting pagelib requirements

pagelib is easy to use, but does require some setup. First, we need to define a local pagelib.php file. This is where we will define the new page type. This is done by extending the appropriate base class. Within this local copy, we need to include the main /lib/pagelib.php file. Next, we must override at least two of the base class member functions: get_type and quick_init. After we have finished creating the file, we must include the local pagelib.php file in the module's lib.php file.

Looking at page setup

When the module's `lib.php` file is included in its pages, the pages gain access to pagelib functions. This include will often be done in either the module's `index.php` or `view.php` file.

We can then create an instance of the class by calling `page_create_instance()`, as follows:

```
function page_create_instance($instance) {
    page_id_and_class($id, $class);
    return page_create_object($id, $instance);
}
```

This function uses the weblib function `page_id_and_class()` to determine and set the page ID and class type of the page to be built. This is then passed into `page_create_object()` in order to generate the actual page object returned. This all works because of some slick object-oriented features of the PHP interpreter. Look at the following example from `page_create_object()`:

```
$data = new stdClass;
$data->pagetype = $type;
$data->pageid   = $id;
$classname = page_map_class($type);
$object = new $classname;
```

The `page_map_class()` function is used to set the `$classname` variable, which is then used to create the correct object type for the page. This is later returned in the function.

In the next section, we dig deeper into the requirements for using pagelib by examining its use in the quiz module.

Examining requirements by reviewing quiz's view.php

Let's have a look in the `/mod/quiz/view.php` file. Around line 47, we see the setup of the page. Note the use of `page_create_instance()`, which is assigned to `$PAGE`. Note the use of all caps for `$PAGE`, as shown in the following code snippet. Moodle coding style convention indicates that this is a global variable:

```
// Initialize $PAGE, compute blocks
$PAGE       = page_create_instance($quiz->id);
```

Next, we see the setup for block support.

Working with quiz blocks

In this same section, we see several lines of code for block setup. One of the biggest benefits of using pagelib is how simple it makes it to add block support to your page:

```
$pageblocks = blocks_setup($PAGE);
$blocks_preferred_width = bounded_number(180,
  blocks_preferred_width($pageblocks[BLOCK_POS_LEFT]), 210);
```

pagelib also handles our edit mode with the following check. This will later be passed into the setup function as a body tag. The global variables, $PAGE and $USER, are checked to confirm whether this user should be allowed to edit this page. If they are, then the inner section of code is run:

```
if ($edit != -1 and $PAGE->user_allowed_editing()) {
  $USER->editing = $edit;
```

In this next section, we see an example of passing body tags to the page object. Body tags are used to pass information into the page such as which page type to use and the access permissions required to be able to view the page. In the following instance, we are checking to see if the user has a capability that will activate a page function that isn't otherwise displayed. This is a useful technique for any pages that will display different types of information or functions depending on the user's role:

```
//only check pop ups if the user is not a teacher, and popup is set

$bodytags = (has_capability('mod/quiz:attempt', $context) &&
            $quiz->popup == 1)?'onload="popupchecker(\'' .
            get_string('popupblockerwarning', 'quiz') . '\');"':'';
```

Now that we have done our page setup, let's look at outputting the page.

Investigating quiz page display

Finally, we call the `print_header()` function to create the page. Note that this also creates the navigation breadcrumb trail for us:

```
$PAGE->print_header($course->shortname.': %fullname%','',$bodytags);
```

In this same section, note the use of `blocks_print_group()` to display all of the blocks for the left-hand side of the page:

```
blocks_print_group($PAGE, $pageblocks, BLOCK_POS_LEFT);
```

pagelib doesn't include a function to explicitly close our page or print the footer function. This is a small inconsistency in an otherwise useful library class. The quiz module defines its own `finish_page()` function to fill this gap. The entire function is as follows:

```
function finish_page($course) {
    global $THEME;
    print_container_end();
    echo '</td></tr></table>';
    print_footer($course);
    exit;
}
```

In the next section, we take what we have learned so far and use it to improve on a prior project, activity Foo!

Converting activity Foo! to pagelib

Why should we convert activity Foo! to use pagelib? It's already a fully-functional activity module. We have already done all of the coding necessary to display a proper Moodle page for our activity. There are actually several benefits of taking the effort to make this change, such as:

- Easier and more consistent page management
- Breadcrumb navigation is automatically generated
- It adds block support
- Easier future upgrades and code maintenance
- It is easier to create additional pages for the module
- Better alignment with Moodle programming guidelines

Creating a local pagelib.php

Let's start by creating our local `pagelib.php` file. We will base our file on examples from the core activity modules. In particular, we will use the quiz module's `pagelib.php` and `view.php` files as a template. We need to make only minor updates in order to get our page working correctly.

In this section of code, note the inclusion of the core pagelib file. Also, note the inclusion of `/course/lib.php`, which is required for block support:

```
require_once($CFG->libdir.'/pagelib.php');
require_once($CFG->dirroot.'/course/lib.php');
```

In this next section, we set up the $DEFINEDPAGES array. This array is used by the pagelib factory functions to create page objects of the correct type:

```
define('PAGE_FOO_VIEW', 'mod-foo-view');

page_map_class(PAGE_FOO_VIEW, 'page_foo');

$DEFINEDPAGES = array(PAGE_FOO_VIEW);
```

After creating our defined pages, we must next extend the base class page_generic_activity:

```
class page_foo extends page_generic_activity {
```

We have to override the init_quick() function, so that we can assign the correct activity name for our page. Note that after assigning $this->activityname, we then call the base class's init_quick() function. This is a common way in object-oriented programming of making a small local change while still leveraging the original base function:

```
function init_quick($data) {
  if(empty($data->pageid)) {
    error('Cannot quickly initialize page: empty course id');
  }
  $this->activityname = 'foo';
  parent::init_quick($data);
}
```

We also have to override the get_type() function for the same reason:

```
function get_type() {
  return PAGE_FOO_VIEW;
}
```

This completes our local pagelib.php file. This is a good example of the minimal definition needed to define a working page type for a module. If we require additional functionality, such as new block positions, we can override additional functions in this file. Remember, we must also include this new file in the module's lib.php file.

In the next section, we update the code for view.php, in order to complete the addition of pagelib support for activity Foo!

Updating view.php

We start by including blocklib, which will work in conjunction with our $PAGE object to add block support. This should be added near the other 'require' statements, near the top of the file:

```
require_once($CFG->libdir.'/blocklib.php');
```

Near line 21, we need to capture the value of the edit parameter. We need to pass this parameter when creating our page. This is needed for proper block support. The edit value is controlled by the block's editing button, which is displayed in the upper right-hand side corner of the page:

```
// Added for page lib support
$edit = optional_param('edit', -1, PARAM_BOOL);
```

Now we are ready to make the major changes to how the page displays.

Initializing $PAGE

We will change from our original manual entries to using pagelib. Around line 57, we need to delete the print page header section that goes through to around line 69. Now, we can insert the page creation code adapted from the quiz module. First, we must create a new page object with our activity ID and then pass this object to set up the page's blocks:

```
$PAGE = page_create_instance($foo->id);
$pageblocks = blocks_setup($PAGE);
$blocks_preferred_width = bounded_number(180,
    blocks_preferred_width($pageblocks[BLOCK_POS_LEFT]), 210);
```

In this section, we set up page editing by checking the value of the $edit parameter and then calling user_allowed_editing():

```
if ($edit != -1 and $PAGE->user_allowed_editing()) {
  $USER->editing = $edit;
}
```

Here, we call print_header() to start our page output:

```
$PAGE->print_header($course->shortname.': %fullname%','');
```

After creating the header, we output a table tag. Note that many of the core modules hardcode this table structure. It provides the basic column structure where blocks are displayed to the sides, and the primary content is displayed in the middle:

```
echo '<table id="layout-table"><tr>';
```

Next, we do our block setup.

Outputting blocks

The following code checks for the $CFG->showblocksonmodpages configuration
value. It's important that our code checks for this value when adding block support
to an activity. If this value is off, which is the default value, then our activity should
not display blocks:

```
if(!empty($CFG->showblocksonmodpages) &&
(blocks_have_content($pageblocks, BLOCK_POS_LEFT) ||
$PAGE->user_is_editing())) {
```

This next section is entirely contained within the condition for blocks being enabled.
We create a column within the table using a td tag, and we identify the column as
"left-column". Note the use of print_container_start() and print_container_
end() to wrap the output from blocks_print_group(), which prints our left-hand
side blocks:

```
echo '<td style="width: '.$blocks_preferred_width.'px;"
      id="left-column">';
print_container_start();
blocks_print_group($PAGE, $pageblocks, BLOCK_POS_LEFT);
print_container_end();
echo '</td>';
}
```

Now we are ready to print our activity output in the middle column.

Outputting the middle column

We can now set up the middle column, which displays the activities content. Again,
we make use of print_container_start(), in order to wrap our output. The
function print_container_start() is defined by weblib, and uses <div> tags to
create the container. If passed as a class type, it will also include this in the <div>
tag, allowing the container to be manipulated by using CSS. Also, note the addition
of print_heading() to display the activity's name in a way that is more consistent
with other Moodle activity modules:

```
echo '<td id="middle-column">';
print_container_start();

print_heading(format_string($foo->name));
```

We must also update the code for closing the page so that is has a matching `print_container_end()` call. We then close the table and print the theme footer:

```
print_container_end();
echo '</td></tr></table>';
print_footer($course);
```

Viewing the results

The end result of the new activity Foo! can be seen in the following screenshot. To reproduce the output below, the **Show blocks on module pages** setting must be enabled under **Theme Settings**. Note the addition of the left-hand side blocks to the sample activities page display. Using pagelib and blocklib in combination made it easy to add this powerful functionality:

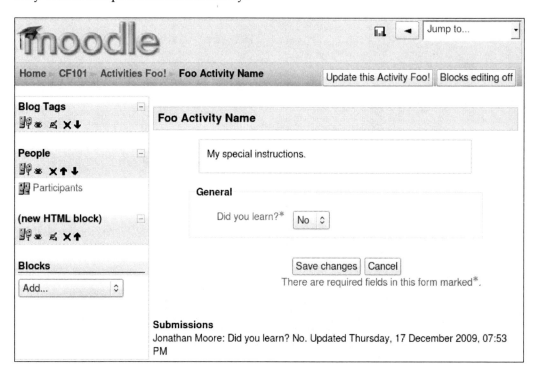

In the next section, we have a look at some related libraries.

Related libraries

There are several Moodle libraries that are related to pagelib. All of these can be of use while working with pagelib and page output.

weblib

weblib provides basic output functions. weblib functions are called in the creation of page objects in pagelib as well as for providing functions to create navigation breadcrumb trails. weblib also provides support for building tabbed interfaces. These are created by using the `print_tabs()` function. An example of a tabbed interface can also be found in `/mod/quiz/view.php`, which was used to develop code samples throughout this chapter. The official documentation for weblib can be found at `http://docs.moodle.org/en/Development:lib/weblib.php`.

blocklib

The blocklib library provides all of the functions necessary to support side blocks in Moodle course pages, the Moodle front page, My Moodle, and other areas of the Moodle interface that support blocks. There is no official Moodle Docs page for blocklib.

graphlib

graphlib provides a graphical object library for creating graphs. It is used primarily in reporting screens, such as for Moodle statistics. The official documentation can be found at `http://docs.moodle.org/en/Development:lib/graphlib.php`.

Summary

In this chapter, you have learned about the basic purpose and usage of the pagelib library. You studied the three basic page classes: `page_base`, `page_course`, and `page_generic_activity`. You looked at the definition of each member function. You examined pagelib's use in Moodle core modules. Finally, you updated the activity Foo! module to use pagelib and to display blocks.

In the next chapter, you will learn about the formslib library, which is used to create, submit, and process forms.

13
Building Forms with formslib

formslib is the preferred Moodle way of creating and processing forms in the Moodle system. It provides easy mechanisms to:

- Define specific form elements for your form
- Ensure that your output complies with XHTML Strict DTD and 508 accessibility
- Customize display format with standard CSS
- Process data securely without extra processing
- Validate data and provide user feedback according to your definitions
- Easily add Help pop-ups to any form element
- Display shortcut form element groups for specific Moodle functionality

formslib uses the PEAR QuickForm libraries, and extends these for specific Moodle functionality. It can likewise be used to add more specific form elements, through extension.

In most cases, using it is simply a matter of creating a new class that extends the Moodle class, `moodleform`, and then adding your own definitions. Once defined, you can instantiate an object of the new class, initialize it, load data into it, extract submitted data from it, and display it.

In previous chapters, we used formslib for things such as our own modules. The standard settings for a module are kept in the file `mod_form.php` in the module's directory. Look back to the modules we created previously, and you will see where we have used these before.

This chapter will discuss the use of Moodle's formslib functions to build and process web forms. We will:

- Examine exactly how formslib is used
- Look at each element type and how it is used
- Learn about rules and validation

Using formslib

To use Moodle's formslib to define a form, you need to extend the class `moodleform`:

```
require_once("$CFG->libdir/formslib.php");
class myproject_form extends moodleform {
```

The `moodleform` class does not extend a QuickForm class, but rather contains one in one of its properties. The `moodleform_form` property contains the specific QuickForm object.

When you extend the `moodleform` property, you typically set a variable to the `_form` property so that you can access the formslib functions. You will almost always see this code in a class that extends the `moodleform` class:

```
function definition() {
    $mform    =& $this->_form;
```

This makes the formslib object available in the easier-to-use `$mform` variable for the remainder of the function.

To create a form, your class only needs to provide the `definition` function. This function adds all of the form elements that you require for your form. There are many other functions that you can provide, but `definition` is the only one that you need to create a form.

To use your form, you need to instantiate an object of your class in some code, and then call the `display` method. So, if your form class was called `myproject_form`, then you would need:

```
$mform = new myproject_form();
$mform->display();
```

Again, there are many more functions that you will use to make things useful, but this describes the basics. We will now look at the details.

Form definition and elements

In the previous section, we skimmed over creating a form and using it without going into any specific details. Now, let's look at what we actually do to define and use a form.

As described in the previous section, we begin by creating a class that extends `moodleform`. Then, we add a `definition` function so that we can create all of our form elements. Next, we will describe the functions that we can use to create our form.

addElement and createElement

A form element is a standard HTML form structure, such as a drop-down menu, text entry box, or radio button, which can be used to extract information interactively from a web user. A form element object is a code structure that contains all of the data and code to display, validate, and extract from a form element.

The two main functions to add form elements to your form are `addElement` and `createElement`. These are essentially the same function, except that `createElement` returns the created form element object without adding it to the form, while `addElement` creates the form element object and adds it to the form. You should typically use `addElement`, unless you need to perform extra processing on the element before adding it to a form (see the section on *Groups* later in this chapter for more information).

These functions take a string argument as their first argument, which defines the name of the element being created. The remainder of the arguments are variables that depend on the type of element being added. In Moodle, the type of element can be any standard HTML form element, as well as any one of several custom Moodle elements.

The elements that are available are defined in the file `/lib/pear/HTML/QuickForm.php` or in `/lib/formslib.php`. The former are the standard definitions supplied with QuickForm, while the latter contains the ones added or overridden by Moodle.

Let's examine the elements that we can add. The next section includes the description, code, and what gets rendered on screen for the most common form elements that you will need. Wherever we use `$attributes`, it is an array that can contain any valid HTML attributes for the input type being created (for example, `$attributes = array("class" => "newclass");`).

Buttons

The following functions add buttons to a form:

Button function

The button function inserts a standard general purpose form button. The first parameter specifies 'button'. The second parameter is the name of the input type to use. The third parameter specifies the text to display on the button. The fourth parameter specifies any extra HTML attributes.

Usage

```
$mform->addElement('button', 'intro', get_string('Press Me'),
                   $attributes);
```

Display

Submit, reset, and cancel functions

These functions insert submit, reset, and cancel form buttons, respectively. The first parameter specifies the type of button that you are inserting. The second specifies a name for the form element. The third specifies the label to display on the button.

Each button will be displayed on its own line (unless otherwise styled). To put these all on the same line, use addGroup.

Usage:

```
$mform->addElement('submit', 'submitbutton', get_string('Submit
              Label'));
```

Display:

Usage:

```
$mform->addElement('reset', 'resetbutton', get_string('Reset Label'));
```

Display:

Usage:

```
$mform->addElement('cancel', 'cancelbutton', get_string('Cancel
              Label'));
```

Display:

add_action_buttons function

This function inserts the standard submit and cancel action buttons, already formatted in a horizontal line. If no parameters are passed to it, both buttons will be output (as shown previously) and the submit label will be the 'savechanges' language string. If you set the first parameter to `false`, no cancel button will be output.

Note that the `add_action_buttons` function is a method of your main form class and not of the `_form` subclass.

Usage:

```
$this->add_action_buttons(true, get_string('Submit Label'));
```

Display:

Checkboxes

The following functions add checkboxes to a form:

Checkbox function:

This example inserts a *single* checkbox element. You can see that both specified labels are displayed.

Usage

```
$mform->addElement('checkbox', 'check1', get_string('Left Label'),
                   get_string('Right Label'), $attributes);
```

Display

In the next example, the checkboxes are output as a group. In this case, you can see that only the checkboxes' right labels are displayed. The group's left and right labels are displayed. You probably would only want to use the elements' right labels and the group's left label for this case.

Usage

```
$group = array();
$group[] =& $mform->createElement('checkbox', 'check2',
        get_string('Left Label'), get_string('Right Label '));
```

```
$group[] =& $mform->createElement('checkbox', 'check3',
        get_string('Left Label'), get_string('Right Label '));
$group[] =& $mform->createElement('checkbox', 'check4',
        get_string('Left Label'), get_string('Right Label '));
$mform->addGroup($group, 'group1', get_string('Group Left Label'),
        get_string('Group Right Label'), false);
```

Display

Group Left Label ☐ Right Label Group Right Label ☐ Right Label Group Right Label ☐ Right Label

With a standard checkbox element, the value '1' will be returned if the checkbox is selected. If it is not selected, the element will not be returned at all. You will need to check for the absence of the element to detect that it is not selected.

Advanced checkbox and checkbox controller

The advanced checkbox is a special element that allows two new features for checkboxes.

The first is the ability to specify values for both the selected and deselected states. This is done by passing an array in the sixth parameter. This also means that unlike a standard checkbox, a value is always returned, regardless of whether the box is selected or not.

The second is the ability to specify a group for use with a checkbox controller. The fifth parameter allows this in the attributes array by specifying a 'group' index and a numeric value for the group.

When you add a checkbox controller to a specified group number, an optional link is displayed that allows the user to quickly select all or none of the grouped checkboxes.

Usage:

```
$mform->addElement('advcheckbox', 'acheck0',
        get_string('Left Label'), get_string('Right Label'),
        array('group' => 1), array('no', 'yes'));
$mform->addElement('advcheckbox', 'acheck1',
        get_string('Left Label 1'), get_string('Right Label'),
        array('group' => 2), array('no', 'yes'));
$mform->addElement('advcheckbox', 'acheck2',
        get_string('Left Label 2'), get_string('Right Label'),
        array('group' => 2), array('no', 'yes'));
$mform->addElement('advcheckbox', 'acheck3',
        get_string('Left Label 3'), get_string('Right Label'),
        array('group' => 2), array('no', 'yes'));
$this->add_checkbox_controller(2, get_string('Select all/none'),
        $attributes);
```

Display:

Uploading and/or choosing a file

The following functions add file selection elements to a form:

choosecoursefile function

This function displays a text box with a file selection button, to allow a user to load a file to the form. Clicking on the button displays the pop-up form. This form allows the user to select a file from the corresponding course file area. The pop-up form also allows the upload of files and the selection of uploaded files.

The first parameter of the function is `choosecoursefile`.

The second parameter is the name to give the element. The third is the label to display on the left-hand side of the form element.

The fourth is an array of options, which can include a course ID number (if excluded or NULL, then the global `$COURSE` variable will be used), options such as the width and height of the pop-up window, and other HTML attributes to apply to the window. Note that if an `options` index is included, then any required `width` and `height` values must be included in that string. The `width` and `height` indexes will only work without the `options` index.

The fifth parameter is an array of appropriate HTML attributes for the element.

Usage:

```
$options = array('courseid' =>null,
                 'height'   =>600,    // height of the popup window
                 'width'    =>800,    // width of the popup window
// 'options'   =>'menubar=0,location=0,scrollbars,resizable'
                 );
$mform->addElement('choosecoursefile', 'cf1',
       get_string('Left Label '), $options,
       array('maxlength' => 255, 'size' => 48));
```

Display:

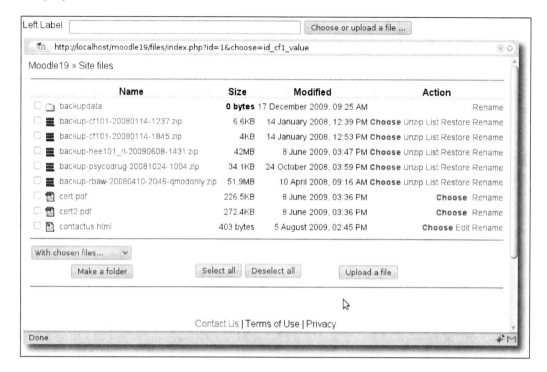

Date and time

The following functions allow date and time selection functions to be added to a form:

date_selector function

This function provides a combination selector that returns a timestamp integer value to the form code.

The first parameter is the function name `date_selector`. The second parameter is the form element name. The third parameter is the label to display on the left-hand side.

The fourth parameter is an array that allows you to specify specific parameters to affect what is displayed. You can have the form display a range of years between start and end years (`startyear` and `stopyear`), whether to allow for daylight savings time (`applydst`), whether to use a specific time zone (`timezone`), and whether or not to ignore the selections (`optional`).

If you provide a `true` value for `optional`, a **Disable** checkbox will appear next to the selector, which will allow the selector to be disabled and ignored.

The fifth parameter is an array of appropriate HTML attributes for the element.

Usage:

```
$options = array('startyear' => 1990,
                 'stopyear'  => 2020,
                 'timezone'  => 99,
                 'applydst'  => true,
                 'optional'  => true
                );
$mform->addElement('date_selector', 'date1',
                get_string('Date Label'), $options, $attributes);
```

Display:

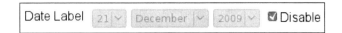

date_time_selector function

This element is pretty much identical to the previous one, except that it also displays time selectors for hours and minutes. Its options parameter (the fourth one) allows one extra index called `step`. The `step` index specifies the increments for the minutes on the minute selector.

Usage:

```
$options = array('startyear' => 1980,
                 'stopyear'  => 2010,
                 'timezone'  => 99,
                 'applydst'  => true,
                 'optional'  => true,
                 'step'      => 15
                );
$mform->addElement('date_time_selector', 'datetime1',
                get_string('Date Time Label'), $options, $attributes);
```

Display:

htmleditor, textarea, and text

The following functions add text entry elements to a form:

htmleditor function

Use this function to display a text area in which a user can enter large amounts of text. If HTML editors are enabled, and you allow them to be used, the standard HTML text area element will be replaced with a JavaScript powered editor that will allow WYSIWYG style formatting controls. You can also choose to display a text-only standard element, as well.

The first parameter is `htmleditor`, the second is the unique name of the form element, and the third is the label to display above the editor area.

The fourth parameter is an array of options that control what gets displayed. The key index for this function is the `canUseHtmlEditor` index. If this is `true`, then the full HTML editor is displayed. Set this to `detect` to allow the form element to use system and user settings.

Usage:

```
$options = array('canUseHtmlEditor'=>'detect',
                           'rows'  => 10,
                           'cols'  => 65,
                           'width' => 0,
                           'height'=> 0,
                           'course'=> 0,
                          );
$mform->addElement('htmleditor', 'htmleditor1',
        get_string('Left Label'), $options);
```

Display:

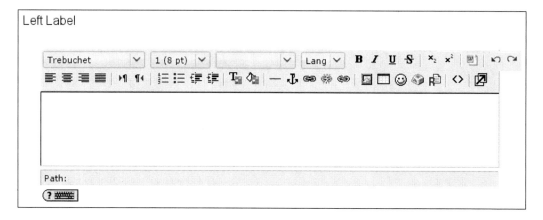

text function

This function displays a small text area for user-supplied text.

The first parameter is `text`, the second is the unique name of the form element, and the third is the label to display next to the text box.

The fourth parameter allows you to supply HTML attributes that affect the form element, such as `size`.

Usage:

```
$attributes=array('size'=>'20');
$mform->addElement('text', 'text1', get_string('Left Label'),
                    $attributes);
```

Display:

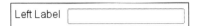

modgrade

This function is a special Moodle function that will insert a grade selector that includes scales, and possibly **No grade** choices.

The first parameter is `modgrade`, the second is the unique name of the form element, and the third is the label to display next to the selector.

The fourth parameter is a Boolean that determines whether a **No grade** option should be in the selector as well. Set it to `true` to include this option.

Usage:

```
$mform->addElement('modgrade', 'grade1', get_string('Left Label'),
                    true);
```

Display:

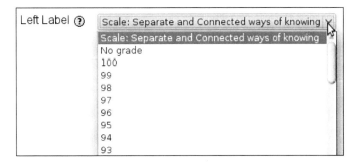

password and passwordunmask

These functions provide a password form element to allow users to enter a password. The first one always hides the text entered. The second one provides a checkbox that when selected, will unhide the text entered by the user.

The first parameter is either `password` or `passwordunmask`, depending on which element you want to use. The second is the unique name of the form element, the third is the label to display next to the selector, and the fourth is an array of HTML attributes.

Usage:

```
$mform->addElement('password', 'password1', get_string('Left Label'),
                   $attributes);
$mform->addElement('passwordunmask', 'password2',
                   get_string('Left Label'), $attributes);
```

Display:

radio

This function provides radio buttons for a single option choice within a group of choices. Radio button elements have to be grouped together to provide any useful functions. As such, only the right label parameter for the element provides anything meaningful. Use the group left label parameter to provide left text.

The first parameter is `radio`.

The second parameter is the unique name of the form element, and must be the same for all radio buttons in the group.

The third parameter is the left-hand side label and does not get displayed when the radio buttons are in a group.

The fourth parameter is the label to display on the right-hand side of the radio option.

The fifth parameter is the value returned when that radio option is selected.

Usage:

```
$radioarray=array();
$radioarray[] = $mform->createElement('radio', 'radio1',
    get_string('Left Label'), get_string('Right Label'), 0,
    $attributes);
$radioarray[] = $mform->createElement('radio', 'radio1',
    get_string('Left Label'), get_string('Right Label'), 1,
    $attributes);
$mform->addGroup($radioarray, 'radioar', 'Group Left Label',
        array(' '), false);
```

Display:

Group Left Label ⦿ Right Label ○ Right Label

select, multi-select, and selectyesno

All three of these functions provide drop-down selectors for the user. The first provides a single choice selector, the second a multiple choice selector and the third is a binary yes/no selector.

For all three, the first parameter is the function name (`select` or `selectyesno`), the second is the unique name of the form element, and the third is the label to display next to the selector.

For `select`, the fourth parameter is the array of options to display, indexed by the returned values. `selectyesno` does not need this array as it only ever shows two options: 0 for "no" and 1 for "yes".

The fifth parameter for `select` and fourth for `selectyesno` are the HTML attributes for the element type.

Note that a single select selector and a multi-select selector have exactly the same code except for one extra call to `setMultiple(true)` for the multi-select. This function turns a single-select into multi-select.

Usage:

```
$options = array(1 => 'option1',
                 2 => 'option2',
                 3 => 'option3'
                );
$mform->addElement('select', 'select1', get_string('Left Label'),
                $options, $attributes);

$select2 = $mform->addElement('select', 'select2',
            get_string('Left Label'), $options, $attributes);
$select2->setMultiple(true);

$mform->addElement('selectyesno', 'select3',
                get_string('Left Label'), $attributes);
```

Display:

hidden, html, and static text

These three elements do not display visible form elements.

In the following image, you can see the "html" and the "static" elements, but the "hidden" element is invisible.

The hidden element is used to generate standard "hidden" form elements that can contain information that needs to be passed to the form, but should not be specified by the user.

The html element can output any arbitrary HTML code in the location in which it is placed. It should not be used unless absolutely necessary for formatting. For example, you can enclose form elements in a new, named <div> or <span> section in order to gain more control over the formatting, through CSS, by using this technique.

The `static` element displays the supplied text where it is called. Use this instead of `html` when all you need to do is put extra text on your form.

Usage:

```
$mform->addElement('hidden', 'hidden1', 'value1');

$mform->addElement('html', '<br /><div align="center"
                    style="color: red;">Free Text</div>');

$mform->addElement('static', 'static1', get_string('Left Label'),
                    get_string('Static Text'));
```

Display:

Groups

Adding a group to a form allows you to group other form elements together into a single display line, with one label for the entire group. This is a nice way to create combinations of elements that really are performing one function.

We used this in the previous example to group radio buttons together (review the radio button example to see how it is coded). It is also used behind the scenes for the date selectors and action button functions.

Rules and validation

Now that we've learned how to create specific form elements, let's explore what else formslib can do for us.

Rules

You can add rules to perform validation of the data entered into form elements. These rules can be applied either during the entry process, or after submission.

addRule

Rules provide an easy and reusable way to apply common data checks without having to rewrite code every time.

To add a rule to a form element, use the following code syntax:

```
$mform->addRule($elementname, $errorstring, $ruletype, $ruledata,
                $validation);
```

The first parameter is the name of the form element to apply the rule to. The second parameter defines an error string to display if the rule fails.

The third parameter is the name of the rule. This name must be a valid rule already registered with the form.

The fourth parameter contains any optional data that needs to be passed to the rule for this element; for example, the maximum length of the data for a `maxlength` rule.

The fifth parameter is either `client` or `server` depending on where the rule should be processed. If 'client' is specified, the rule will be tested when the element has been entered in the form, and failures displayed immediately. If 'server' is specified, the data will not be tested until the form is submitted.

Note than you can add several rules to any form element. All rules will be applied to the data entered.

Moodle comes with several predefined rules available for use. These are specified as strings for the `$ruletype` parameter. These are:

- `required`: Specifies that the element must be entered
- `maxlength`, `minlength`, `rangelength`: Specifies a length restriction, passed in the `$ruledata` parameter
- `email`: Specifies that the entered value must be a valid e-mail address
- `regex`: Specifies that the entered value must match the provided regular expression
- `lettersonly`, `alphanumeric`, `numeric`, `nopunctuation`, `nonzero`: Specifies specific character restrictions on the entered data
- `callback`: Specifies a function to be called to validate the data, entered in the `$ruledata` parameter
- `compare`: Allows for the comparison of two fields' values by using a specific comparison rule specified as the `$ruledata` parameter

registerRule

You can register your own rules to add to the list of rule types mentioned previously. When you register your rule, it becomes available to any form element in the same way as the previous types.

The code syntax to add a rule is:

```
$mform->registerRule ($ruleName, $type, $data);
```

The first parameter is the name of your new rule. This is the name that will be passed as the $ruleName parameter to addRule.

The second parameter is generally callback. It can also be regex or NULL, but we'll focus on the first. The callback argument means that the rule will call a supplied function for validation.

The third parameter is the name of the function to call. The function must exist when the form is used or it will generate an error.

Once you have registered this rule, it can be used in any form as an argument to addRule.

Here is an example of using the registerRule construct:

```
$mform->registerRule('hexdigits', 'callback', 'check_hexdigits');

function check_hexdigits($string) {
    $hexdigits = '0-9A-F'; // Allowed hex characters
    $regex = '/^['.$hexdigits.']+$/';
    if (!preg_match($regex, $string)) {
        return false;
    }
    return true;
}
```

This rule will check that the entered data is a valid hexadecimal number. The check_hexdigits function will be called with the entered data, and validated. If the data entered includes any characters other than valid hexadecimal ones, the rule will fail and return false.

Validation

Another way to perform validation on your form data is through the use of the validation function. This function, when defined in your form class, is called once data has been submitted. The entered data is then validated on the server and if any errors are returned, the form will be redisplayed, along with any provided error messages. As long as a validation function exists, the form cannot be processed until that function returns no errors.

Typically, you use a validation function when the validation rules are more complex than can be performed by an addRule function. Typical examples of this would be when more than one field entry has relationships that need to be tested first.

To return validation information from the function, you need to return an array, indexed by the form element names with error messages to be displayed. These messages will then be displayed with the field that they are indexed by.

Here is an example, taken from the forum module:

```
function validation($data, $files) {
    $errors = parent::validation($data, $files);
    if (($data['timeend']!=0) && ($data['timestart']!=0)
        && $data['timeend'] <= $data['timestart']) {
        $errors['timeend'] = get_string('timestartenderror',
            'forum');
    }
    return $errors;
}
```

This particular function checks two fields, one specifying a starting time and one specifying an ending time, in order to verify that the ending time does not come before the starting time. If it does, an error message indexed on the ending time field name, is returned. So if an invalid ending time is entered, the form will not be processed, and the error message will be displayed in the form (see following screenshot).

Summary

There are many features of formslib that can be used to simplify the management and processing of your Moodle forms. The best reference for what can be done and what new features have been added is at the Moodle wiki page at `http://docs. moodle.org/en/Development:lib/formslib.php`. You have looked at the basics here, and you can see many examples of formslib in use in the code from previous chapters. Review those chapters to see the actual uses of formslib.

Please use this chapter as a good reference guide to help you with your form creation and processing.

In the next chapter, we will look at web services.

14
Development for the Adventuresome: Web Services

Moodle currently has two popular implementations for web services: Remote-Learner Web Services library, and Moodle Networking. Remote-Learner Web Services are SOAP-based and Moodle Networking is XML-RPC-based. The SOAP library allows remote manipulation and the creation of courses, users, user enrollments, grade passing, and SSO. It is also a great example of what you might accomplish by leveraging the techniques covered in this book. The XML-RPC library provides a secure channel, SSO, and full Moodle API exposure (with serious caveats) to the trusted site.

During the writing of this book, we had to make what some may consider a controversial decision to focus more pages on the RL Web Services library than on Moodle Networking. Moodle Networking is the official core Moodle method for web services. So this would be the argument in favor of its importance. Or even that it is more important than the RL WS library. However, in practice, while working with our client base, we have developed only one implementation of Moodle Networking (for Jaspersoft) versus 10—12 implementations with the RL WS library. Looking through the Moodle forums gives an impression that developers needing web services access were generally choosing the non-core library. There is a new Web Service implementation in Moodle 2.0 that doesn't require Moodle Networking to be used. This new library is more similar to the light-weight approach of RL WS, but is a totally new library.

This chapter will explore in detail the basic concepts and programming of Remote-Learner Web Services. It will also give an overview of the pluses and minuses of each library. The following topics will be covered:

- Remote-Learner Web Services pluses and minuses
- Web Service user management
- Web Service user enrollments
- Web Service Single Sign On (SSO)
- Web Service grade passing
- Moodle Networking pluses and minuses
- Moodle Networking security model
- Moodle Networking exposing functions
- Moodle Networking SSO

Using Remote-Learner Web Services

The Remote-Learner Web Services library was originally called OKTech Web Services. It was the first web service library to be developed for Moodle. It was developed for client projects, to provide a simple, flexible, and cross-platform method of remotely controlling Moodle. It was donated to the Moodle community as a GPL software and is available from the plugins database at `http://moodle.org`. A more recent version is included in this chapter's source code. The following sections list the library's pluses and minuses.

Advantages

The Remote-Learner Web Services library has several advantages, which are listed below:

- Easy-to-use access to users, SSO, courses, and grade management
- SOAP-based
- WSDL file is easy to use in popular development platforms, such as Visual Studio, Flash, PHP, and Java.
- No core modifications needed to use it

Disadvantages

The Remote-Learner Web Services library also has several disadvantages, which are detailed as follows:

- Not as inherently strong a security model as Moodle Networking
- Not part of core Moodle
- Doesn't provide modular extensibility as well as the Moodle Networking model
- Many individual versions tailored to specific sites needs; that is, forks.

Installation

There are two parts to the installation of this library. The first part is installing the server side of the installation. The second part is installing the client side. The library is contained in the Web Service.zip file. Once expanded, the library contains the library code, along with two important subdirectories: documentation and clients. The documentation directory contains the official documentation for the library, along with an example WSDL file. **WSDL** stands for **Web Service Definition Language**. It is an XML schema that defines both the data structures and functions provided by our web services. The clients directory contains sample code in various languages that implement clients for the library. These included PHP, Python, and Java clients.

Server-side setup

To set up the server side of the library, unzip the Web Service.zip file and copy the Web Service folder to the root of the Moodle installation. You can confirm that the code is functioning by navigating to the following URL in your browsers:

```
http://moodlesite.domain/Web Service/wsdl.php
```

If the installation is functioning correctly, the URL will open an XML document containing the WSDL file for the web services library.

Once the basic code has been copied, we need to run the command-line tool wsdl2php.php in order to generate the proxy classes required for the proper operation of the web services server, as follows:

```
cd [moodle_root_dir]/ws
php ./wsdl2php.php http://moodlesite.domain/ws/wsdl.php server
```

If successful, the script will generate a series of PHP files in the current directory. These are used to provide the server side for the web services. Note that if your user account does not have appropriate permissions to write the files, you may need to run the script with `sudo`, as in the following example:

```
sudo php ./wsdl2php.php http://moodlesite.domain/ws/wsdl.php server
```

Let's have a look at how to set up a PHP client.

Client setup

Our example code for this chapter will be done in PHP. However, the library can be used with any one of a variety of programming languages. Making use of the library, either locally or on a remote server, doesn't actually require any software installation. This is one of the benefits of a web service library, either can be consumed entirely remotely. We can, however, set up a local copy of the proxy classes for our client to use. This is not required, but it helps to provide access to the data structures defined within the WSDL file. This can be done as follows. If running on the same server as the Moodle site, call the `wsdl2php.php` file by using the path to the Moodle installation. Otherwise, copy the `Web Service.zip` file to the client server and unzip it:

```
cd [client_root_dir]/ws_client

mkdir proxy_classes

cd proxy_classes

php /path_to_Web Service_folder/wsdl2php.php http://moodlesite.domain/Web Service/wsdl.php
```

Again, creating the local proxy classes is optional. Creating the proxy classes is really required only for data type mappings. In practice, this doesn't always benefit us that much. We still have to know the structure for assigning and manipulating the data provided by the web services.

Let's test our web service setup.

Testing with ppdemo_trace.php

A quick way to test and confirm that everything is set up correctly on both the server and client ends is to use the test script `ppdemo_trace.php`. This is an informal test script used by the developers of the library to help test new functionality. The script contains several commented sections of code from various generations of the library. Its output is in HTML, and is meant to be viewed from a web browser. The `ppdemo_trace.php` file can be found in the `Web Service/clients` folder. In particular, we want to confirm that the log in worked correctly. Before running the script, we need to enter a valid administrator login into the `auth.php` file. Now we can navigate to the URL in our browser and review if the output is sensible. Note that at any given time some of the commented sections may not work with the current version of the library. A version of the file with the basic functionality activated is included in our chapter's sample code. Following is a sample output from a working login:

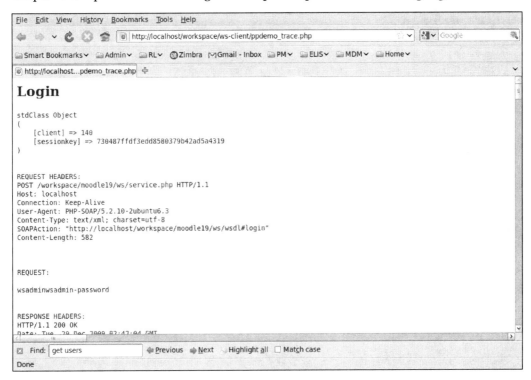

Our development team also recommends the following website for a good web service testing tool:

```
http://www.soapui.org/
```

Setting up your Web Services connection

This chapter will include several examples of using the Web Service library. All of these will have the same basic connection code in common. The following example illustrates how to connect using the proxy class code. In the first line, we have included the MoodleWS.php file, which includes the proxy classes generated by the wsdl2php.php script. Next, we set the URL for the WSDL file on the server. Finally, we create a new SOAP object and log in:

```
require(dirname(__FILE__) . '/proxy_classes/MoodleWS.php');
$wsdl = 'http://localhost/workspace/moodle19/Web Service/wsdl.php';
$client = new MoodleWS($wsdl, $wsdl, array('trace' => 1));
// Login to service
$session = $client->login("wsadmin","wsadmin-password");
```

The next example shows the same type of connection, but without using the proxy classes. This type of connection can be used without the local installation of the Web Services library, and without generating the local proxy files. Note the optional use of the class mappings for the `SoapClient` class, which are created by the `$opts` variable assignment. These can be used in a similar way to the proxy classes, but without the need to install a local copy of the library:

```
class PHPuserDatum {}; // stub class for mapping
class PHPuserRecord {}; // stub class for mapping
$opts = array('classmap' => array('userDatum' => 'PHPStockType',
              'userRecord' => 'PHPuserRecord') );
$client = new SoapClient('http://localhost/workspace/moodle19/Web
                          Service/wsdl.php', $opts);
$session = $client->login("wsadmin","wsadmin-password");
```

PHP also provides several built-in SOAP functions that you can investigate to learn more about the library. The `var_dump` function outputs a simple text representation of the object passed to it. This can be a very handy tool for determining the complex structures used in some web service functions. We combine this function with `__getFunctions` and `__getTypes` to learn about which functions and which types are defined in the WSDL file. This can be used with any SOAP-based web service, in order to investigate how it works.

```
var_dump($client->__getFunctions());
var_dump($client->__getTypes());
```

Let's have a look at some additional options that are available to aid in debugging.

Debugging setup

We can use the following options to enable debugging, which can be useful for finding problems. The first line turns off WSDL caching. This can be useful if we need to make changes to the server-side services. The other two lines control error and debugging output:

```
ini_set('soap.wsdl_cache_enabled', '0');
ini_set('error_reporting', E_ALL);
ini_set('display_errors', 'On');
```

In our next section, we dig into user management.

Managing users

The Web Service library includes functions to create, update, and delete users. In this section, we will create a series of command-line utilities to make use of these functions. Generally, we would embed our web service functions directly into the third-party application. However, such integrations are not always possible, especially if the third-party system doesn't support web services. Command-line tools can also be very useful for system administrators. For example, in our hosting operation, we have automated the creation of Moodle sites via batch scripts. As apart of the site set up process, the scripts create a new administrator account. Command-line tools, such as the ones developed in this section, can be handy for such use cases.

Creating users

We will call our create user script, `createuser.php`. It will use command-line arguments to set up the new user's profile. All of the user fields will be set, in order to prevent the user profile from being displayed the first time that the user logs into Moodle. The format for our command-line tool will be:

```
createuser.php username idnumber password first last email city country
description
```

Processing arguments

The first thing that we need to do is to confirm that we have received the correct number of arguments via the command line. We can do this using the built-in PHP variables `$argc` to get the argument count, and `$argv` for the argument array—including the command name, we need to receive ten arguments. If we get the wrong count, we should display the correct usage for the command:

```
if( $argc != 10 ) {
  echo("Usage: $argv[0] username idnumber password first last email
        city country description\n");
  exit();
}// if
```

Connecting to Web Services

Next, we perform our standard web service connection set up:

```
require(dirname(__FILE__) . '/proxy_classes/MoodleWS.php');
$wsdl = 'http://localhost/workspace/moodle19/Web Service/wsdl.php';
$client = new MoodleWS($wsdl, $wsdl, array('trace' => 1));
$session = $client->login("wsadmin","wsadmin-password");
```

Now let's write the code to create a user.

Using edit_user() to create a new account

We use the `edit_user()` function to create the user. This accepts an array of user objects, along with an action command for each user. Valid actions include: Add, Update, and Delete.

We will use the proxy classes in this next section to create the correct structure for our user information. First, we create an instance of `editUsersInput`, as follows:

```
$users = new editUsersInput();
```

Then, we assign to the object the correct values from our command-line arguments. This section of code is a good illustration of the mixed utility of the class mappings. We still have to know the internal structure of the `$users->users` array in order to make the correct variable assignments. There are a few areas of note in this assignment. First, the `action` element is assigned the value `'Add'`, because we are creating a new user. This value will be changed for each of our sample scripts to denote the appropriate action. We also need to note the assignment of the `auth` element to the value `'webservices'`. The SSO functions require this authentication type to be set. However, if you want users to be able to log in directly, then they should be assigned `'auth' => 'manual'`:

```
$users->users = array(
    array(
        'action'        => 'Add',
        'confirmed'     => 1,
        'policyagreed'  => 1,
        'deleted'       => 0,
        'mnethostid'    => 1,
        'username'      => $argv[1],
        'auth'          => 'webservices',
        'password'      => md5($argv[3]),
        'idnumber'      => $argv[2],
        'firstname'     => $argv[4],
        'lastname'      => $argv[5],
        'email'         => $argv[6],
        'icq'           => '',
        'skype'         => '',
        'yahoo'         => '',
        'aim'           => '',
        'msn'           => '',
        'phone1'        => '',
        'phone2'        => '',
        'institution'   => '',
        'department'    => '',
        'address'       => '',
        'city'          => $argv[7],
```

```
        'country'     => $argv[8],
        'lang'        => 'en_utf8',
        'timezone'    => '',
        'lastip'      => '',
        'description' => $argv[9]
    )
);
```

Now we are ready to call the `edit_users()` function. We have to pass both the `$session->client` and `$session->sessionkey` values from our login to the web service. Lastly, we pass the `$users` object, with the values for the new user assigned to it:

```
$response = $client->edit_users($session->client,
                    $session->sessionkey, $users);
```

Although the `createuser.php` file is a usable and potentially valuable script, there are conditions that can cause it to fail. For example, if the user already exists, a database error will be generated. In our sample code, we do not error check for this condition. In a true production script, we should wrap our call to `edit_users()` with a `catch/try` combination, or use other error checking methods.

Let's have a look at the results of our work so far. Let's open a command line and run our script to create a new user. Enter the following:

php ./createuser.php janes 1234388398 mypassword Jane Student janes@ sample.com Paris FR "Test Student from web service"

From Moodle, we should now be able to browse for our new user, which should look similar to the following screenshot:

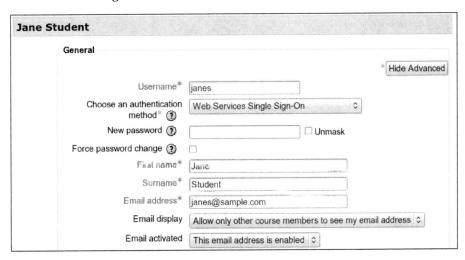

Let's start working on the update script.

Updating users

We will call our update script `updateuser.php`. Luckily, we can reuse almost the entire `createuser.php` script for the update function. The only functional change needed is to edit line 20 of the file. Line 20 assigns the action for the user. You just need to change the action to `'Update'`, as follows:

```
'action' => 'Update',
```

You should make one more cosmetic change in order to clean up the output to the user at the end of the script:

```
echo("Updating user\n");
```

It's always great as a programmer when you can reuse code to save time!

Let's have a look at the results. Let's run the update script from the command line to modify the user **janes** that we created earlier. Enter the following into the shell:

```
php ./updateuser.php janes 1234388398 mypassword Jane Smith janesmith@
sample.com Paris FR "Updated test student from web service"
```

One downside of this method is that the fields are hardcoded into the script. It would be very easy to enter them out of order and damage an existing account. Or, it may be that for a particular use case, it's not necessary to edit all these fields. These scripts do a good job of illustrating consumption of the web services, but again will probably need some adjustments for production use. This should result in the account being modified to look like the one in the following screenshot. Note how both the **Surname** and **Email address** fields have been changed from our original:

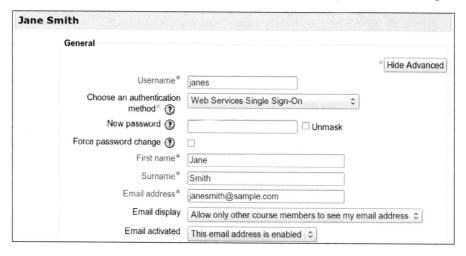

In our next section, we will implement user deletion, which will round out our user management set.

Deleting users

The `deleteuser.php` script will also be based on the `createuser.php` file. We have to make a few more changes, but the basic setup and logic are the same. First, we only need one argument for deleting a user—the `idnumber`. This results in the following new code that will handle the script's command-line arguments:

```
if( $argc != 2 ) {
  echo("Usage: $argv[0] idnumber\n");
  exit();
}// if
```

As we eliminate eight command-line arguments, we need to update our user profile assignments as well. This will prevent an 'unknown object' error. Every line in the user setup with a `$argv[]` assignment needs to be removed, except the one for the `idnumber` field. For example, we should blank out the `username` assignment as follows:

```
'username' => '',
```

Each field assigned to a `$argv[]` value needs to be assigned a blank value.

We also need to change our action to `'Delete'`, using the following change to line 20:

```
'action' => 'Delete',
```

We can wrap up by changing our output to the user, at the end of the script:

```
echo("Deleting user\n");
```

These short scripts provide a great set of administrative tools, and do an excellent job of illustrating the power of the web services library. In our next section, we tackle web services based SSO.

Creating a Web Services based Single Sign On

The Remote-Learner Web Service library includes functions to support Single Sign On (SSO). This makes use of the ability to hook into the user login function, just as our earlier example in the chapter on external integrations illustrated. However, the Web Service library implements a much more secure method of authentication. When used in combination with connections over HTTPS, this library provides a production-ready SSO methodology.

To implement SSO, the library requires the installation of the **Web Services Single Sign On** authentication plugin, which is included in the code samples for this chapter. The plugin can be installed by copying it into the `/auth` folder of the Moodle installation. To complete the setup, we need to enter an **SSO Ticket** in the settings screen. Also, note the option to automatically create a user, which can be very useful for simplified system integrations. The following screenshot shows the settings screen:

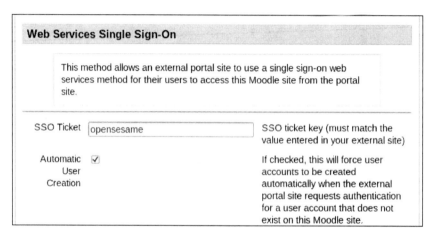

This chapter describes an example implementation that uses the Web Services SSO functions. Although the Web Service library can be used to create secure logins, the example in this chapter would still need additional work to make it secure. The example implements a web page that creates an SSO login link directly into a course. To be production-ready, the page would need to be secured by using the remote site's login and permission checking. If we were programming a page such as this in Moodle, we would protect it with both a login check and a test against a particular user capability in the appropriate context. For illustration, this script simply takes GET arguments as part of its URL. These arguments specify both the specific user and the course. We will call our example SSO script `ssologin.php`.

Let's get started.

Creating our HTML wrapper

First, we need to create a basic HTML page wrapper. This is simple when using one of PHP's built-in features—the ability to put arbitrary HTML code inside the script file:

```
<html>
<header><title>WebServices SSO</title>
<body>
```

Web service connection setup

At the start of the script, we perform our basic web service connection setup. This is the exact same setup that we have used throughout the chapter to authenticate our script to the service.

Processing SSO parameters

Now we are ready to process our SSO parameters. We need to capture both the username and the courseid. We use the standard PHP array $_GET to capture the parameters. First, we check with the isset() function to confirm that the parameters were passed. If these were passed, we assign these to the variables $username and $courseid:

```
if (isset($_GET['username']) && isset($_GET['courseid'])) {
  $username = $_GET['username'];
  $courseid = $_GET['courseid'];
```

Note that as we are simulating an external system; we are not making use of the more secure param() functions included in Moodle. This is just a simple and insecure example web page to demonstrate how to consume the SSO capabilities. In a production environment, we should use the equivalent parameter cleaning functions of the portal software. If parameters are not well-checked, then this can lead to Cross Site Scripting exploitation and SQL injection exploitation, among other security problems.

In the next section, we attempt authentication.

Using authenticate_user()

Now that we know the user, let's attempt to authenticate. We will use the authenticate_user() function. This function takes four arguments. The standard first two parameters are client and sessionkey. The third parameter is the user to log in. The final argument is the SSO ticket. This should be set to match the value entered in the Web Services Single Sign On authentication module settings screen. The SSO ticket value provides an extra layer of security to confirm that a trusted authority is using the service:

```
$authentication = $client->authenticate_user($session->client,
                    $session->sessionkey, $username,'opensesame');
```

Let's process the results of the function call. If the login was successful, we will receive a status of 'ACK':

```
if($authentication->status == 'ACK') {
```

If successful, the `authenticate_user()` function will also return a single-use session identifier. This value is stored in `$authentication->info`. To make use of the session, we simply have to pass it to the Moodle site as a parameter in a URL. Because the session is of single use and is cryptographically generated, it is much more secure than our original URL SSO. We don't have to be worried about the user copying and pasting the URL, or about users guessing the pattern and logging in as other users. The following code generates a link to our test site, with a direct link to the `courseid` that we passed as a parameter:

```
echo("<a href=http://localhost/workspace/moodle19/course/
    view.php?id=$courseid&wssid=$authentication->info >Go to My
    Course</a>");
}
```

Closing wrapper

Let's finish our SSO page by outputting the close to our HTML document.

```
</body>
</html>
```

In this section, we have created a fully-functioning SSO implementation in less than 30 lines of code! Next, we will implement some additional command-line scripts, to control user enrollments.

Enrollment management

Earlier, we created three command-line scripts to control user management. Let's flesh these out by creating two additional scripts: `enrollstudent.php` and `unenrollstudent.php`. Our scripts will have the following usage:

enrollstudent.php idnumber courseid

unenrollstudent.php idnumber courseid

The `idnumber` is used to identify the user account, and should be set to the `idnumber` value in the user's profile field. The `courseid` should be set to the `idnumber` of the course. Let's get started!

Creating enrollstudent.php

The `enrollstudent.php` script adds an enrollment for a student to a course. Again, we can use the same basic template from our earlier scripts. At the start of our script, we need to change only the number of arguments, and the text of our usage description:

```
if( $argc != 3 ) {
    echo("Usage: $argv[0] idnumber courseid\n");
    exit();
}// if
```

Using enrol_students()

The `enrol_students()` function takes four arguments: client, `sessionkey`, user array, and course `idnumber`. Because the function takes an array of users, one or more users can be assigned an enrollment at the same time. In the case of our command-line script, we just need to pass a single user.

```
$response = $client->enrol_students($session->client,
                $session->sessionkey, $argv[2], array($argv[1]),
                'idnumber', 'idnumber');
echo("Enrolling student\n");
```

In the next section, we modify the `enrollstudent.php` file, to remove a student from a course.

Creating unenrollstudent.php

We can create our unenroll script by copying our enrollment script. Completing the transformation requires a few simple changes. We use the `unenrol_students()` function instead of the `enrol_students()` function. Both functions take exactly the same arguments, so all we need to change is the function name. Finally, we change the output to the user, to indicate the new function:

```
$response = $client->unenrol_students($session->client,
                $session->sessionkey, $argv[2], array($argv[1]),
                'idnumber', 'idnumber');
echo("Unenrolling student\n");
```

This completes our enrollment management scripts, and rounds out our set of command-line tools using web services.

In the next section, we take on grades!

Grade passing

Clients using Moodle will often want to pull a complete list of all user grades. Typically, this will be done so that the data can then be passed into another system. Often, these are legacy systems that are not compatible with new technologies, such as SOAP, or XML. The lowest common denominator in these situations is a **Comma Separated Value (CSV)** or flat file. In this next section, we will implement a script to bridge between our web service library and a system that can accept a flat file. The flat file will contain all of the course grades for all of the users enrolled in courses across the entire site. The format of the file will be:

Example CSV File:

```
"Course","Course ID Number","Student Name", "Student ID Number",
"Grade"
"Course Fullname 101","1234","tom happy", "", "100"
"Course Fullname 101","1234","Web Service Student", "wsuser3", "0"
```

Let's start coding.

Creating the CSV grade script

We will call our new script `listgrades.php`. We again use the same basic structure that we have used previously in the chapter. The heart of this script is the `get_grades()` function. The function parameters for `get_grades()` are as follows:

```
get_grades(client, sesskey, courseids, userids,
          cidfield = 'idnumber', uidfield = 'idnumber' ).
```

The `courseids` argument should contain an array of courses. The returned results will be limited to grades from the courses listed in the array. If left null, the function will return grades for all courses on the site. The `userids` argument contains an array of users for which to generate grades. If left blank, the function will return grade data for all students in the requested courses. The final two arguments control the field mappings to use for identifying courses and users. These default to the `idnumber` field. Because we want to pull all of the grades for the site, we are going to pass NULL values for both `courseids` and `userids`. This will result in a list of all of the grades for the site. This is accomplished with a single function call:

```
$listgrades = $client->get_grades($session->client,
                    $session->sessionkey, NULL, NULL, '', '');
```

For sites with large numbers of users and/or courses, it may be necessary to generate the list on a course by course basis, in order to prevent PHP or Apache timeouts.

Generating the header line

To provide appropriate labeling of the CSV file, let's generate a header line that denotes which columns are assigned to which fields:

```
echo("\"Course\",\"Course ID Number\",\"Student Name\", \"Student ID
    Number\", \"Grade\", \n");
```

Course loop

The results from the `get_grades()` function are structured as a set of nested arrays. These are nested as follows:

```
main object -> grades (by course) -> users -> activities
```

We start by defining a loop to iterate through our list of courses. This can be a bit confusing because the class is defined as `->grades`, but contains a list of courses and associated grade setups:

```
foreach ($listgrades->grades as $grade) {
```

In the next `foreach` loop, we iterate through the list of users:

```
foreach ($grade->users as $user) {
```

Within this loop, we can now start to output data to our flat file. We are going to create our output by using `echo`. This will use the standard output stream, and can be piped to a file of our choosing, by using command-line shell operators. In this line of code, we output the appropriate variable for each column of our CSV file. Note that the Web Service library does not filter out users or courses with missing ID numbers. These are included in the file. So, if missing, they are output as blanks:

```
echo("\"$grade->longname\",\"$grade->idnumber\",\"$user->fullname\",
    \"$user->idnumber\", \"$user->coursegrade\", \n");
```

If we want activity-level detail, we can add another `foreach` loop, and cycle through the activities array structure in our result set. For our example, we only want the overall course grade, so we don't need the additional loop.

We now have a fairly complete implementation of a web services client in PHP, which includes: user creation, user editing, user deletion, user enrollment management, Single Sign On, and grade passing.

Let's move on to a discussion of Moodle Networking.

Using Moodle Networking

Moodle Networking, or MNet, is the built-in web services library for Moodle. It was added to Moodle in version 1.8 and has been improved for version 1.9. It is a library, an API, and a feature of Moodle. As a feature, MNet is the method provided to connect one or more Moodle sites together for Single Sign On integration. As a library, it provides basic functions for creating trust relationships between other Moodle sites or third-party applications. As an API, MNet supports the definition of wrapper functions, in order to safely expose core Moodle functionality via XML-RPC. MNet has a more complex setup than other web service offerings, and a limited built-in set of XML-RPC wrapper functions. MNet's strength is its security architecture, which implements a robust public key encryption model. Note that whereas the core web service protocol is XML-RPC, MNet allows for it to be extended by using other web service protocols, such as SOAP and REST. Extensions for these protocols are placed in the `mnet/soap` and `/mnet/rest` folders respectively. The following sections list the detailed advantages and disadvantages of Moodle Networking.

Advantages

Using Moodle Networking for development has the following advantages:

- Includes encryption and trust management
- Implements a standardized SSO mechanism
- Exposes the Moodle API
- Provides standardized methods for wrapping any internal functionality into a web service

Disadvantages

Using Moodle Networking for web services has the following disadvantages:

- More complex to use than RL web services
- Must define wrapper functions to access API via XML-RPC
- Limited documentation
- No active maintainer for most of its life after initial release (note that as of the update on 01/28/2010, there is now a maintainer)

The rest of this section will dig into some of the details of Moodle Networking and its web service library.

What is XML-RPC?

XML-RPC (`http://www.xmlrpc.com/`) is a remote procedure call that uses HTTP as the transport and XML for the encoding. XML-RPC is designed to be as simple as possible, while allowing complex data structures to be transmitted, processed, and returned.

There are many supporters on either side of the XML-RPC versus SOAP debate. SOAP is derived from XML-RPC, adding additional features. Some say that SOAP's additional features come at the cost of too much complexity (see `http://weblog.masukomi.org/writings/xml-rpc_vs_soap.htm`). Others say that SOAP's additional features make it easier to use.

Moodle's implementation of the XML-RPC protocol relies on the PHP library, `xmlrpc`. Note that in older versions of PHP this library was not enabled by default. From the phpinfo screen of your Moodle installation, you should see a section labeled 'xmlrpc' to indicate that the library has been installed. Without this library, Moodle Networking will not function. More information about this library can be found at `http://us3.php.net/manual/en/book.xmlrpc.php`.

MNet XML-RPC supported service types

The web service functions are limited to system services and three module types. The system-level services provide helper functions, which expose lists of methods supported by the library. The three module types that can be extended to provide web services are authentication, enrollment, and activity modules. Note that at the time of writing Penney Leach, the new MNet maintainer, has begun to add support for additional types.

MNet XML-RPC security model

As mentioned earlier, MNet uses XML-ENC and XML-DSIG standards to implement a Public Key encryption standard, in order to protect access to its web services. From a system administration point of view, this is implemented as a site trust system. The administrator of the system on either side of an MNet connection designates which sites are to be trusted and which services are available. The Public Key encryption system exchanges keys during the setup process for these trusts, and periodically thereafter. Once the trust is created, services are exchanged by using the encrypted channel.

Moodle has a related open-source project called Mahara. Mahara is an open-source ePortfolio system, which implemented the Moodle Networking Protocol (see `http://mahara.org`). The source code for Mahara is a good place to review an implementation of this security model and MNet in general.

See the following links for the official specifications for XML-ENC and XML-DSIG:

- `http://www.w3.org/TR/xmlenc-core/`
- `http://www.w3.org/TR/xmldsig-core/`

Let's have a look at how to extend the Web Service library.

Using MNet in activity modules

MNet allows for functions within activity modules to be exposed as a web service. This requires a wrapper function to be created. Wrapper functions are stored within a file called `rpclib.php`, which should be placed in the root directory of the module. The `rpclib.php` file must contain an `mnet_publishes()` function. For activity modules, this must be prefaced with the activity's name. So, for example, activity `foo` would need a function named `foo_mnet_publishes()`. This function must create an array structure that defines the services to be offered. Make a special note of the `['methods']` array, which defines the actual mapping of functions from the module. Here is an example from the Moodle Docs site that shows the service definitions for MNet's SSO:

```
/**
 * Provides the allowed RPC services from this class as an array.
 * @return array  Allowed RPC services.
 */
function mnet_publishes() {

    $sso_idp = array();
    $sso_idp['name']        = 'sso_idp'; // Name & Description go
                                         // in lang file
    $sso_idp['apiversion']  = 1;
    $sso_idp['methods']     = array('user_authorise','keepalive_
                              server', 'kill_children', 'refresh_log',
                              'fetch_user_image', 'fetch_theme_info',
                              'update_enrolments');

    $sso_sp = array();
    $sso_sp['name']         = 'sso_sp'; // Name & Description go
                                        // in lang file
    $sso_sp['apiversion']   = 1;
    $sso_sp['methods']   = array('keepalive_client','kill_child');

    return array($sso_idp, $sso_sp);
}
```

Note that the `@return` and `@param` values are utilized for XML-RPC introspection. Therefore, it's a good practice to include this commenting.

Let's do a quick recap of the required elements for exposing activity module functions as a web service.

- Create the `rpclib.php` file
- Create the `<module_name>_mnet_publishes()` function
- Create a services array defining wrapped functions
- Create the required language file entries
- Enter the `<service_name>_name`
- Enter the `<service_name>_description`

XML-RPC services are published with function names as follows. For example, function `my_function()` in module `foo` becomes:

```
mod/foo/rpclib.php/my_function
```

Let's have a look at how MNet works with authentication and enrollment plugins.

Using MNet in auth/enrol plugins

Exposing web services for these plugin types is similar to the process for activity modules, with a few changes needed to deal with the object-oriented nature of these plugin types (see *Chapter 9, Integrating Moodle with Other Systems* for more information):

- Class constructors must not require arguments
- Create `mnet_publishes()` as a member function to the extended object class, rather than `rpclib.php`

If we expose a function named `sync_activity()` for the authentication module `myauth`, an example function name for an exposed authentication service would be:

```
auth/myauth/auth.php/sync_activity
```

In the next section, we cover SSO.

MNet SSO model

MNet provides a robust Single Sign On facility that allows users to pass between trusted systems in a Moodle Network. MNet's SSO creates two service types:

- Identity Provider (IdP)
- Service Provider (SP)

An IdP is the user's primary or home site. This is the original site that the user logged into. The service provider is the remote site that the user is logging into via SSO. The MNet SSO has the following work flow:

1. The user clicks on the link to SP displayed on the IdP site
2. `/auth/mnet/jump.php` is called on the IdP site, and passes the `hostid` parameter for SP
3. IdP creates token and MNet session
4. User is redirected to SP landing URL
5. User visits the SP landing page
6. `/auth/mnet/auth.php/user_authorise` is called by SP on IdP via XML-RPC
7. IdP verifies session and returns user data
8. SP optionally gathers more information on the user via XML-RPC
9. SP redirects to original link request

Other MNet Documentation

The official documentation for MNet can be found at `http://docs.moodle.org/en/Moodle_Network`.

The official documentation for Moodle Networking's web services API can be found at `http://docs.moodle.org/en/Web_Services_API`.

Several PDF documents detailing the programming interface and error codes for Moodle Networking can be found in this chapter's source code folder.

Summary

In this chapter, you have learned about the Remote-Learner Web Services library and its pluses and minuses. You have implemented the following functions via web services in PHP: user management, user enrollment management, Single Sign On, and sitewide grade passing. You reviewed the pluses and minuses of Moodle Networking. Finally, you took a quick tour of MNet's web service library, including the security model, exposing activity module functions, exposing auth/enrol functions, and the SSO model.

With this chapter, we have come to the end of our journey together in learning how to program and extend Moodle. Thank you for coming along on this grand adventure!

Index

Thank you for buying
Moodle 1.9 Extension Development

About Packt Publishing

Packt, pronounced 'packed', published its first book "*Mastering phpMyAdmin for Effective MySQL Management*" in April 2004 and subsequently continued to specialize in publishing highly focused books on specific technologies and solutions.

Our books and publications share the experiences of your fellow IT professionals in adapting and customizing today's systems, applications, and frameworks. Our solution based books give you the knowledge and power to customize the software and technologies you're using to get the job done. Packt books are more specific and less general than the IT books you have seen in the past. Our unique business model allows us to bring you more focused information, giving you more of what you need to know, and less of what you don't.

Packt is a modern, yet unique publishing company, which focuses on producing quality, cutting-edge books for communities of developers, administrators, and newbies alike. For more information, please visit our website: www.packtpub.com.

About Packt Open Source

In 2010, Packt launched two new brands, Packt Open Source and Packt Enterprise, in order to continue its focus on specialization. This book is part of the Packt Open Source brand, home to books published on software built around Open Source licences, and offering information to anybody from advanced developers to budding web designers. The Open Source brand also runs Packt's Open Source Royalty Scheme, by which Packt gives a royalty to each Open Source project about whose software a book is sold.

Writing for Packt

We welcome all inquiries from people who are interested in authoring. Book proposals should be sent to author@packtpub.com. If your book idea is still at an early stage and you would like to discuss it first before writing a formal book proposal, contact us; one of our commissioning editors will get in touch with you.

We're not just looking for published authors; if you have strong technical skills but no writing experience, our experienced editors can help you develop a writing career, or simply get some additional reward for your expertise.

Moodle 1.9 Multimedia

ISBN: 978-1-847195-90-6   Paperback: 272 pages

Engaging online language learning activities using the Moodle platform

1. Ideas and best practices for teachers and trainers on using multimedia effectively in Moodle

2. Ample screenshots and clear explanations to facilitate learning

3. Covers working with TeacherTube, embedding interactive Flash games, podcasting, and more

4. Create instructional materials and design students' activities around multimedia

Moodle Administration

ISBN: 978-1-847195-62-3   Paperback: 376 pages

An administrator's guide to configuring, securing, customizing, and extending Moodle

1. A complete guide for planning, installing, optimizing, customizing, and configuring Moodle

2. Secure, back up, and restore your VLE

3. Extending and networking Moodle

4. Detailed walkthroughs and expert advice on best practices

Please check **www.PacktPub.com** for information on our titles

Moodle 1.9 Theme Design

ISBN: 978-1-849510-14-1   Paperback: 310 pages

Customize the appearance of your Moodle Theme using its powerful theming engine

1. Create your own Moodle theme from the graphic design stage right through to the finished complete Moodle theme

2. Offers design examples and ways to create appropriate themes for different student age groups and styles

3. Effective planning for creating and modifying new themes, customizing existing themes, and enhancing them further

4. Clear focus on beginners with ample screenshots and clear explanations to facilitate learning

Drupal for Education and E-Learning

ISBN: 978-1-847195-02-9   Paperback: 400 pages

Teaching and learning in the classroom using the Drupal CMS

1. Use Drupal in the classroom to enhance teaching and engage students with a range of learning activities

2. Create blogs, online discussions, groups, and a community website using Drupal.

3. Clear step-by-step instructions throughout the book

4. No need for code! A teacher-friendly, comprehensive guide

Please check **www.PacktPub.com** for information on our titles

www.ICGtesting.com